Conversations with Nadine Gordimer

Literary Conversations Series

Peggy Whitman Prenshaw
General Editor

Conversations
with Nadine Gordimer

Edited by
Nancy Topping Bazin and Marilyn Dallman Seymour

University Press of Mississippi
Jackson and London

Library of Congress Cataloging-in-Publication Data

Gordimer, Nadine.
    Conversations with Nadine Gordimer / edited by Nancy Topping Bazin
and Marilyn Dallman Seymour.
        p.   cm. — (Literary conversations series)
    Includes bibliographical references and index.
    ISBN 0-87805-444-8 (alk. paper). — ISBN 0-87805-445-6 (pbk. :
alk. paper)
    1. Gordimer, Nadine—Interviews.   2. Novelists, South
African—20th century—Interviews.   3. South Africa—Politics and
government—20th century.   4. South Africa—Intellectual life—20th
century. I. Bazin, Nancy Topping, 1934-   .   II. Seymour, Marilyn
Dallman.   III. Title.   IV. Series.
PR9369.3.G6Z465   1990
823—dc20   90-12555
                                                        CIP

British Library Cataloging-in-Publication data available

Books by Nadine Gordimer

Face to Face: Short Stories. Johannesburg: Silver Leaf Books, 1949.

The Soft Voice of the Serpent and Other Stories. New York: Simon and Schuster, 1952; London: Gollancz, 1953.

The Lying Days. London: Gollancz; New York: Simon and Schuster, 1953.

Six Feet of the Country. London: Gollancz; New York: Simon and Schuster, 1956.

A World of Strangers. London: Gollancz; New York: Simon and Schuster, 1958.

Friday's Footprint and Other Stories. London: Gollancz; New York: Viking, 1960.

Occasion for Loving. London: Gollancz; New York: Viking, 1963.

Not for Publication and Other Stories. London: Gollancz; New York: Viking, 1965.

The Late Bourgeois World. London: Gollancz; New York: Viking, 1966.

South African Writing Today. Edited with Lionel Abrahams. London: Penguin, 1967.

A Guest of Honour. New York: Viking, 1970; London: Jonathan Cape, 1971.

Livingstone's Companions. New York: Viking, 1971; London: Jonathan Cape, 1972.

The Black Interpreters: Notes on African Writing. Johannesburg: Spro-Cas/Ravan, 1973.

On the Mines. With David Goldblatt. Cape Town: Struik, 1973.

The Conservationist. London: Jonathan Cape, 1974; New York: Viking, 1975.

Selected Stories. London: Jonathan Cape, 1975; New York: Viking, 1976.

Some Monday for Sure. London: Heinemann, 1976.

Burger's Daughter. London: Jonathan Cape; New York: Viking, 1979.

A Soldier's Embrace. London: Jonathan Cape; New York: Viking, 1980.

Town and Country Lovers. Los Angeles: Sylvester and Orphanos, 1980.

What Happened to Burger's Daughter; or, How South African Censorship Works. Johannesburg: Taurus, 1980.

July's People. London: Jonathan Cape; New York: Viking, 1981.

Something Out There. London: Jonathan Cape; New York: Viking, 1984.

Lifetimes: Under Apartheid. With David Goldblatt. London: Jonathan Cape; New York: Knopf, 1986.

A Sport of Nature. London: Jonathan Cape; New York: Knopf, 1987.

The Essential Gesture: Writing, Politics and Places. Edited by Stephen Clingman. London: Jonathan Cape; New York: Knopf, 1988.

My Son's Story. London: Bloomsbury; New York: Farrar, Straus & Giroux; Cape Town: David Philip; Johannesburg: Taurus, 1990.

Contents

Introduction

"I'm reckless when I write, and I always have the feeling that,oh well, it doesn't really matter, I'm *going* to do it. It's got to be done completely, or not at all." So Nadine Gordimer told Stephen Gray in 1980. She is reckless in that she ruthlessly tries to write the truth as she sees it without considering personal or public consequences. Gordimer asserts in the interviews that a writer cannot afford to be self-conscious or fearful. Honesty is absolutely essential.

Reading the interviews selected for this volume will increase almost every reader's admiration for Nadine Gordimer. The interviews convey very clearly the pressures she has been under at various times during her career. The apartheid government, for example, banned three of her works during the sixties and seventies and put temporary embargoes (which were detrimental to sales) on several others. At the opposite end of the political spectrum in the 1970s, some radicals insisted that whites could not know blacks well enough to write about them or they exacted that any blacks depicted be without flaws or ideological misgivings. Pursuing "*any* truth that comes to mind" as she writes, Gordimer has woven a precarious path among the conflicting demands and complex tensions that surround her.

The interviews in this book are arranged chronologically from 1958 through 1989. They carry us through her writing career as well as through a recent history of events in South Africa. The two interviews that focus most strongly on political events are those by Bernard Sachs (1961) and Claude Servan-Schreiber (1979), but politics have necessarily permeated her life, her work, and, therefore, all of these interviews. Gordimer has emphasized that she was not by nature political; however, the revolution that has been in progress through-out this 1958–1989 period forced her to become so. She explained to Alan Ross in 1965: "I have come to the abstractions of politics through the flesh and blood of individual behaviour. I didn't know what politics was about until I saw it all *happening to people.*" As she told Claude Servan-Schreiber (1979): "Because the society in which I live is so permeated with politics, my work has become intimately connected with the translation of political events, of the way politics affect the lives of people." "Their lives, and I believe their very personalities, are changed by the extreme political circumstances one lives under in South Africa" (Hurwitt). She clarifies to her interviewers that she is a radical, not a liberal, and demonstrates the inadequacy of liberal attitudes in her novels *Occasion for Loving* (1963) and *The Late Bourgeois World* (1966). From early on, she wished to disassociate herself from the liberals. They had failed because, confronting what was, in fact, not just a political but also an economic structure, their strategies were too moderate to bring about significant change. Gordimer supported the African National Congress openly, risking persecution, all through the years when it was a crime to do so. Black majority rule, a major issue in 1990, she had already endorsed as natural and inevitable thirty years earlier. The color of the government does not matter as long as it "will care for justice and be capable of setting up an efficient and incorruptible administration," she told Sachs in 1961.

These interviews contain frequent references to historical events—the Sharpeville massacre (1960), the Soweto uprising (1976), the death of Steve Biko (1977)—and to those shaping history—Winnie Mandela, Desmond Tutu, Nelson Mandela—the same kind of historical material that enhances her ninth novel, *A Sport of Nature*. She rarely revises her fiction but, as she said in 1987, she makes sure that "whatever stays must be right in terms of the external reality, history, and topography." The facts must be as accurate as the truth that emerges from her fiction. She is interested in history—the external reality that shapes personal lives. But ultimately it is, for example, what the Soweto uprising meant to people that fascinates her, and it is fiction or poetry that can tell that story. In 1979 she spoke to Alex Tetteh-Lartey about Soweto: "You can understand the events—that so many people were killed, that this happened, that that happened. You can read the newspaper reports, but the psychological process within people, how it changes them, how they examine themselves and their own position vis-à-vis their own people as well as the white man, this is stuff for the novelist, not for the journalist." Similarly, she stated in her powerful 1982 talk "Living in the Interregnum" what she would probably say of these interviews: "nothing I say here will be as true as my fiction."

Indeed, interviews are problematic. Nadine Gordimer does not even save them. She wrote to me in a letter dated 21 April 1989: "Most of them annoy me too much and are too full of inaccuracies brought about by selectivity for me to wish to read them over again." In any interview with Gordimer, there is another personality involved, each one with perspectives or agenda other than her own or simply different ways of understanding what she says. A number of the interviews lie cradled within articles or commentaries by the interviewer. In one of these, published in 1978, Nesta Wyn Ellis successfully conveys to her readers what life was like in South Africa: Soweto is "where a million blacks crowd a dismal location of prefabricated two-room rented huts and the murder rate is the highest in the world." In contrast, "whites live in new, supermarket-studded, jacaranda-shaded islands of whiteness, where blacks never come except as servants, carrying their passbooks like visas, in the dawn." Some interviewers' questions draw new material from Gordimer. Others invite a repetition of statements made in earlier interviews, in part because Nadine Gordimer is amazingly consistent over the years in some of her attitudes and beliefs, especially in regard to her writing. But since evidence of consistency is important, repetitive material has not been cut; each interview has been printed in its entirety. Also, individuals who had not done the interviewing typed the transcriptions of several of the radio and television conversations; therefore, these had to be edited for intelligibility. Thus, in the interviews taped for the mass media, sometimes Nadine Gordimer shares her power over the printed page not only with the interviewer but also with the typist and the editor.

Nevertheless, however fallible, interviews do add a great deal to our understanding of a writer's views and personality and this, in turn, helps us understand her work. Reading the interviews, like reading nonfiction pieces by an author, enriches our reading of her texts. Conversely, reading Gordimer's novels and short stories enhances our understanding of what she says in the interviews. Just as Gordimer says her creative work is like a "jigsaw puzzle," a "mosaic," so too the study of an author must fit all the pieces together in order to attempt to comprehend or intuit the whole. The pieces include everything she has written (novels, short stories, essays, articles) as well as what she has said—to the extent that that can be captured in interviews or in memoirs or anecdotes supplied by her friends.

The primary focus is always on the writer's art, for it is through the art that we can try to understand human behavior and the significance of what we experience. As Gordimer told Diane Cassere in 1972: "What the writer is piecing together is his view of the world." In 1987, she explained to Carol Sternhell, "I began writing out of a sense of wonder about life, a sense of its mystery, and also out of a sense of its chaos." She reiterated in 1988: "The function of the writer is to make sense of life. . . . to make something coherent out of it. Isn't all art doing that?"

Gordimer assured Cooper-Clark (1983) that "the form and style of a book come about through the demands of the content." Each book is different and "there is only one way" to write each of them. All of her novels and some of her short stories are discussed in these interviews. A few of the interviews discuss several of her works. Margaret Walters leads the dialogue through nine of her novels— from *The Lying Days,* published in 1953, through *A Sport of Nature,* published in 1987. Other interviews focus primarily on one book. In 1979, for example, Alex Tetteh-Lartey focused on her essays in *The Black Interpreters*; in 1987, he talked with her about *A Sport of Nature.*

Perhaps the book discussed most in the interviews is *Burger's Daughter.* Despite Gordimer's prominent international reputation, it was banned in South Africa for being "obscene, blasphemous, pernicious in the area of race relations, offensive to certain parts of the population, and detrimental to the security of the state" (Servan-Schreiber). Throughout her interviews, she talks about the problem of censorship. Although she herself was often its victim, she emphasizes that black writers have been still harder hit. In 1969 she stated that no black writer or intellectual was likely to stay in South Africa. Nevertheless, she struggled constantly to aid and coach young writers and to form professional associations where black and white writers could meet for mutual support.

Nadine Gordimer chose not to go into exile, instead to accept the risk and daily stress of staying in South Africa. As Servan-Schreiber noted, the difference between the white person in Algeria and the white in South Africa is that "the white South African has no mother country." Gordimer definitely sees herself as African, and she has read widely in African literature. In the interviews one finds her opinions of such writers as Chinua Achebe, brief histories of literature by blacks and by whites in South Africa, and comments on the development of literature throughout Africa.

She discusses throughout the interviews many authors who influenced her; for example, Upton Sinclair's *The Jungle* made her see the situation in South Africa as one of class struggle. As a young writer, she particularly admired D. H. Lawrence's *Sons and Lovers* and E. M. Forster's *A Passage to India*. She also held in high esteem the short stories of Eudora Welty and visited her once in Jackson, Mississippi. However, the writings of Marcel Proust influenced her the most: "Proust has been an influence on me, all my life—an influence so deep it frightens me . . . not only in my writing, but in my attitudes to life" (Hurwitt). She identifies with writers in the Soviet Union and especially with outstanding writers from Eastern Europe such as Czeslaw Milosz of Poland and Milan Kundera of Czechoslovakia. They, too, have had to struggle against repression and censorship. In her opinion, the best contemporary fiction is coming from Latin America (Carpentier, García Márquez, Fuentes, Puig, Vargas Llosa, Borges).

Another reason to read her interviews is for the autobiographical material and insights that they offer. Most interesting perhaps among the many conversations about her early life are the ones with Jannika Hurwitt and Jill Fullerton-Smith in which Nadine Gordimer discusses her complex relationship with her mother. Gordimer's life as a young woman in the 1950s is described in her interview with the Junction Avenue Theatre Company. This was a stimulating period of her life, and she learned a great deal through her friendships with black writers and artists. Yet she labels this same period that of the Toy Telephone: "It was a toy because while there were committees and groups all talking about what needed to be done for the blacks, there was no one listening at the other end" (Ellis). However, a few factual errors appeared in the interviews. For example, all the interviews cite Luthuania as her father's country of origin, but she corrected this item in our chronology to read Latvia! We left that reference unchanged but did correct two other errors. Some of the interviews had referred to her daughters, but she has only one daughter and one son. Some confusion existed, too, about her husband's profession; he is an art dealer.

The interviews cover still other topics. In Jan Askelund's, Gordimer speaks of her concerns with translations of her works. In several others she points out admiringly the existence in her country of heroes—those political activists (black and white) who make enormous personal sacrifices for the cause of black liberation. In Gardner (1980), Boyers (1982), and elsewhere, she clarifies why feminist issues are not one of her priorities. In her most recent interviews, she talks about another important aspect of her novels—that of sexuality. She has concluded that sex and politics are the "two greatest drives in people's lives." In a discussion of her puzzling and extremely sensual character Hillela, she says: "I think there may be a particular connection between sexuality, sensuality, and politics inside South Africa. Because, after all, what is apartheid all about? . . . It's about black skin, and it's about woolly hair instead of straight, long blond hair, and black skin instead of white skin. The whole legal structure is based on the physical, so that the body becomes something supremely important. And I think maybe subconsciously that comes into my work too" (Fullerton-Smith).

Certain of the interviews in this volume have never before appeared in print. These include the two interviews by Alex Tetteh-Lartey, those by Hermione Lee and Terry Gross, and except as noted those by Margaret Walters and Jill Fullerton-Smith. A strangely-combined, although smooth-reading version of excerpts of the Margaret Walters and Jill Fullerton-Smith interviews appeared as if it were an interview by Olga Kenyon in *Women Writers Talk: Interviews with 10 Women Writers*. New York: Carroll & Graf Publishers, 1989. The interview with Jan Askelund (originally in Norwegian) is appearing in English for the first time, and the interview with Claude Servan-Schreiber (originally in French) is appearing in English for the first time in its entirety. Excerpts from it appeared earlier in *World Press Review* 21.1 (January 1980), 30–34; however, many of the most interesting sections had been omitted, and it has been totally retranslated. Most of Nadine Gordimer's available interviews have been included in this collection.

My coeditor Marilyn Dallman Seymour and I would like to thank, in particular, the many interviewers whose work appears here and without whom this volume would not have been possible. We are grateful to those interviewers, editors, publishers, producers, administrators, and agents in many different countries who gave us permission to use material over which they have jurisdiction. We are also especially grateful to Stephen Clingman, whom Gordimer described in her 1989 letter as "the only interpreter I trust," for his help in locating interviews. I would like to thank Mariejo Wornom for help with a few difficult spots in my translation of the Servan-Schreiber interview. Anthony Roland facilitated our getting approval to use the Margaret Walters interview; we appreciate his time and telephone calls. We also thank Margaret Chatfield and the reference and interlibrary loan staff of the Old Dominion University library for their assistance. Eloise Skewis and Carolyn Rhodes generously helped in the early stages of indexing and proofreading. Very special thanks go to Ernest Rhodes for long hours spent entering the proper names for the index into the computer. Through the editorial process, we have appreciated the patience and support of our editors, Seetha Srinivasan and Ginger Tucker.

I also wish to thank Charles Burgess, Dean of the College of Arts and Letters, and my colleagues in the English Department at Old Dominion University who awarded me a semester's leave to do research. I am grateful to the College of Arts and Letters for a grant that covered a number of research expenses.

Going back many years, I wish to thank an old friend, Jan Carew, who through hours of conversation during the '60s and '70s introduced me to African and Caribbean writers and first told me about a wonderful writer, Nadine Gordimer, in whom I should take an interest.

We extend our deep appreciation to David Goldblatt for granting us permission to use his photograph of Nadine Gordimer for our book.

Most of all, of course, we appreciate the generosity of Nadine Gordimer in entrusting us with the compilation of this book. Through these interviews, as well as through her fiction and essays, she has kept alive—and made vivid for many people—her dream of a just, nonracial society in South Africa.

NTB
March 1990

Chronology

1923   Born, 20 November in Springs, a small mining town in the Transvaal, South Africa. Second daughter of Isidore Gordimer, Jewish watchmaker and jeweler who had emigrated from Latvia at age 13, and Nan Myers Gordimer, a native of England.
Educated at Convent of Our Lady of Mercy in Springs

1937   13 June, "The Quest for Seen Gold," Gordimer's first published fiction appears in the children's section of Johannesburg's *Sunday Express.*

1939   First short story that was not juvenile fiction, "Come Again Tomorrow," appears in *Forum,* a Johannesburg weekly.

1945   Attends the University of the Witwatersrand in Johannesburg for one year; no degree.

1949   6 March, marries Dr. Gerald Gavron
Face to Face: Short Stories published by Silver Leaf Books, Johannesburg.

1950   6 June, birth of daughter Oriane

1952   *The Soft Voice of the Serpent and Other Stories.* New York, Simon and Schuster; London, Gollancz, 1953.
Divorced from Dr. Gerald Gavron

1953   *The Lying Days.* London, Gollancz, and New York, Simon and Schuster.

1954   Marries Reinhold Cassirer

1955   28 March, birth of son Hugo

1956   *Six Feet of the Country.* London, Gollancz, and New
            York, Simon and Schuster.

1958   *A World of Strangers.* London, Gollancz, and New York,
            Simon and Schuster.
            A World of Strangers is banned for the next 12 years.

1960   *Friday's Footprint and Other Stories.* London, Gollancz,
            and New York, Viking.

1961   Visiting Lecturer, Institute of Contemporary Arts, Wash-
            ington, D.C.
            W.H. Smith Literary Award for *Friday's Footprint*
            The New York Times listed *Friday's Footprint* among 200
            best works of fiction in the world.

1963   *Occasion for Loving.* London, Gollancz, and New York,
            Viking.

1965   *Not for Publication and Other Stories.* London, Gollancz,
            and New York, Viking.

1966   *The Late Bourgeois World.* London, Gollancz, and New
            York, Viking.
            The Late Bourgeois World is banned for the next 10
            years.

1967   Edits with Lionel Abrahams, *South African Writing Today*

1969   Visiting Lecturer, Harvard University, Cambridge, Massa-
            chusetts; Princeton University, Princeton, New Jersey;
            Northwestern University, Evanston, Illinois
            Thomas Pringle Award (South Africa)

1970   *A Guest of Honour.* New York, Viking, and in 1971
         published by Jonathan Cape, London.
         Visiting Lecturer, University of Michigan, Ann Arbor

1971   *Livingstone's Companions.* New York, Viking, and in
         1972 published by Jonathan Cape, London.
         Adjunct Professor of Writing, Columbia University, New
         York
         A Guest of Honour is nominated as best novel of 1971 by
         the *English Sunday Telegraph* and *The Observer.*

1972   African Literature Lectures, University of Cape Town
         Foreword to Oswald Mtshali's *The Sound of a Cowhide
         Drum*
         James Tait Black Memorial Prize (England) for *A Guest of
         Honour*

1973   *The Black Interpreters: Notes on African Writing.* Johan-
         nesburg, Spro-Cas/Ravan.
         On the Mines (essay to accompany photography by
         David Goldblatt) Cape Town, Struik.

1974   *The Conservationist.* London, Cape, and New York,
         Viking, 1975.
         Booker Prize (England) for *The Conservationist*
         CNA Prize (South Africa) for *A Guest of Honour*

1975   *Selected Stories.* London, Cape, and New York, Viking,
         1976.
         Visiting Gildersleeve Professor at Barnard College, New
         York
         CNA Prize (South Africa) for *The Conservationist*
         Grand Aigle d'Or Prize (France)

1976   *Some Monday for Sure.* London, Heinemann.

1978   Penguin issues *Selected Stories* under the title *No Place
         Like: Selected Stories.*

1979   *Burger's Daughter.* London, Cape, and New York, Viking.
        11 July, *Burger's Daughter* is banned by censorship
        committee under the South African Publications Act of
        1974.
        August, Director of Publications appeals decision of his
        committee and *Burger's Daughter* is reinstated.
        Honorary member, American Academy and Institute of
        Arts and Letters

1980   *A Soldier's Embrace.* London, Cape, and New York,
        Viking.
        Town and Country Lovers. Los Angeles, Sylvester and
        Orphanos.
        *What Happened to Burger's Daughter; or, How South
        African Censorship Works.* Johannesburg, Taurus.
        CNA Prize (South Africa) for *Burger's Daughter*
        Honorary member, American Academy of Arts and
        Sciences

1981   *July's People.* London, Cape, and New York, Viking.
        "A Terrible Chemistry" (Writers and Places Television
        Series, England)
        Screenplays for four of the seven television dramas
        collectively entitled "The Gordimer Stories," 1981–1982
        ("Country Lovers," "A Chip of Glass Ruby," "Praise,"
        and "Oral History")
        Scottish Arts Council Neil M. Gunn Fellowship
        Common Wealth Award for Distinguished Service in
        Literature (USA)
        D. Litt., University of Leuven, Belgium

1982   Modern Language Association Award (USA)

1983   Coscripts and coproduces "Choosing for Justice: Allan
        Boesak" with her son, Hugo Cassirer

1984   *Something Out There.* London, Cape, and New York,
        Viking.

1985   Premio Malaparte, literary award from Italy
        D. Litt., Smith College, Northampton, Massachusetts
        D. Litt., Mount Holyoke College, South Hadley, Massa-
        chusetts
        D. Humane Letters, City College of New York

1986   *Lifetimes: Under Apartheid* (Text consists of excerpts from
        novels and stories; photographs by David Goldblatt).
        London, Cape, and New York, Knopf.
        Nelly Sachs Prize (West Germany)
        Officier de l'Ordre des Arts et des Lettres (France)
        Brockport Writers Forum International Award (State
        University of New York, Brockport)
        D. Litt., Harvard University, Cambridge, Massachusetts
        D. Litt., Yale University, New Haven, Connecticut
        Assists in organizing the Anti-Censorship Action Group
        (ACAG)

1986–87 Vice President of P.E.N.

1987   *A Sport of Nature.* London, Cape, and New York, Knopf.
        Bennett Award (USA) for 1986
        D. Litt., Columbia University, New York City
        D. Litt., New School for Social Research, New York City
        D. Litt., York University, England
        Assists in planning a National Writers' Conference:
        "South Africa - Beyond the Platitudes"
        July, Patron and Regional Representative, Congress of
        South African Writers (COSAW)

1988   *The Essential Gesture: Writing, Politics and Places* (essays
        edited by Stephen Clingman). London, Cape, and New
        York, Knopf.

1989   Scripts and narrates a film in the BBC series "Frontiers."

(Subject: frontier between Mozambique and South Africa).

1990   *My Son's Story.* London, Bloomsbury; New York, Farrar, Straus & Giroux; Cape Town, David Philip and Johannesburg, Taurus, 1990.

Conversations with Nadine Gordimer

"I'm Not So Observant," Says Nadine—
But Johannesburg Sees Itself in Her Book
The Man on the Reef/1958

From *The Star* (Johannesburg), 11 July 1958. Reprinted by
permission of *The Star.*

Before I was half-way through Nadine Gordimer's new novel, *A
World of Strangers,* I made up my mind to meet her and introduce
her to readers who know her only as a writer and not as a person.

Miss Gordimer, an authoress with an international reputation built
up on three previous books and numerous short stories in British and
American magazines, is known personally to a comparatively small
group in Johannesburg, where she lives in a rambling, old-fashioned
but comfortable house.

Yet in her latest novel—already in its third impression in Britain
and shortly to be published in America—she has given what is
probably the most penetrating, incisive account of Johannesburg and
its people ever written.

"I don't think I'm particularly observant," she told me. "In fact,
whenever I do see something which I think will make a plot for a
story, it never comes to anything. But when I'm writing, I often
remember some incident which happened months or years ago and I
fit it in."

In private life, Miss Gordimer, short, dark and slim, is Mrs.
Reinhold Cassirer with two [children] and three dogs—a Dachshund,
an English setter and a bulldog named Bongo which snored in a
resounding bass throughout the interview. Mr. Cassirer is a business
man with no literary pretensions.

"I never see a thing my wife writes until she's finished it," he says.
"I had to wait two years to see *A World of Strangers.*"

Miss Gordimer says: "I'm afraid I don't consult anybody, but rely
entirely on my own judgment. I write the way I want, and though I
could have made a lot more money if I had angled my stories, that's
the way I want it."

She wanted to be a writer from the time she learned to write.

"As a very small girl I used to make up my own newspapers. I would laboriously copy the layout of *The Star*—even to the small black stars which used to be on the front page—and fill it with my own stories."

Her first piece of writing was a laudatory poem on President Kruger. She was nine and received a prize at school for it. At 12 she wrote her first short story and it was published.

For years she wanted to be a journalist.

"What changed my mind?" She looked me straight in the eyes. "I decided that I wanted to be a writer."

In those early days, she admits, she was a painfully slow writer and would rewrite a story many times before she was satisfied.

"I'm still not fast—1,000 words on a good day, 600 on a bad one—but I rarely have to rewrite now."

Uys Krige was the first person of note to recognize her talent and, through his recommendation, she was invited to submit a story for *The Saturday Book*. This brought her instant recognition and a contract with the *New Yorker* for a first sighting of every short story and article written by her.

She owes a large part of her success to a dedication to routine.

"It took me years to develop my own style. One week I would try to copy Hemingway after reading him; then I would imitate another writer whose work I admired. Now I'm just myself."

Having established a style, she determined to devote every morning to writing.

"I'm not at home to anybody before 2 p.m. on any day of the week."

Although a popular party game in Johannesburg just now is identifying characters in *A World of Strangers* with this city's socialites, Miss Gordimer denies that her characters are real.

"Naturally a writer often draws on experience of human behaviour, but none of my characters is based on any one person I know or have met."

The Literary Scene: Nadine Gordimer
Bernard Sachs/1961

From *The Road from Sharpeville* (London: Dennis Dobson, 1961), 174–78. Reprinted by permission of Tessa Sayle Agency.

Bernard Sachs: What steps would you take to bridge the yawning gulf between black and white in South Africa?

Nadine Gordimer: I think any realistic policy of integration must begin at the beginning—with schools. All barriers of race and colour should be removed in education, from kindergarten to university. Children should enter the non-racial community life at school-going age, and be educated in mixed classes, with an undifferentiated syllabus and educational standard for all. If this had been done after the war, for example, our country would by now have been able to make use of the best African brains of a generation—they would have been just about ready to emerge, qualified, from the universities at this time, when African nationalism is causing the African people to reach out for responsibility whether they are qualified for it or not. Those of the same generation who, by the limits of their own capabilities, are not fitted for higher education, would at least have reached what is now (in the actual situation) the general average of white education, and this would have made reasonable, even from the African point of view, some form of qualified franchise for all races. I believe that the various education Bills that have created one standard of education for black and another for white are the most evil and disastrous of all *apartheid* legislation.

Concurrently with the integration of education, there should be a qualified franchise for Africans, Indians, Coloureds and whites at once, with a firm date for universal franchise. These two fundamentals—education and the vote—must come first, and together; though ideally, the one should be a preparation for the other. But it is clear that so far as the non-Europeans are concerned, they will never get the horse unless they put the cart first; the only safeguard they can secure to themselves against the long-term consequences of this wrong order of things is a—strictly temporary—qualified franchise.

That is why I should introduce such a franchise immediately, for though I agree it would put the Africans at a disadvantage temporarily, it would give them a loud and growing voice while, under a stepped-up educational programme, they are preparing themselves for the responsibilities of the inevitable African majority to come. I do not worry about the colour of future governments—only about whether they will care for justice and be capable of setting up an efficient and incorruptible administration.

B.S.: Would a policy of concessions result in the swamping of the whites by the Coloureds and Africans—a colonialism in reverse, as seems to be indicated by events in the Congo?

N.G.: The steps outlined above are the only measures that, in my opinion, can hope to prevent 'colonialism in reverse.' Integration is the only answer; and it depends on the active consent of both black and white.

B.S.: Has the situation in the Congo brought about any change in your outlook?

N.G.: None.

B.S.: Most South Africans, even Dr. Jan Steytler, think that it would be wrong to allow outside interference to influence South African internal affairs. Do you agree?

N.G.: I find it difficult to answer this question with a straight yes or no. I should say it all depends what this country does, and goes on doing. Overwhelmingly, I feel that I should like to see this country right itself—and by that I mean do away with racial discrimination—from within, and by the efforts of its own people. We suffer enough from moral ambiguities as it is; if interference were to mean occupation by force, international policing, or something of that nature, I think we might then achieve justice without having secured to ourselves the touchstone of justice—the knowledge (and strength) of having done the right thing by our own decision and choice. You can stand a man on his feet, but his own sense of balance is deep inside him. I am in favour of interference in the form of moral pressure of all kinds. There are thousands of white South Africans, for example, to whom it would never have occurred that *apartheid* might be considered a disgrace if their favourite sporting team had not been boycotted in some international contest.

B.S.: The view has been advanced that the English section here has in the past deferred too much to so-called Afrikaner moderate opinion, and has on that account failed to establish more vital bonds with progressive African opinion—to the detriment of the country. The people who hold this view believe that moderate Afrikanerdom as a decisive force is irrevocably lost to Verwoerdism. Do you agree?

N.G.: I think that it is not only to so-called Afrikaner moderate opinion that the English section has deferred, but to the mass of so-called moderate opinion speaking both languages, a mass that is kept apart only by the diversion of schoolboy loyalties—putting up and taking down each other's flags—but that belongs solidly together on the one question that has reality in our situation: its attitude to the Africans. The average English-speaking South African does not have to defer to the average Afrikaner on questions of African policy, because he is in perfect agreement with him. It simply suits the average English-speaking South African to assert a non-existent moral superiority over the Afrikaner by pretending to 'defer' to an attitude that the English-speaking South African secretly endorses, but that he would be ashamed to admit openly. The whole business of 'bringing the two white races together'—given so much space in the English as well as the Afrikaans press—has long seemed to me so much cant. The two white races do stand together on the one issue that counts—against the blacks. While this cant has been going on, the really vital bringing together—of black and white—has been ignored. Only the defunct Communist Party, the Congress of Democrats and the Liberal and Progressive Parties have understood the need to establish bonds with progressive African opinion.

B.S.: What is your opinion of the quality of the literature turned out in recent years by the Africans?

N.G.: I presume this question refers to literature in English. The quantity has been so small that there is not really sufficient to be judged as something as portentous as a separate literature, but if it must be so considered, it takes its standard from one or two outstanding books that have achieved overseas publication. Personal records such as Ezekiel Mphahlele's *Down Second Avenue* and Peter Abrahams' *Tell Freedom* have style and quality of a high order. (Taken, as I prefer to think of them, as part of South African English writing in general, they are the best that has been done in this genre by anybody.) So far, no imaginative writing by Africans has matched this standard, though there have been some good short stories.

B.S.: Certain people hold the view that the Africans will in the years to come dominate the literary field here, since they are best placed to give expression, in all its subtlety, to the racial tensions which make more of an impact on them. Do you agree?

N.G.: Novelty of subject-matter or point of view may give a fillip to mediocre writing, but the truly creative imagination is not dependent on the novelties but on the deep underlying sameness of all human experience. If Africans do dominate South African literature in the future, it will be because they have produced among their millions some great writers who will not be limited to the expression of the novelty of being black. No one can say at this stage what the contribution of the modern Africans will be to the creative arts: whether they will find their medium in painting, sculpture, music, or literature. Many people think that their outstanding contribution will be to music, since their tradition in this medium is very old, continent-wide, and already (through the work of American Negroes) an important stream in twentieth-century musical development. There is at least as much evidence that a great new movement in art might come from them. Both music and, to a lesser degree, art have remained a living tradition throughout the experience of colonialism. But the fact that there is no African literary tradition does not imply that the Africans' talents are unlikely to lie that way; their oral tradition of story-telling is richly imaginative both in ideas and the use of words, and seems to have come down to Western-educated Africans beautifully unimpaired—most of those I know are brilliant talkers. This oral tradition may flow into the mould of the written word.

Author: Nadine Gordimer

John Barkham/1962

From *Saturday Review*, 12 January 1963, 63. Reprinted by permission of Omni Publications International Ltd. for *Saturday Review*.

Explain it as you will, the flowering of talent among South African writers since World War II is something of a miracle. A literate population not much larger than that of the city of Philadelphia has produced a whole crop of writers like Alan Paton, Nadine Gordimer, Dan Jacobson, Peter Abrahams, and Laurens van der Post, whose names are known wherever the English language is read. Can it be that the race tensions endemic in their country are responsible for this extraordinary burgeoning of talent?

Only partly so in her case, replies Nadine Gordimer, South Africa's unchallenged First Lady of Letters. We discussed the question on my visit to South Africa last August, when, as luck would have it, she had just completed her third and most ambitious novel, *Occasion for Loving*. For herself, Miss Gordimer is convinced that no exterior stimulus, however strong, was needed to make a writer of her.

"I believe I am a natural writer," she said to me. "I started from the inside. It wasn't the impact of events around me which drove me to express myself. I was doing that anyway, even as a child. Only later did I become conscious of my situation as a white South African. Then, of course, it began to affect me as a writer to the point where I had to break out of the color cocoon."

She smiled at my puzzlement. "First, you know, you leave your mother's house, and later you leave the house of the white race. Since then the fact that I am a white person has strongly affected my writing."

This is no overstatement, as is clear from her books, and particularly so from her latest novel. In South Africa color-consciousness is the fulcrum on which the uneasy relationship of the races is balanced. It is the country's writers, as much as its politicians, who have brought this situation to world attention. Not, mark you, as propagandists, but in terms of creative literature.

With six books to her credit (three novels and three collections of tales), Nadine Gordimer strikes one as an artist now approaching her prime. To look at, she is a small, fine-boned woman in her late thirties, aloof of expression, with a rare smile that lights up her face like a lamp. Her voice is soft, her articulation precise, her conversation eloquent. Reared in a drab, dusty gold-mining town called Springs, some thirty miles east of Johannesburg, she spent much of her life within earshot of the noisy batteries that crush auriferous rock. For some years past, her home has been in a pleasant suburb of Johannesburg, where she lives with her husband and two young children.

Miss Gordimer has been writing stories since childhood and selling them since her teens. Thirteen years ago she broke into *The New Yorker* and has been appearing in its pages ever since. Her lapidary style, coupled with the unerring flashes of insight in her best tales, have made her preeminent as a short story writer in South Africa. She takes naturally to the form, working out the entire story in her mind before committing it to paper.

The novel doesn't deter her, but—as she emphasizes—it is content that dictates form. "A story to me is like a piece of music, with its distinctive movements, rhythms, and cadences. Only when I have worked these out to my satisfaction do I write them down, and, once on paper, I rarely have to change anything. Every story presents its own technical problems, and I confess that I enjoy grappling with them.

"The novel," she went on, "is more flexible—and more demanding. Things alter shape as you go along. The plot remains the bone, as it were, but the flesh is sometimes unwieldy. Sometimes, too, a character will disappoint by failing to emerge as I had hoped. These are problems familiar to all novelists." She considers *Occasion for Loving* to have been the most exacting of her books, in that its contrasting rhythms and varied viewpoints required her to explore new narrative techniques and structural forms.

Miss Gordimer works in the mornings in a small room overlooking her garden. At such times she is incommunicado to all callers. "Then

I live in the interior world which is private to all imaginative writers. This world is, in fact, the great line of continuity in my life. Whatever else may change for me, this interior world is always there waiting for me to enter."

Nadine Gordimer
Studs Terkel/1962

From *Perspective on Ideals and the Arts*, 12.3 (May 1963), 42–49. Reprinted by permission of Studs Terkel.

The author of six books, NADINE GORDIMER, South Africa's "First Lady of Letters," is perhaps that country's most distinguished living fiction writer—the *Atlantic Monthly* called her "one of the most gifted practitioners of the short story anywhere in English." Her work, over the years, has come more and more to mirror the political and psychological tensions that grip South Africa. "I'm an apolitical person," she says, "in a situation where to be effective you have to be political. All I have to offer is my ability to write." *Occasion for Loving*, her new novel, was published last January by The Viking Press: "Its main theme," Miss Gordimer says, "is that the liberal attitude has become meaningless. We have to accept that we cannot live decently in a rotten society." Miss Gordimer was born 39 years ago in the small gold-mining town of Springs, 30 miles from Johannesburg. Her father was a Jewish refugee from Lithuania who ran a jeweler's shop in Springs, where she grew up. Though she began writing very young, she had to wait until she entered the university in Johannesburg before receiving any encouragement. She wrote her first novel, *The Lying Days,* after an unsuccessful first marriage; she married a second time—she has two children—and began to travel—to Europe and America. *The Soft Voice of the Serpent*, her first collection of short stories, was published in 1950; her second, *Six Feet of the Country,* in 1956. *A World of Strangers,* another novel, came out in 1958, and was banned in the soft cover edition in South Africa to prevent its being read by Negroes. Miss Gordimer's third collection of stories, *Friday's Footprint* (1960), won the W. H. Smith and Son Literary Award of £1000 in London in 1961.

Terkel: Nadine Gordimer could easily be described as South Africa's First Lady of Letters. A very distinguished novelist and short story writer, America knows of her through a number of works, the most recent being the novel, *Occasion for Loving*. We're seated in her home in a very pleasant part of Johannesburg, a city of fantasy as well as fact; more about this perhaps in our conversation. Miss Gordimer, we hear a good deal about South Africa and writing—a country with not too many people who are literate, at the moment—and yet it's produced so many important writers: Alan Paton, yourself, Peter Abrahams, Dan Jacobson, others. Do you have any theory about the reason for this?

Gordimer: Well, no, I'm afraid I haven't. It seems really a bit of a mystery. What people do say is, it's because of the racial conflict in this country, the political conflict. But I'm not sure that that's the answer.

Terkel: People think, perhaps, that these tensions might make for a certain creativity on the part of someone who's in the middle of it?

Gordimer: Yes. While I'd think that's true in my case, certainly I think I would have been a writer *anyway*. I don't think I've been motivated *primarily* by the situation here, because I was writing long before I was consciously aware of the racial tensions.

Terkel: Let's start from the beginning: you say you wrote before you were aware you were writing. . . .

Gordimer: I simply wrote about South Africa because that is my home; it's the thing I know; and because I've always lived here. And the conscious preoccupation with our particular situation, I think, came quite a long time after I'd begun to write.

Terkel: Let's start with the unconscious preoccupation. The other day I was visiting a mine—Vlakfontain—and when I told you about it earlier, you laughed and said that that's the very area where you lived as a girl—Springs, South Africa. What about this area, this place, and you?

Gordimer: Well, I was born there. It was a town in the gold-mining area, the richest gold-mining area in the world: Witwatersrand. I was born in one of the small towns there, a town that existed *for* the mines, that existed to cater to the needs of the mine. So this was my background.

Terkel: One of your books, *The Lying Days,* dealt with this particular time in your life?

Gordimer: Well, I used that background, yes.

Terkel: When did you first become aware that you were a writer? When did you first begin to write, physically, kinesthetically?

Gordimer: I think I became aware at the same time as the actual *act* of writing. I started very young, very young, indeed. I don't quite remember when. I was quite a child . . . when I began to write. But I don't think that my *particular* background—in fact, I'm quite sure my particular background had very little to do with it. On the contrary, it was a background that would mitigate against it. It was *culturally* a very thin background. I mean there were no other people that *I* knew who were trying to write. There was very little music; there were no pictures to look at; but of course there was a public library, where you could always read.

Terkel: The environment around you was not one that was conducive to creativity on your part.

Gordimer: There was no *cultural* stimulus. Of course, one doesn't know whether a cultural stimulus is *needed* to make a writer or a painter. It seems to come from inside as often as from outside.

Terkel: What led you to the library? From what you say, there was nothing around you, whether it was a teacher, or a parent, or a figure in the community who told you about a certain book, or showed you a certain painting, or let you listen to a certain piece of music: you had none of this apparently.

Gordimer: I mustn't exaggerate: it was an ordinary small town, middle-class background, and people read the Book of the Month and the *Reader's Digest* and so on, but there wasn't any serious reading going on around me, and there was not a library in anybody's house.

Terkel: What led you, a young girl, to the library?

Gordimer: I don't know, I suppose . . . some sort of feeling . . . some instinct that there were *other* things in life that I had an instinct towards but that I really didn't know about.

Terkel: Do you remember the early subjects that attracted you?

Gordimer: Yes, they were far away from South Africa. There was this curious split in the life of a person like myself—living in a small town in South Africa—between the life we lived and the life we read about. If you live in Europe or you live in America, the books you read are set in the scenes you know, more or less. But this was not so for people like myself because the literary world referred to countries we'd never seen, and a kind of life we didn't know. This is not only my own experience, it's one that I have in common with people like Dan Jacobson and others. We've discussed it from time to time, and we've come upon a very curious thing: we had one life which we lived in books and another life that we lived in reality.

Terkel: There came a time, though, did there not, when the reality of the life you lived and what you wrote merged?

Gordimer: Well, no, I don't think it ever did. What happened was this: I found that my own background provided a vast, really untouched experience that had hardly been written about at all. You know how Africa had been written about during the 19th century—as a kind of place for adventure and explorers. And in South Africa itself we were known for *Jock of the Bush Veld*. This story about a dog was far better known than perhaps our first great piece of imaginative work, Olive Schreiner's *The Story of an African Farm* [1883].

Terkel: I remember, as a boy in high school, a teacher gave me a copy of *The Story of an African Farm* by Ralph Iron. I believe that was Olive Schreiner's nom de plume. You read that, then, as a young girl.

Gordimer: Well, no. I must say that when an adolescent—a great reading time—I hardly noticed at all that we *did* have a small literature here. We had Olive Schreiner and William Plomer and Sarah Gertrude Millin, but I was reading literature from Europe and America. And it was really a little later that I began to read about my own country, even, as I say, though there was so little. But there did come the consciousness that one could break out. One didn't have to write about . . . . One didn't have to know Europe in order to be able to write or to think or to have ideas—that one could apply this to one's own background and explore *that* in writing.

Terkel: I must ask you this question—it was John Barkham who asked you this, too, for his *Saturday Review* piece—you, living in a certain country, South Africa, a white woman in this country, certainly a country of great tensions, at the moment unique among other countries of the world, do you feel this must, of necessity, determine the content of what you write?

Gordimer: No, I don't. In the beginning in my writing I was obsessed with myself as most youthful writers are, and with my own emotions, and so on, and it was only when I turned from this to the world around me—related myself to my background, as it were—that I began to realize that this was in many ways unique, and full of unanswered things, and full of things that I had taken for granted, so that when I began to doubt myself, emotionally, in every way, then the doubts about the color thing—which is what you mean—began to come, too.

I don't know whether I said this to John Barkham; I know I've said this to someone else in some interview, but it's so important to me that I'll repeat it to you: I think that people like myself have two births, and the second one comes when you break out of the color bar. It's a real rebirth when you break out of your background, the taboos of your background, and you realize that the color bar is not valid, and is meaningless to you.

Terkel: Nadine, do you remember—this is a difficult question to answer—do you remember generally the time when you broke out; you were conditioned to a certain prejudice, were you not?

Gordimer: Yes, indeed, I was.

Terkel: Have you an idea when it was?

Gordimer: Yes, roughly, I do. I was brought up in a home where we had black servants. It was a very patriarchal atmosphere, so much so that I can tell you that my nanny—the one I had when I was two years old—is still with my mother. So, it's this very close family thing. *But,* she was a servant; and she's always remained a servant. And even though we were close—in this way that children and the people who look after them are, a situation that you're familiar with in your own South—it was quite without question that she could never sit down with us at the table or be received in any social way—or anyone else who was black. We had no black friends, though we were kind and decent to our black servants—and I grew up in this kind of atmosphere.

But then, as I began to read, and to read a bit of philosophy, and to read creative thinkers in various fields, I began to question the whole idea of man, and to learn about the brotherhood of man, and so on, and to apply this eventually to my own life. And to ask myself, well, why? *Why* hadn't we any black friends? *Why* are these people different? *Why* are black children called pickaninns, whereas we were always called children? Where does this whole division come about?

And, of course, once you start to doubt, then your world begins to collapse. And you have to build a new one for yourself, one way or another.

It began like that. In my writing it began with what I call the master-servant stories. Some writers never get past them; thank God I did. Anyway, I wrote some stories, early stories . . . no, quite late ones, really, when I was 18 and 19, that reflected this conflict in my mind: how I could accept these people, the Africans, for certain purposes and reject them as human beings. And it wasn't a thing that came entirely from the outside; it never can. You can't really take these things from the outside. It was confirmed by my own *feeling* that I loved these people, that they were just people the same as I was: some of them I loved, some of them I didn't like, some of them I would never want to speak to or be friendly with, and others I would.

So it began that way. Then, later on, when I left the small town where I lived and moved in a wider, less confined society, when I came to live in Johannesburg, I had the opportunity to meet Africans who had the same interests as I had, who were on the same educational level—people I could meet on my own level. Then, of course, the whole thing was confirmed for me. So, it happened, really, pretty naturally.

Terkel: There was a double development here: outside, and to some extent the people you met, the books you read; but, in addition, and perhaps most important—because you speak of the interior life often, deep inside you—was this particular restlessness on this particular subject, or not quite contentment in accepting what was.

Gordimer: Yes, indeed, otherwise I might have stayed all my life accepting the conventions into which I had been born—our kind of kindly, patriarchal attitude. I felt it was false. Something in me told me it was false, and things outside me, as I grew older, confirmed that it was false, and cruel, and absurd.

Terkel: I'm sure that we'll return to this particular subject—the one, the great, obsession of South Africa. I would like to, now, stick to this matter of you and writing. You probably would have been a writer no matter where you were, whether it was Kenosha, Wisconsin, or Paris, or Johannesburg. . . .

Gordimer: Yes, I think so. I think so for the simple reason that I began writing, not stimulated by my particular situation, but just out of—well, it sounds pompous, but—the *human* situation.

Terkel: Your interior life, then, is the firmest thread of continuity in your life. Each day . . . are you with yourself a good portion of the time?

Gordimer: Yes, I suppose so. It always sounds odd when one talks about the interior life. It sounds snooty and ivory tower. I don't mean it that way at all. What I mean is: the interior life is something, I think, that has an uninterrupted continuity. All sorts of things happen to you in your outward life. But this interior life is something you're constantly working out for yourself and that remains with you through all sorts of changes and ups and downs.

Terkel: Is there a steady flow of writing on your part each day? Do you have a habit, or is it done improvisationally?

Gordimer: No. I think it's a habit. It's a kind of discipline, so that I do work regularly, and when I don't *seem* to be working, then probably I still am, too. You tend to measure yourself—all writers do—by what you actually have put down on paper, how many words. But I don't think that's when the work's really done. It's done at other times. It's happening sometimes at the back of ordinary, everyday living, while you're talking to someone, or while you're going about some daily chore you have to do—meeting the world in some way. Then you're carrying on your work behind it. I think the two run concurrently.

When it comes down to how incidents in life directly influence what you write, I find, myself, that very often it's a terribly delayed process. You have some particular experience; you may not even notice that it strikes you heavily at the time. And then it takes months, sometimes even years, before it sinks down into your being and then comes up again, rises up again sufficiently for you to use it to write.

Terkel: The only work of yours I've read—and I apologize—is *The Soft Voice of the Serpent and Other Stories.* These stories, to me, in reading them, almost all of them have this common theme of the hurt, the unexpressed, the inchoate hurt. . . . The very first story, the title story, about the couple. He has lost a leg. They are very much involved with one another, and yet when he sees the locust— which has lost a leg, too—they josh about it, seemingly in a jocular fashion. Then when he realizes, even though the locust *has* lost a leg, the locust can fly, and he can't, we suddenly sense the wall between the husband and wife again. Even though she tries to reach him, she can't quite make it. And it ends on this note of slight bitterness. Is this theme of man's lack of communication, this wall that separates people—one wonders, if it could be hurdled, it would be marvelous—would you say that this is a recurring theme in your work?

Gordimer: Yes, I'm afraid it is. I must admit it. It seems to recur again and again. In the highly personal things like the one you've mentioned, with the locust, and also when I've written about black and white in this country—because I've written usually about the borderland, the kind of frontier where black and white *do* meet, to a certain extent, and more or less as equals, though you can never be equal in an unequal society, you can not make up by any kind of personal ethic for the set-up around you—but anyway, I have dealt *mostly* with this kind of half-world where people do meet—black and white—and because of the general set-up around them, and other inequalities forced upon them, they tend *just* to go past, *just* to miss. I must admit I have written again and again about the moment of communication that doesn't *quite* come off.

Terkel: I think the second story in *The Soft Voice of the Serpent* is perhaps a better example; it's called "The Catch." It deals with the Indian, and we should point out that in South Africa the Indian is considered non-white, a non-European. This is about a couple in Durban, as I recall, vacationing. They meet this Indian who has a big fish, and they're friendly with him, but they never quite make it. They give him a lift in their car, yet we know that there is a wall that separates them. This theme again. You live in a country where this question is paramount. They—the couple—can't avoid being patronizing.

Gordimer: I remember in that particular story they'd been friendly with the Indian every day on the beach, but then one day their white friends come to see them, and it's on that day that he makes his big catch, and rushes up full of pleasure because he's got this big fish, and *this* time they're embarrassed by his company. They really don't want him. I *have* written about that sort of thing quite often.

Terkel: You said a moment ago that one could have a personal ethic that ignores the color bar, but even this will fail if the society itself is based upon an unethical premise. Would you mind expanding on this a bit?

Gordimer: This is something I've been coming to think about lately, and that I've written about in this latest book of mine, *Occasion for Loving*. And that is: the inevitable discrepancy between, for want of a better word, what one calls "the liberal attitude" and the decencies implied in a sort of liberal way of life, with an accent on decent personal relations and, I would say, the almost impossibility of making a go of it in a society that is opposed to this sort of thing. You can say, well, I don't see any difference between black and white people. I choose the people that I like, and I have a certain standard of behavior that is general, no matter what color or creed or anything else. But, it doesn't work in a society where, in the general framework, people *are* judged by the color of their skin.

Terkel: When I first landed here—it seems years ago, but it was just about six days ago—at the Jan Smuts Airport, I don't know what it was, maybe reading your short stories, maybe it was a precon-ceived notion, somehow I had this feeling in landing: an air of unreality. Everybody was gay and charming and gracious. There was a party for us. There were toasts made. And I thought—among all the white faces—that these people were on a reserve, that these people were those who were isolated, rather than those they thought they were putting on the reserve. Is this fact or fantasy on my part? This feeling.

Gordimer: The feeling that the happy, comfortable life of the whites was somehow unreal . . . .

Terkel: Yes.

Gordimer: It's very curious—and one doesn't want to be stuffy about it—but that's one of the strange things about South Africa, it's such a beautiful country, and it's somehow a *climate* for happiness—this is very ironic when you think of the things that go on here. But on the physical level, one can't help enjoying this, and responding to it. I'm sure you felt it yourself, being here. But, of course, there *are* people who live *only* on that level. Who don't come off it; who never look around; who happen to be white, and so don't feel. They only get the advantages—so-called advantages—of the color bar and nothing else.

Terkel: I think the point I was trying to make, was the fact that a great deal of development is taking place here now, and more and more the government is putting the African, the black man, away from the white man through the policy of apartheid, in which the city will be all white and the townships all black. I read in the papers, your papers—the *Daily Mail*—about the movement of blacks out of Johannesburg, who are being put in townships or reserves in rural communities. But, somehow, I had the feeling that the *white* man was putting *himself* in a reserve.

Gordimer: Yes, I think the white man *has* put himself in a reserve, and is doing so more and more. That, of course, does give you this feeling of unreality. Especially when you arrive in an official place like the airport where they really *do* apply apartheid. Where you don't even see a black waiter. You get the idea this is a completely white country until you step outside, and the black man comes along to carry your baggage to your car.

Terkel: What I thought was more unreal, and strange, was taking the bus through town. The very genial guide is telling us about Johannesburg. We're all whites—a number of VIP's, so-called, in this bus—and there are all these black faces staring at us along the streets. They weren't smiling, though the guide was telling us these are a very happy people, irresponsible, childlike, and happy. Neither were they hostile. The look, I say, was bland. It's hard to tell what was being thought as they saw this bus going through, but I'm sure it's a sight they see many times.

Gordimer: It's a familiar one. And if they had to stop and register some emotion every time they saw a bus full of white people going through the town, it would be very trying. That's the paradox. In the town itself, as you probably noticed, despite all the doorways divided—one for black and one for white—and the buses for white and the ones for black: in the streets you're mingling *all* the time. And, even despite job reservations at work, black and white are working together all the time. They may not use the same recreation facilities, and they don't have the same cloak rooms and lunch rooms and so on, but they are working together. So it's always a contradiction.

Terkel: It's this crazy contradiction that seems to tie people up in one way or another. It seems to keep them from being more natural, more themselves.

Gordimer: They are always having to observe limits that aren't really laid down. You're perhaps working in a shop, and you've got a handyman. Or in a woman's dress shop, you've got someone doing the ironing or have an alteration hand who is black, and a kind of friendly feeling, a comradeship comes up between the people, and all the time they have to keep up—it's bred in them, and they're conditioned to it—they have to keep up this separateness, they have to block off their own feelings of friendship toward each other. This happens all the time.

Terkel: An unnatural kind of law, let's say. Unnatural behavior. . . . You mentioned climate earlier: it's incredibly beautiful and exquisite here. I wonder if there isn't a connection in one way or another between the sudden storms, the exquisite sky: whether this hasn't something to do with making this whole thing so unrealistic. The unnatural social set-up and the most natural and beautiful of climatic set-ups.

Gordimer: Yes, I should think it probably has got something to do with it. Certainly it's striking, isn't it, when you come from some-where else. I didn't leave South Africa until I was 30, something which now astonishes me because I've been around a lot since then. But I really only realized when I got out and came back again the contrast between this very strange life that we live here and the innocence, one might say, of the landscape around us.

Terkel: Isn't it as though there's an innocence at work, too, perverse though it might be, an innocence in applying a law which we call apartheid. Deep down isn't there a realization this can't quite make it, even by those that seek to apply it? I'm asking you to probe into the minds of others, which is an unfair thing to ask. . . .

Gordimer: I wouldn't use the word "innocence" in this connec-tion at all. I don't think that the ideology of apartheid or its application is innocent. I think it's evil. It's evil in its concept and it's evil in its application. And it can't even be excused on the grounds of naïveté.

Terkel: The authorities who apply this law: do you feel they are a lost people who seek to retain a certain way of life that is no longer pertinent to a society, and no longer relevant?

Gordimer: I think they are people who refuse to face up to historical fact, quite apart from anything else. They are simply trying to preserve a way of life that suits them—at whatever cost to anyone else.

Terkel: This evil has other implications, doesn't it? Apartheid itself must lead to other kinds of repressions. I notice, for example, there are different regulations concerning the arts. Censorship. Repressions of one sort or another. They *do* go hand in hand, I suppose?

Gordimer: You can't devise laws which will operate only against one section of society. It seems to be a queer kind of law-of-returns that these things come home to roost; and there's a very good example of this now in the Censorship Bill, which, it seems, will definitely go through this present session in Parliament—because the people, the artists and writers, it will hit hardest will be the Afrikaners. In particular the writers. There they are, writing in this youngest language in the world, and it's a wonderful achievement—Afrikaans [South African Dutch]—make no mistake about it. Things like the Censorship Law will kill it because it prevents the free growth and experimentation of Afrikaans writers. People who write in English can command an audience wherever English is spoken, presupposing that they are good enough: but no matter how good you are if you're an Afrikaans writer, no matter how brilliant, you are confined to your particular audience. This language is spoken in only one part of the world. And if your views don't suit the government—and con-sequently they won't suit the publisher either, because he cannot sell your work anywhere else—you're simply shut up, your mouth is closed.

Terkel: These Afrikaans writers: are there some who come to mind?

Gordimer: Well, I'm not really qualified to talk about them except in a very general way because I'm a very poor linguist, and I've read very very little in Afrikaans. But, I do know a couple, and I have kept in touch generally with the trends in Afrikaans writing. I hear, on good authority from friends of mine—from a distinguished Afrikaans poet, who is a friend of mine, who was one of the first people to encourage me when I began to write—that there's a new develop-ment among Afrikaans fiction writers.

The poets, let me say, have always been good. Exceptional. But the fiction writers tend to turn out a lot of cheap historical romances and so on; they kept well off the questions of the day, well off any color question or anything like that. But now they seem to be changing: so my friend tells me. Not only in the political sense, but just in the general sense of literary experimentation. There's even a kind of coming Beat Generation of Afrikaner writers. As you can imagine, this will not go down well with the strict prudery, the Calvinist laws of the new Censorship Bill, which hits out not only against political outspokenness but any other kind. So these people are really in great trouble because, as I've said before, there is no where else they can be published.

Terkel: Are there a number of black *African* writers who come to mind? who have something fresh to say about their country, about the world?

Gordimer: It's a very curious situation. It seems—I'm prepared to stick my neck out over this—that the literary language of South Africa, for black South Africans, is going to be English. It *is* English for those who have begun to write in any serious sort of way, apart from purely scholarly things, the odd epic poem, or the historical legends, and so on. The modern writers and the urban writers write in English. Most of them begin as journalists on the one or two magazines and papers here that are published in English. This is a kind of apprenticeship to using the language, and from there on they go on to write.

There have been two or three. It sounds very very little, out of this vast black population, but when you consider that English is a second language and that their education could be better, and so on—it's not bad. And there are two or three who really are good, and who have something to say, and who know how to say it. They have been accepted as capable writers in the outside world, in England, in America, and have been published there. What they have to say is naturally about their particular situation as intellectuals in a society that provides for people of their own color only as peasants and workers. There's no room for African intellectuals in this society.

Theirs is a miserable lot, as you can imagine. You get this situation: you get people like Peter Abrahams and later Ezekiel Mphahlele, and one or two others, who have left this country because as African intellectuals there was no place for them here, no suitable job for them, and no possible life for them at all. Having left the country, or even while they were here, they wrote about this situation, usually in the form of autobiographical books. I call them escape books because that's what they are. They are books about breaking out of the limitations of their life: and not in just a physical sense. These books—apart from the fact that they have literary merit—show how intellectual Africans feel, and how articulate Africans express what other Africans feel.

Now these books, without exception, are banned in this country. Peter Abrahams' *Tell Freedom* [Knopf, 1954], which was the story of his life as a young boy, and how he grew up and began to write: that is banned here. Mphahlele's book called *Down Second Avenue* is also banned. Alfred Hutchinson, who was a journalist, wrote *his* escape book, more of an escape book in the physical sense, which was called *The Road to Ghana* [John Day, 1960] and that was banned.

The government, on the one hand, talks about Bantustans, and allowing the African to develop along his own lines, and civilizing him and giving him culture, but whenever the African people produce somebody articulate, somebody with talent and creativity, they don't permit his work to be available to people here, white or black. So you get this paradox, from which you can draw your own conclusions.

Terkel: This leads us to the subject of Bantustans and to the matter of the new education laws, which, as I understand it, ostensibly are designed to help black Africans to recognize their roots, to return to their heritage, to speak their language, whether it be the Zulu or whatever. In truth, however, they're pointed toward cutting Africans off from the mainstream of what's happening in the world. You spoke of English as being the language of the new African writer, but English is de-emphasized in this whole new educational approach, or am I wrong in this?

Gordimer: The accent in the educational approach—which incidentally is not so new, it came in the early 50s, the Bantu Education Act—put a ceiling on African education. It seems, I think, such a tragic paradox that we have in this country the highest literacy rate in the whole continent. And that's something to be proud of. But, unfortunately, this pride is cut right off because the education goes so far and no further. You can matriculate and can go to a Bantu university; once you get to university level, however, there's no

getting away from it, the educational opportunities are *not* the same.
And now, since the Bantu Education Act, the educational opportunities even at secondary schools are not the same: the standard of
Bantu education is lower than the standard of education applied to
whites. So it's a way of creating a second-class nation, isn't it? It
seems so to me. And it's a very effective way of doing this. It prevents
people from attaining a certain educational standard simply because
they are black.

Terkel: You spoke of books that were banned, books that deal
with very pertinent themes, and perhaps may or may not offend the
authorities or frighten them. Have you had difficulties—because you
are outspoken in these matters, your novels deal with life as it is, not
as some think it should be—have you encountered difficulties on this
score?

Gordimer: I've had one novel of mine banned in the paperback
edition. It was not banned in the hardcover edition.

Terkel: You're batting 500, then, on that book. Now we come to
your recent novel, *Occasion for Loving,* published by Viking [in
America].

Gordimer: This book hasn't yet come to South Africa. The
English edition comes here; the American edition doesn't. So I don't
know what the reaction will be in this country to this particular book.

Terkel: What is the theme of the novel?

Gordimer: Well, it's got a number of themes, but I'm very bad at
talking about my own books. I get tripped up in my own
complexities. . . . Well, I'll try. It's about liberals. And it's about what
we were talking about before, the attempt of people to apply a
personal standard of values, to oppose it to the social set-up within
which they live: in this case, liberals who have no color feeling and
who don't really mind the color-bar, who decide that within their
private lives they will live the way they want to live, the decent way.
I've tried to show how this works out in conflict with the situation
here, and whether, indeed, it can be successful. Whether it is
successful, or whether it is a failure. Whether a personal liberal
attitude is a failure.

Terkel: What do you think?

Gordimer: As it works out in the novel, it's a failure. So you can
draw your own conclusions.

Terkel: We're back to this theme, and I suppose it's the theme of the world today: of the individual and society; the individual who seeks what he feels is a decent way of behavior, and yet the society in which he lives may be somewhat indecent in nature. Here, then, is the problem: how can he operate within this framework? And this, basically, is the theme of *Occasion for Loving.*

Gordimer: Yes. But one opposes things like the color-bar not only and not necessarily politically but from within, from the strength of personal values. The novel explores how far one can succeed with this.

Terkel: Often we hear the case being stated for the writer to live away from the world, that is, to live in his ivory tower—I'm not referring to art for art's sake, now, just being away from the turbulence of things—yet you are, what's the French word, *engagé,* you are involved.

Gordimer: Yes, but—how should I put it, I'm not really a very politically-minded person, but living perhaps not just in South Africa and that situation, but I think in the whole world today—you simply cannot be an aware person without being involved. It's so closely involved in one's life. And so far as political issues are concerned, I've really approached them from the inside. They are implicit in my life and in my values, and that is how I've come to write about them. I wrote about them from that point of view not out of any hope that I could persuade anybody to change their minds, nor to make any kind of propaganda; I couldn't do that, I wouldn't know how to.

Terkel: Clearly, then, your writing is that of a person who is emotionally and intellectually involved with the world in which she lives, yet who is not on a platform stating a certain position. Someone has said that South Africa's problem has perhaps been best dramatized by its writers and not by its politicians.

Gordimer: Yes, I must say I think that's true. It *certainly* is true. There's another dimension added by a poet or a writer. It's a dimension that a newspaper report, or anything of a purely factual nature, never quite gives.

Terkel: Earlier you spoke of people scarred by a circumstance or by a law: in one of your stories, "The Train from Rhodesia," the little indignities that the blacks suffer at the hands of the whites are dramatized.

Gordimer: I think when you live here you become very conscious
of them, you suffer from them, as this girl did: she suffered from
seeing her husand or lover demean himself by falling into this black-
white cliché of beating down the African, who had made this little
artifact which he wanted to buy, and getting it from him for less than
it was worth. She suffered really from seeing herself demeaned
through her lover. But, of course, when you live here, *you* often deal
out these things, too, and then you suffer from that as well. You *are*
white and you deliver these hurts, sometimes unwittingly, to Africans
and they deliver them back to you. So you cannot be unaware of
them.

Terkel: This is a key point, right here, when you say that he
demeans himself and she as well is demeaned. The white man who is
demeaning the black man in truth cuts himself down, does he not?
I'm thinking of apartheid. If there is a chief sufferer, it probably is the
white child. In America at Little Rock there was a photograph, a very
celebrated photograph, of a little Negro girl being led into the school
by the National Guardsmen, while on the side the white adults are
spitting at her, or shouting at her. And it occurred to me that *she* is
not as big a loser as they are, or their kids are, the kids who are being
taught to be *Ubermenschen,* in a sense, different. It's these white kids
who are the real losers rather than the little Negro girl who—to use a
phrase by James Baldwin—knows her name, knows who she is. I
wonder whether this isn't, in a very dramatic way, the story of South
Africa?

Gordimer: I think it is in the long run. I can't say it is *now* because
the white children are still lapped in this false security of white
supremacy. To put it absolutely coldly, from the most self-seeking
point of view it's an absurd preparation for future life in Africa. It's an
absurd preparation for one's growth as a human being. And, believe
me, I speak of this with conviction because in my generation one of
the great experiences for us—or people like myself—was this second
birth that I mentioned. In a more liberal time than there is now,
fifteen or ten years ago, we broke out of the color-bar—out of our
old feelings and our old convictions. But now, because of the laws of
the country, we see our children being brought up in the same white
supremacy convention, and they will have to go through it all over
again in a much more difficult time. They will be totally unfitted for
life in Africa, and life generally will be more difficult for them.

Terkel: So they are more the losers than the African child.

Gordimer: That much less human.

Terkel: This is connected with what I said when I disembarked that day at the airport, that day so long ago, eight days ago: it was the whites who were on the reserve, and not the black men. They put themselves on this island themselves; there they were toasting one another, and yet I felt this tremendous insecurity. Earlier you called it evil. You think, then, there is this awareness on their part that what they're doing is evil?

Gordimer: I think we're talking now of two different things: I'd like to draw a distinction. We were talking before of apartheid and of people who genuinely believe in it and who are applying it, and now we are talking about the great mass of white people who may not be actual supporters of the policy of apartheid but who live in a kind of indifference, a terrible kind of indifference, who just want to see the status quo maintained, who just want to see white supremacy maintained. They're prepared—in a shamed kind of way—to back whoever they feel has a strong enough hand to keep it going another twenty years, another ten years, however long they can make the time.

Terkel: Apparently there isn't the slightest care, then, for the next generation.

Gordimer: I don't think so. *They* wouldn't believe this—because you will see that they send their children to good schools, and they provide nice homes for them, and, within the white ethic, they tell them to behave decently, to be kind, and honest, and so on. But— that big *but* is that—it does not extend to humanity in general; it doesn't extend across the color-bar.

Terkel: We've been talking about apartheid; it seems to come in automatically. Someone has said that the subject of any cocktail party, any party to be held anywhere, in South Africa—it can start out carefree, gay—inevitably returns to the subject referred to as "the great South African obsession."

Gordimer: Yes, it does. It's quite true. It seems very hard to get away from: for the simple reason that it is so closely intertwined with our lives.

Terkel: You said earlier you'd be a writer no matter where you were, yet living here do you find that your themes are determined by the fact that you live in South Africa?

Gordimer: Well, yes, I suppose so, because they're implicit in my writing: just as writers in the South in America . . . they cannot help it; they've lived and have been brought up in this situation. What else shall they write about? It creeps in.

Terkel: A Carson McCullers, a Flannery O'Connor, a Tennessee Williams . . . .

Gordimer: Yes. And even if it doesn't come in directly, even if there is no conflict between black and white, no meeting place between black and white, the way the whites are, the way the blacks are, is shaped by the way the blacks and whites have lived together.

Terkel: There's a title of one of your short stories that I find very attractive: "Is There Nowhere Else Where We Can Meet?" Somehow this title seems to have an *overall* symbolism. A white girl is going into a suburban golf course and is accosted by a black man who steals her purse.

Gordimer: She's attacked by a black man. That is their point of meeting; this is the only thing that could bring them together.

Terkel: "Is There Nowhere Else Where We Can Meet?" Doesn't that seem to describe the whole white-black relationship? Is there nowhere else we can meet? No other way? Here are these repressive laws that are being instituted, and as a result of which, I'm sure, there's a reaction, one way or the other. I suppose the more repressive the laws are, the more emphatic the reaction will be the other way. I'm asking you this question now, Nadine Gordimer, as a writer and a South African: Is there nowhere else we can meet?

Gordimer: I think that the way things are going now, there *isn't* any other place . . . where we can meet. It's getting, it seems, to the stage where there's *no* civilized meeting place between black and white anymore. None that is recognized.

Terkel: Don't you see any *modus vivendi* anywhere here?

Gordimer: Do I think that we could have a non-racial society here? That such a thing would work?

Terkel: I'm asking you this.

Gordimer: Well, I'm thinking about it. It's very difficult to answer because this is a question with *so* many emotional overtones. I don't know whether I could trust myself to tell you the truth, or even admit to myself the truth. . . .

I'm not sure it would work anymore. I honestly believe that it could

have worked even as late as after the war—if things had gone
politically differently, if the whites had behaved differently. Even as
late as after the war, I think we might have managed it in this country.
But, then again, I *wonder* when I look at the picture of the whole
continent of Africa becoming more and more the black man's
continent. So, I don't know. But something in me still makes me
believe that it *could* have worked.

Oddly enough, there are points of meeting between South African
whites and their fellow South African black men that you don't meet
with in other parts of Africa. And to me, that's the great tragedy: that
this opportunity—it might have been a unique one on the continent
—has been brutally thrown away. Cynically thrown away. I don't
think the Africans want it anymore.

Terkel: You don't think the black man, the African wants it
anymore?

Gordimer: No. And that's the deciding factor in the end. It won't
be for us to say anymore what *we* want. And I don't think that *they*
want it anymore.

Terkel: You mean that they have *had* it.

Gordimer: Yes.

Terkel: There were the attempts, and eventually a time came. . . .

Gordimer: It was too little and too late. But I may be wrong.

Terkel: Is there any way out that you see?

Gordimer: One can't begin to think of a way out now. Supposing
one could get rid of the apartheid government and put in its place—
what? . . . It's very difficult to say: a non-racial government? some
kind of coalition between moderate black and white elements. It's
very, very difficult to say whether there would still be time even now,
today, or tomorrow, for such a thing to come about.

Terkel: Is there something else in the works for you that you care
to talk about? In writing?

Gordimer: You mean something that I'm busy with?

Terkel: Yes.

Gordimer: No, no. Not at the moment. But I don't think one's
come to the end of writing about life here anymore than life
anywhere else.

Terkel: It sounds as though there's a new stage you're entering.
You, yourself, don't know what that stage will be. . . .

Gordimer: No. You only know it as you live it. It's your situation, and then it goes along—you live it.

Terkel: Now it amounts to day to day discoveries, doesn't it?

Gordimer: Yes. Yes, I suppose one could call it that.

Nadine Gordimer: A Writer in South Africa

Alan Ross/1965

From *London Magazine*, 5.2 (May 1965), 20–28. Reprinted by permission of *London Magazine*.

Nadine Gordimer, whose new volume of short stories, *Not for Publication,* appears later this month, was born and brought up at Springs, an indeterminate mining town thirty miles from Johannesburg. Its sprawling hideousness is redeemed only by the huge tawny mine dumps whose crumbling ramparts are to the gold towns of the Rand what the Pyramids are to Cairo. Most of Miss Gordimer's working life has, however, been spent in Johannesburg. There, in a jacaranda-surrounded house whose garden overlooks the shiny corrugated-iron roofs of the tilting northern suburbs, she now lives with her husband, Reinhold Cassirer, their children and various dogs.

The basis of her remarks in the following pages was a trip we made together to Swaziland in January. In no sense an interview, the resulting dialogue, as I have formalized it, is merely a one-sided and much simplified version of various conversations spread over several days, the consequence of my own curiosity about the actual hazards of functioning as a writer in contemporary South Africa. Nadine Gordimer's story, "The Worst Thing of All," appeared in our February issue, and a biographical piece, in our *Leaving School* series, in May 1963.—A.R.

A.R.: There is, perhaps, a difference in the nature of your allegiance to South Africa as a writer and to it as a person?

N.G.: I have no allegiance to SA as a writer. Like any other writer, my allegiance is to what Proust called 'That book of unknown signs within me no one could help me read by any rule, for its reading consists in an act of creation in which no one can take our place and in which no one can collaborate.' He goes on to say—significantly for me—'And how many turn away from writing it, how many tasks will one not assume to avoid that one! Every event, whether it was the Dreyfus affair or the war, furnished excuses to writers for not deciphering that book; they wanted to assert the triumph of Justice, to recreate the moral unity of the Nation, and they had no time to think of literature. But those were only excuses because either they did not possess or had ceased to possess genius, that is, instinct. For it is instinct which dictates duty and intelligence which offers pretexts for avoiding it. But excuses do not count, the artist must at all times follow his instinct, which makes art the most real thing, the most austere school in life and the last true judgment.' This does not mean to say that I think I should turn my back on 'my' Dreyfus affair (bannings and detentions without trial), or 'my' war (against apartheid), but that their significance should be nothing less than deeply implicit in whatever I write, since it is *there:* part of the substance of life within which my instinct as a writer must struggle. Unlike Sartre, I believe a 'writer's morality' is valid, and the temptation to put one's writing at the service of a cause—whether it is fighting the colour-bar or 'the momentary renunciation of literature in order to educate the people', etc—is a betrayal. Similarly, I should turn back upon him his question 'In a country lacking leaders, in Africa, for instance, how could a native educated in Europe refuse to become a professor, even at the price of his literary vocation?' How should he not? As much as increased crops and more schools and universities, Africa needs an articulated consciousness other than that of newspaper headlines and political speeches.

As a person, my allegiance to South Africa is responsibility toward the situation to which I was born. A white South African, brought up on the soft side of the colour-bar, I have gone through the whole packaged-deal evolution that situation has to offer—unquestioning acceptance of the superiority of my white skin, as a small child; acceptance of the paternal attitude that 'they' are only human, after all, as an older child; questioning of these attitudes as I grew up and read and experienced outside the reading and experience that formed my inheritance; and finally, re-birth as a human being among other human beings, with all this means in the face of the discrimination that sorts them into colours and races. Whether I like it or not, this has been the crucial experience of my life, as the war was for some people, or membership of the Communist Party for others. I have no religion, no political dogma—only plenty of doubts about everything except my conviction that the colour-bar is wrong and utterly indefensible. Thus I have found the basis of a moral code that is valid for me. Reason and emotion meet in it: and perhaps that is as near to faith as I shall ever get.

A.R.: Although none of your books is formally political, would you agree that the South African situation has conditioned you as a writer to an extent that could not have happened in any other country? Or put another way, that the uniqueness of your situation has meant that, almost regardless of natural tendencies, you have developed one way rather than another?

N.G.: Yes, through the extraordinary way in which the political situation has moulded the lives of the people around me. Not only obvious confrontations of black and white are affected; whites among themselves are shaped by their peculiar position, just as black people are by theirs. I write about their private selves; often, even in the most private situations, they are what they are because their lives are regulated and their mores formed by the political situation. You see, in South Africa, society *is* the political situation. To paraphrase, one might say (too often), politics is character in SA. I am not a politically-minded person by nature. I don't suppose, if I had lived elsewhere, my writing would have reflected politics much. If at all. As it is, I have come to the abstractions of politics through the flesh and blood of individual behaviour. I didn't know what politics was about until I saw it all *happening to people*. If I've been influenced to recognize man as a political animal, in my writing, then that's come about through living in South Africa.

Is this a limitation? How can I say? I honestly don't think I've ever sacrificed the possible revelation of a private contradiction to make a political point. My method is to let the general seep up through the individual, whether or not the theme can be summed up afterwards as 'Jealousy', 'Racial Conflict' or what-have-you. Despite what I've said above, quite a lot of my writing could have come about absolutely anywhere—the stories in particular; some of the stories are even set in other countries. My private preoccupations remain, running strongly beneath or alongside or intertwined with the influence of the political situation. I don't think I should allow myself to blame any limitations on the impingement of politics; in another situation, I should probably have developed other limitations and found other factors to take the blame.

A.R.: In South Africa the writer walks a fraying tightrope: do you think that the literature of protest has little meaning there or that South African writers could have been more effective as a group than they have?

N.G.: I don't think so. Of course, the country has thrown up a number of people who have climbed on the bandwagon of interest in this country as a 'problem'; they seize upon the most sensational aspects of life here, the most obvious, and concoct something calculated to be a best seller. Then there are others, people of sincerity and intelligence, who genuinely are moved to write by a sense of outrage. They produce neat documentary novels. Neither the former nor the latter are writers, and one mustn't look to them for a literature of protest any more than any other kind of literature.

Here, again, I think that the protest can only be as good as the writing. And there is only a handful of writers, despite the numbers of people who are writing.

Does 'effective' mean the same as 'good', in this context? I take it that it does, since the effectiveness—in terms of provoking direct action, bringing about change in legislation—of any protest literature is surely doubtful. If effectiveness is measured by whether or not a novel, or story or poem makes people doubt, where they were complacent, then I should say that within South Africa itself, protest literature has made little mark, although it is widely read among white people. They seem to read it as if it were all happening somewhere else, to some other people. Abroad, I think it's at least made people realize where the wretched country *is*, if nothing else . . .

A.R.: Have any particular writers influenced you either technically or in the way you have tried to use political material unpolitically or vice-versa? Whom among contemporary writers do you admire most?

N.G.: I find it's very hard not to lie when answering this question. In fact, I don't think one ever answers it twice with the same names. You outgrow writers, as you outgrow friends, and out of shame, 'forget' them. Then, of course, there are the writers who influence you profoundly, forever, and whose influence has disappeared, become something new of your own; and there are writers—perhaps of a single story or poem—who make a brief revelation and then drop away.

If I think about it, I find I can more or less sort out the specific way in which certain writers influenced me. Lawrence was one (like almost everyone else in my generation I went on a great Lawrence bender round about the age of seventeen). He influenced my way of looking at landscape and the natural world in general—his sensuousness dilated my senses and brought up close to me rocks, petals, and the fur of animals around me. Henry James made me conscious of form—a single sentence as much as an entire novel—as something other than what I had taken for granted as dictated by the sense and story themselves. He also gave me a predilection for circumlocutory sentences whose numerous clauses, in my hands, adhered to each other like scotch tape. It's taken me years to extricate myself, and I still find odd examples cropping up here and there in my writing.

From Hemingway I learnt to leave things out. Or rather, to hear the essential in dialogue. E. M. Forster influenced my handling of human relationships and, indeed, my conception of them. Yeats, Auden, Rilke and Donne, Virginia Woolf, *Middlemarch*, André Gide, *Dubliners*, Proust and Eudora Welty, all influenced me at the most formative time. Later came Conrad; and latest, Camus. His thinking has influenced my attitudes in the way that E. M. Forster's once did; there has been nothing comparable in between. But here I am drawing the distinction between writers who influence one's thinking and writers who influence one's writing. I don't think my writing can be influenced any longer.

Among story writers I greatly admire Patrick White and Bernard Malamud. Among novelists, V. S. Naipaul, Saul Bellow, Graham Greene. And single works, like Muriel Spark's *Memento Mori,* Günter Grass's *Tin Drum.* Natalia Ginzburg's first two books, Golding's early works. Not-so-contemporary, but read by me contemporarily—Italo Svevo, Malcolm Lowry.

A.R.: You began, and one tends to consider you essentially, as a short-story writer. Do you feel, because of economic or other pressures, that you will find yourself increasingly writing novels?

N.G.: I don't consider myself a short-story writer primarily— whatever other people may think—because I really do want to write novels. That is, I want to write both. I have written a few stories that satisfy me but I've not written a novel that comes anywhere near doing so.

A.R.: You are married to a European, have travelled in Europe and have many friends there. Suppose it became possible, would you like to move, and to where?

N.G.: I shouldn't like to leave Africa. If I did, I think I could live happily in England in the country.

A.R.: Have you any immediate writing plans?

N.G.: They are always very vague. I want to write a good novel. I'm interested in attempting only very complex things in a novel, things I probably shan't be able to bring off. I think people who write stories, as well, are likely to feel this about novels; they know how much can be done within the compass of a short story—they're not interested merely in opening the same thing out like a concertina.

More generally—I've become interested lately in self-esteem as a motive for human behaviour, and I'd like to go into it. The desire for it seems to me often to be stronger than the drive of sex, money, or power.

A.R.: Do your books develop from imaginary characters in real situations or real characters in imaginary situations?

N.G.: Both. Sometimes one, sometimes the other.

My stories often originate in what might be called the tail-tip of a situation as it is whisked out of sight. A look, a sentence hanging in mid-air (I'm a great unconscious eavesdropper, always have been, on street corners, in restaurants, planes, etc). A train of associations begins to play out; the story begins to form about the fragment. When stories arise out of actual experiences of my own, there is usually a lapse of months or even years between the happening and the writing, a lapse during which the experience lies dormant, gathering like a magnet those characters, phrases, ideas, ancillary events, that belong with it in kind, and will transform it. Time means nothing in that part of the mind where this takes place; something that happened ten years ago on the other side of the world coexists with something observed yesterday.

A.R.: Could you define for us the several layers of Johannesburg society?

N.G.: Officially, white-black. Within the overall white hierarchy, a division into English-speaking, and Afrikaans-speaking. Politically, the

Afrikaners at the top, but social standing did not come to them commensurately with the rise of political power, and you won't meet many of them in the smart country clubs. (To do them justice, they are free of social snobbery, and probably wouldn't want to be members, anyway, even if they were welcome.) Socially, then, English-speaking company directors and industrialists on top, the professions next, then *white* white-collar workers, builders, then plumbers, miners, electricians, and lastly taxi-drivers, bus conductors and postmen. Lower than that the white hierarchy doesn't go; our dustmen are all black. And our road-workers and sweepers.

In the black—or rather shaded—population, the hierarchy measured by colour-bar restrictions goes something like this: Coloured (mixed blood) and Indian (no passes carried); African. Within the three groups, the social hierarchy tends to follow an educational hierarchy: teachers, lawyers, doctors, journalists, writers and (in the case of women) social workers and nurses; clerks; domestic workers and labourers. The Indians would include business men in the first category, and they rarely work as nurses and never as domestic servants.

Political leaders have a special status among Africans and Indians, and this status is maintained across the colour-bar in the small white minority which identifies itself with, or at least respects, the African struggle for equal rights.

A.R.: Are your physical surroundings important to you?

N.G.: Yes. Though, as for working conditions, I can put up with practically anything except cold feet, and a radio playing anywhere within hearing.

A.R.: O'Hara once remarked that the people who interested him most, jockeys, billiard players, footballers, etc, somehow never got into his stories. Is that at all true of yourself?

N.G.: No. There's nothing remotely like a literary life in South Africa and so one is constantly moving (undetected, as it were, and naturally) among people doing all sorts of jobs and living all sorts of lives outside the intellectual context. You may get lonely for your own particular kind, but you don't lose touch with your general kind.

And yet—yes. The appalling language barriers in South Africa keep one deaf to certain people's lives—specially country people. They don't get into my stories much because I don't know enough about them. And African gangsters. They don't get in either, for obvious reasons. And heaven knows when their Genet will appear.

A.R.: Where were you first published, and by what stages did your relationship with *The New Yorker* develop?

N.G.: I was first published in South Africa when I was fifteen, at the beginning of the war, in a liberal fortnightly started, I think, by the politician J. H. Hofmeyr. My contribution was a story, and I kept the secret of my age out of the vanity of wanting to be taken for a grown-up writer. During and just after the war, quite a few politico-literary magazines had a short life in South Africa. I was completely uninterested in politics but I was writing stories, and they published them. One of the best and longest-lived of the little magazines was a monthly published by some curious brotherhood called the Society of Jews and Christians, and the editor, Amelia Levy, encouraged me in the best way by publishing those stories in which I was forgetting the writers I'd read and really beginning to find my own voice and themes. Doris Lessing was another of her protégées. Then I met Uys Krige, the Afrikaans poet—also through having a story published in a little magazine, a purely literary one that he was editing—and when the editor of an anthology approached him for a contribution of his own work, he reproached the man for always publishing stuff from the same old names, and insisted that he read a long story of mine. It went into the anthology; I was about twenty-two by then and had no need to conceal my age. Then Uys Krige suggested that I should send some stories overseas, and dug up the name of a girl he'd been friendly with in Italy, an American who had said she was a literary agent, at home. My stories began to appear in American little magazines, and in *Harper's Magazine;* to my amazement I had letters from several American publishers, asking me if I had a novel to offer them. I didn't. In the meantime, a small, new publishing house in Johannesburg brought out a book of my early stories.

One day I got a cable from my American agent to say that the *New Yorker* had bought a story called "A Watcher of the Dead." That was in 1950, and the proofs were the only ones I ever had with Harold Ross's famous comments on them; he died soon after. From the beginning my particular editor was Katharine White, wife of E. B. White. She was a marvellous editor, she knew what you could do and she wouldn't let you fumble anything, and on my subsequent visits to America I began a friendship with the Whites that has outlasted the other relationship—she is retired, now. I get irritated when people say: 'You write for the *New Yorker*, don't you?' I've never written a line *for* anyone or any magazine in my life (I'm not talking of commissioned articles, of course); I write what I want and if the *New Yorker* has wanted to publish it, they have done so. I haven't had a story in the *New Yorker* for more than two years, because they haven't been getting what they had learnt to expect from me. That's the only criticism I would make of the much-maligned *New Yorker*: it's not that there is a *New Yorker* 'formula' to which writers are encouraged to conform (a sort of plot-theme machine, with levers marked Aged Grandmother, Crummy Child-hood, Suburban Suffering?) but that once having bought a particular kind of story from you because it was something fresh and original, they seem to yearn to have you go on writing the same kind of story for the rest of your life. They are not interested in growing pains over something new; but who wants to go on doing successfully what he can do with one hand tied behind his back? You begin to feel much more excited about your near-misses and to want their interest granted.

A.R.: If you consider your new stories in relation to your first book, do you see much change?

N.G.: Much more complex in organization, I want them to *do* more in the space of the attention they take up when they are read, if you know what I mean. More intellectual in approach. Less concerned with catching the surface shimmer; preoccupied not so much with the how, but the why. When I look at the good stories in my first book (some of them are awful) I realize that I have lost something, too; the eye that sees everything as if for the first time, sensuousness, a dancing nervous tension that I shan't find again.

A.R.: Do the terms romantic/realist have any meaning to you in regard to your work, or to yourself as a person?

N.G.: I suppose I am a romantic struggling with reality; for surely this very engagement implies innate romanticism? Do realists question the meaning of reality and their relationship to it? No— because they identify with it. I find it difficult to put a label on myself. One's much more likely to be accurate at finding one for someone else!

A.R.: Do you find that, within South Africa, whatever you write gets measured by the various political yardsticks?

N.G.: Oh yes. And the measurements never tally. The Right finds you're way out Left, and the Left finds you fall short. You get shot at from all sides. It doesn't matter. All writing is posthumous, in this sense, isn't it?

Nadine Gordimer Talks to Andrew Salkey

Andrew Salkey/1969

From *The Listener,* 7 August 1969, 184–85. Reprinted by permission of *The Listener.*

Nadine Gordimer, it has been said of you that you write from a position of intense social involvement. As a South African, what does this mean?

I think it means that I'm totally opposed to apartheid. I've always had this position and defended it at home and abroad. In my own life it means nothing to me and I've lived my life, insofar as one can, ignoring it.

And have you been able to protest in spite of the society in which you live?

I think so. It has been a modest protest. One always feels inadequate and I'm not really a political person. I've never belonged to a political party. So mine has been a little private war.

You have said that a writer must never allow himself to become a propagandist. Yet doesn't the political situation in South Africa intrude and offend as it becomes more and more a part of your consciousness: aren't you forced to protest in your writing?

I suppose if one analyses it, then one calls it protest, but it comes about from inside, as it were. A writer puts his hand down into the great mass of life around him and pulls up all sorts of extraordinary things. He uses the substance of the life around him—that's all he has—and if he does so truthfully, then of course political things come into it, especially in South Africa. Politics, the effects of politics, permeate even the most private sector of people's lives, and this comes into your writing if you're an honest writer, which I hope I am. There is protest there, but it's implicit. I have drawn it from the substance of the society around me.

Have you been banned?

43

Two of my books have been banned and an anthology that I edited was also banned.

You've had, I think, nine books published and yet you've said that they're really all one book. What did you mean by this?
This is a theory I have about most writers, not only about myself. I think that in effect we all write one book, but we write it piecemeal and often from very different points of view throughout our lives. You move on, you change, and your writing changes with this advancement. Or sometimes you regress and the writing appears to go back too. But in the end, for a writer, your work is your life and it's a totality.

You were born in a gold-mining town; educated at Witwatersrand University; you've been writing for about 20 years; you have a daughter and a son; you're a fiercely independent spirit, self-critical, and someone who obviously needs all the diversity of a balanced society to help feed your writing. One wonders why you haven't left South Africa.
All these things, this analysis of what one needs, is fascinating, but one doesn't feel it oneself. I've never lived anywhere else and it seems to me that there's no particular formula for a writer's needs. A writer deals with the situation to which he was born and he deals with it according to the talents that he has—as long as he isn't suppressed entirely and hasn't got to put his writing into a bottom drawer. I haven't left South Africa because of my feeling of commitment to the place as a human being rather than as a writer. If I went to live in England, for instance, where I have my cultural roots, I might be very happy there. I might write quite well there. I don't feel that I would lose my identity as a writer because I was born in Africa: I'll carry Africa with me whenever I need to draw on it. But I do feel that as a human being, as a woman, I would then be living on the surface of whatever country I lived in. I could never have the commitment to the society in an adopted country that I have to my feeling of opposition to apartheid in South Africa.

Are you fearful of exile?
I've asked myself this question and I don't think I am any more. All that I could fear in exile would be that I would dry up. But I think that

I've been writing too long now. If I had left Africa when I was very young, this question obviously would have entered into my thinking about going into exile. But now I feel differently.

You have been unwilling to be partisan. You insist on objectivity. Isn't this very nearly anti-South African?

I think it is very anti-South African in the sense that I'm against the system there. I have the feeling that many of my friends and many braver people than I, who've done a great deal more in the political field, feel that we are the real South Africans because we oppose apartheid, we oppose the colour bar, we dislike the system intensely and fight it. But at the same time we love the country and we feel we are the true South Africans.

What if you were a black South African: would you remain?

If I were a black South African writer, I would leave. It's really impossible for any black writer to stay. It's almost impossible for any black intellectual to stay. And I don't think white South Africans realise quite how much this impoverishes our intellectual life, what a loss it is to the white South Africans who are so keen to keep their white supremacy. How, intellectually, this makes a joke of their so-called supremacy.

To what extent are you able to use your writing as a weapon?

To quite a large extent, I think. First of all in my fiction, where I am writing about South Africa in depth, as it were; and more pointedly and more specifically, I use it when either I write articles or appear, as I do occasionally, on a public platform, criticising aspects of the society in which I live.

How free are you to carry out your protest, not only in your writing but in your social action? Aren't you watched rather closely?

Different people seem to be dealt with differently, according to their fields of activity. Writers, more than any other professional group, are a persecuted group in South Africa. Two well-known writers have lost their passports: Alan Paton and Athol Fugard. I have been dealt with rather differently: my books, two of my books, have been banned. The black African writers have been almost totally wiped out. They don't exist in South African literature any more because all the books of the major writers are banned. One can't even quote a paragraph from anything they've written. This is one of the battles I have taken up and feel myself committed to: not to allow the African writers to be forgotten in South Africa.

One of the very important assets of the literary resistance has been the magazine the Classic. *What has been its effect so far?*

I'm afraid very little, because the *Classic* has a very small circulation and it tends to reach peope who are sympathetic to the whole cause of African literature. I consider that South African literature, if it consists only of white writers, doesn't exist any more than it would do if it consisted only of black writers, and I'm very dubious about its existence as a body of literature today. The *Classic* was started by a group of black and white writers who cared only to produce good writing and were not prepared to take into consideration the political and social taboos against people like this working together, or producing their work together. It has been very much hampered over the last few years as black writers have been banned, because, when they're banned, the *Classic* can no longer publish their work. For this reason there is some disagreement with my own point of view, which is that the *Classic* should go on being published as long as it's not suppressed, because however tragic it is when people are banned, one must still look to new writers and give them a place to publish their work as long as we can continue to do so.

Has the emphasis in the Classic *been on literary excellence, or on the political militancy of the writing?*

It has been on literary excellence, but with the situation in South Africa being what it is, literary excellence can carry implicit protest. For example, if a story is written by an African about the sort of life he is living in a resettlement area to which he has been removed, it is at once a piece of literature and, because it is describing a kind of life that is discounted and that people would rather not hear about, it also becomes a social protest.

Authors and Editors: Nadine Gordimer

Barbara A. Bannon/1970

Reprinted from pages 21–22 of the December 28, 1970 issue of *Publishers Weekly,* published by R. R. Bowker Company, a Xerox company. Copyright © 1970 by Xerox Corporation. Reprinted by permission.

Nadine Gordimer impresses as a woman whose spirit is as lovely as her face. Miss Gordimer, who is, with Alan Paton, unquestionably the most talented white writer writing out of South Africa today, recently visited America in connection with her well-reviewed novel, *A Guest of Honour,* published by Viking.

For more than four years, Miss Gordimer told *PW* [*Publishers Weekly*], she has been traveling through the new nations of Africa, lecturing on African writers, and much of what she observed in places like Zambia, Kenya, Tanzania, Malawi and Uganda, she translated into fiction in the book, which deals with an Englishman who returns to the African nation he had tried to help as a revolutionary sympathizer years before it attained independence. "Everything I know I have put into this book," she says.

"The most positive gain that is being made in these states is in the field of education," Miss Gordimer believes. "It is quite moving to see the money being spent on education in these states today. They are really trying to bridge the gap. People always tend to look at the things that have gone wrong in these new nations, not the things that have gone right. If standards have dropped for some of the white people, it means that the bread and jam is being spread that much thinner now to get it down to the lower economic and social levels. The oldest of these new African states is only 12 years old. It is not important what happens to a white élite; it is important that the lot of the indigenous people has improved."

White people coming to Africa today still tend to think that the influences the Africans want are those of the western or specifically American way of life. Africans, on the other hand, do not look at things this way at all, Miss Gordimer pointed out. What they want is

47

what will help their countries improve economically and in learning, whether that help comes from East or West. A stage has been reached in the relationship between Europeans and Africans or Americans and Africans that has gone beyond the color feeling, and many of the new nations are more than willing to bring in foreign teachers to help.

"Very interesting" writing is being done in Africa by Africans right now, Miss Gordimer said, mentioning the work of Wole Soyinka, Chinua Achebe, and a novel by Ferdinand Oyono called *Houseboy*, in which "a white man's life is seen through native eyes from the sweepings under the bed."

The tragedy for her own South Africa insofar as native African writing is concerned is that the tremendous and sudden flowering of promising writers which occurred 10 years ago coincided with police activity to clamp down hard on articulate Africans. Some went into exile and are writing from there. Others "in Orwellian fashion were simply wiped out as writers" while they remain in South Africa.

"If you take away the one or two Langston Hughes or Richard Wrights we might have produced and make it impossible for young blacks today even to read their books, then you set back any possibility of native South African writing emerging soon and force any new young black writers to start all over again," she said.

"In my own country I think of myself as a white African," Miss Gordimer told *PW*, "but in any of these other African territories I am simply white and a foreigner. The paradox is that in my own country I am simply accepted by black friends as an African."

Nadine Gordimer is acutely aware from what she has observed in this country that "many black Americans have lost their identity." She does not really believe they will find it again by trying to "go home" to Africa. If "the American dream has been offered to them too late for their acceptance, calling themselves Afro-Americans and adopting imaginary black names will not help ultimately," she says.

"They do not share the identity that Africans have with Africa, with their own language, with being a man with feet on his own earth. If black Americans haven't any identity, they must somehow forge a new identity of their own in America rather than looking to Africa," she says. "I certainly do not think they will find it by following a black apartheid and separatism. They must work with white Americans."

Africa in the Eleventh Hour: An Interview with Nadine Gordimer

E. G. Burrows/1970

From *Michigan Quarterly Review*, 9.4 (1970), 231–34. Reprinted by permission of *Michigan Quarterly Review*.

Burrows: Miss Gordimer, what led you to become a writer?

Gordimer: I've written *ever* since I can remember. I began writing when I was a little girl, and there was never really anything else that I wanted to do. Even though, at times in my life, it seemed dubious whether I could make a living this way, I was determined not to do anything else. Fortunately, it worked out all right.

Burrows: You were born in South Africa, were you not?

Gordimer: Yes, I was born in one of those small gold-mining towns near Johannesburg and went to a convent school there. I didn't travel outside of Africa until I was thirty and had written a couple of books.

Burrows: Was the life and literature of England the principal influence on your work?

Gordimer: From the beginning, my cultural contacts were with England. Although I read books by American writers, I identified myself primarily with England and people in English literature. On the other hand, my life and the country in which I was living—even the seasons are wrong way around with Christmas in midsummer—seemed to set me apart. I felt that I would be eternally outside this rather magical world on the other side of the ocean. It was a long time before I realized that I didn't have to imitate English writers or their way of life, that I could write about my own life which seemed to me so commonplace but, to the rest of the world, extremely exotic.

Burrows: Is there a feeling of national identity among South Africans?

Gordimer: Oddly enough, very much so, despite the fact that we are such a divided society. There is a strong physical feeling for the country. We may be at each other's throats politically, but nearly all of us share a strong attachment to the country itself.

Burrows: Do the descendants of Dutch settlers in South Africa still relate to Holland?

Gordimer: The Afrikaans-speaking people, those of Boer descent, severed their links with Europe some time ago. They are isolationists by temperament, tradition, and politics. Of course, a percentage of the Boer or Afrikaner population was of Huguenot descent. French names survive, but little else; if France has a glowing image in South Africa today, it is because she is the only great power to break the embargo on the sale of arms to South Africa. The cultural connections with Holland remained for some time until South Africa's color-bar policies became repugnant to the Dutch in Holland itself. The break was instigated in Europe. The Hollanders have more or less disowned the Afrikaners whose language, of course, derives from theirs. The animosity which exists between the two white groups—the English-speaking white South Africans and the Afrikaans-speaking white South Africans—is, in my opinion, a case of tweedle-dum and tweedle-dee, since it ignores the whole issue of the massive black population. There are sixteen million blacks as opposed to only three-and-a-half million whites.

Burrows: From this vantage point, we think of South Africa as being especially blessed in its writers. Is there a real literary ferment there today?

Gordimer: The growth of a South African literature has been a truly wonderful thing. Today, unfortunately, it's in a sad state. Around the end of the last century, we had one or two remarkable white writers. There were as yet no black writers; black South African writing begins with Thomas Mofolo's fine historical novel *Chaka,* published more than twenty years later. Until the missionaries created written languages for the African peoples, the black literary tradition was purely an oral one. The Zulus, a great tribal group, had a rich poetic oral tradition, for instance, but not a written one. So when I speak of literature in the nineteenth century, I am referring to books written by white people. *The Story of an African Farm* by Olive Schreiner is often thought of as being the beginning of South African literature. She stood more or less alone. Of course, there was a lot of Tarzanish writing—exotic South Africa, you know—but little of a serious nature or about real people. The people were described on the same level as the animals and the scenery. But then, in the

1920s, there was a new impetus. We had Pauline Smith, a remarkable short-story writer, Sarah Gertrude Millin, and William Plomer. Plomer left South Africa and is now a famous English poet. Millin and Plomer were the first two writers to touch on the big issues in our country, especially the color-bar. Millin wrote *God's Step-children* and Plomer wrote *Turbott Wolfe*, two novels which took diametrically-opposed points of view, but it was a beginning. It brought to public attention the fact that there were things going on in South Africa that were of great interest and relevance to the western world. After these two writers, there was again a lull. Then, when the entire continent of Africa began to wake up and think about independence after the Second World War, we had a new wave of writers starting with Alan Paton and his *Cry, the Beloved Country* in 1949. Then Dan Jacobson and I began to write. We found ourselves, so to speak, by writing about things we thought the rest of the world wasn't interested in. He wrote about rural communities. I wrote about life on the gold mines with their small closed-off white communities and the hundreds of thousands of Africans coming to labor there. There were a number of other new writers as well: Jack Cope, Jan Rabie, and the playwright Athol Fugard, whose plays are beginning to be performed in the United States. At this time also a most interesting nucleus of black writers was formed around Ezekiel Mphahlele, Lewis Nkosi, Bloke Modisane, and Todd Matshikiza. Actually, although I speak of these two groups separately, we all knew each other, and, in a sense, our work was complementary. We had a new literature going. But then the black writers were picked off one by one by one. Some became banned persons. Nothing a banned person writes, even if it is not political, even if it is only a love poem, can be published. Some writers, like Nkosi and Mphahlele, became frustrated and left. And there were a number of others who fled as political exiles—the poet Dennis Brutus and the novelist Alex La Guma. For years some of us who were left have been trying to edit a small literary magazine in which the work of black and white writers is brought together. But we find it more and more difficult, and I'm afraid the magazine is limping toward its death. Because of bans and censorship, both black and white writers find they cannot write honestly from the substance of life around them—not for publication at home.

Burrows: Are there books not written by banned South Africans which are prohibited in South Africa as well?

Gordimer: Since 1955, when the first censorship act was passed to be followed in 1963 by a more comprehensive act, 11,000 books have been banned. There are ninety-seven definitions of what is undesirable in literature. Two of my own books are banned, and I would say that they were banned because they dealt with political matters in what was considered an "undesirable" way. But many books are banned because they are too frank sexually. Still, in South Africa, politics is undoubtedly a dirtier word than sex. Books by Frantz Fanon and Eldridge Cleaver, for instance, can't be bought in South Africa.

Burrows: Are the laws restrictive not only upon literary works but upon other art forms as well?

Gordimer: Yes, indeed. The censorship act covers entertainments, and there are other laws that cover painting. I often think the painters are lucky—they can be less explicit, more implicit. There has been only one case of a painter getting into trouble. He was charged with blasphemy and obscenity.

Burrows: Has there been much experimentation in the arts?

Gordimer: In painting and sculpture, I would say yes. Although black African literature has been banned almost out of existence, black painters have emerged and are gaining recognition at home and abroad as well. In the theater mixed casts are prohibited. If you write a play in South Africa, it would seem inevitable for you to include black and white characters, because that is the way the country is. But a white man would be forced —and I have seen this—to play a black man's part in "black-face."

Burrows: Most writers and artists in South Africa would seem to express a liberal point of view. Are there conservative writers of any merit?

Gordimer: One hesitates to make value judgments, and, in the long run, writers must be allowed to write what they like. If they choose to ignore a political situation, if they want to write a metaphysical novel, they must be allowed to do it. But, speaking for myself, for them to be able to justify this, they must be extraordinarily talented writers. I doubt whether there is one who could measure up to this condition in South Africa. What else can an honest writer do but draw on the life around him? His work becomes implicitly political. I'm not talking about propagandists; I'm talking about writers who really care about the truth, the sincerity, and the integrity of their writing. I suppose the old Tarzan romantic piece is still saleable on a sub-literary level. And there are some who write only about the animal life. But among the Afrikaans writers, there has been an interesting development. The majority of them have never thrown in their lot with other white writers in protesting censorship, for instance. As Afrikaners, they belong to another language and culture and they find it difficult, with one or two courageous exceptions, to make common cause with the English-speaking writers. An Afrikaans group called "Sestigers" (literally, the people of the Sixties), has done quite a bit of experimenting in form. I must confess I don't find it very revolutionary. It's mainly derivative, some going as far back as Virginia Woolf, some borrowing their techniques from William Burroughs. Much of it is competently written, but I can't help thinking what a mistake it is. These writers refuse to come to grips with the great issues that are around them. In the last couple of years, however, they have begun to write more frankly about sexual matters and *that* bothers the censors, too. The Afrikaans writers are beginning to run into trouble, now and then, and I suspect that before long they will find themselves lined up with the English writers, both white and black, in the fight for freedom of expression. Maybe then, when all the South African writers find themselves in the same boat, we'll get some action.

Burrows: Can you tell us about your new novel?

Gordimer: It's about a non-existent, composite, central African country. Imagine a place somewhere between Kenya, Tanzania, Zambia, Rhodesia, and Angola—you know, just make a hole in the middle of Africa and push it in—that's where it takes place. I am trying to deal with problems of trade unions, who, in an independent African state, find themselves in conflict with the political leadership, which they created in the pre-independence struggle. It was through the trade unions that many political parties got started in Africa; political training was provided by the trade unions. On another level, the novel deals with problems of a white man who began as a colonial administrator and was expelled from the country during

Colonial times for backing African nationalists. It is understood that when independence comes, he will return to help the nationalists rebuild the country. The novel recounts the conflicts of responsibility and commitment that arise on his return.

Diamonds Are Polished—So Is Nadine

Diane Cassere/1972

From *Rand Daily Mail* (Johannesburg), 27 July 1972, Eve & TV
Section, 2,4. Reprinted by permission of Times Media Ltd.

Nadine Gordimer is like a diamond. Small, precise, hard—and she's polished.

Her latest book, a collection of 16 short stories, has recently been released from embargo and it has been well received by the reviewers.

She has also just returned from a holiday in Corsica and the South of France—and a trip to London to receive the James Tait Black Memorial Prize. Miss Gordimer won it for *A Guest of Honour,* her fifth novel published in 1971.

She is the first South African to receive the award, which counts among its winners the celebrated writer, Virginia Woolf.

The personality angle was taboo when I saw Miss Gordimer at her home in Parktown this week. She made it very clear she would not discuss her personal life or her future writing plans.

"If you are going to do something, you do it. You don't talk about it and analyse it."

But she makes no bones about the whole African situation and how it affects the country's writers.

"Censorship is more harmful to the public than to the writers." All Miss Gordimer's books have been embargoed since the establishment of the censorship board and two have been banned in South Africa.

"I find this embargo extremely irritating—it comes at a time when your book has just been published . . .

"I am totally against the whole concept of censorship," she said. "And I feel strongly about the position of the writer in this country—but I must make a clear distinction between the position of the White and the Black writer. The White writer has a bit more freedom.

"There is a fear among Black writers of showing themselves to be articulate and thus suspect.

55

"To believe that there is a specific hidden dynamism among Black writers is, perhaps, too romantic . . . but there are vast areas of their lives that can be expressed only from the inside.

"The last decade has been static. Black artists seemed to suffer from a kind of paralysis and stagnation that has encouraged White proxy in the arts, as in politics—by which I mean White's airing Black grievances and aspirations.

"There have been tremendous changes now of course. I used to regard myself as a liberal, but I now regard myself as a radical.

"There is a healthy movement among Black people to assert their independence of White inspiration.

"What did White liberalism offer them? A share in a new world that liberals did not have the power to help them attain.

"We were putting out a hand that contained only our goodwill. This has been the failure of liberalism.

"Of course some of us are hurt now, but this is natural. I had great faith in personal attitudes, but in the end this has been meaningless to Blacks. In the end we could not change their lives."

She believes a Black Government for South Africa is inevitable—no matter how the Whites feel about it.

"How many Whites could stomach living under a Black Government?" she asks.

"For myself I have no feelings about it. I would as well live under a just Black Government as under a just White Government.

"Without justice, there is nothing to commend one above the other. We have never had a just Government in the history of South Africa because it has always been a Government in which the majority of the people were voiceless."

How about the recent student protests and police and Government handling of the situation? She replied emphatically:

"I have always supported the students. I have a great admiration for them. They are the conscience of White South Africa.

"The way the protests were handled? It was frightful."

While she is outspoken in her political beliefs, Miss Gordimer will not discuss her personal life at all, apart from the obvious facts.

She was born and brought up in Springs and went to university for

a while but did not stay to get her degree. Her first work—a short
story—was published when she was 15 years old.

She has written 10 books in all—"a round number now"—five
books of short stories and five novels.

Miss Gordimer has travelled extensively in Africa, the United States
and Europe. She has a son and a daughter and is married to Mr.
Reinhold Cassirer.

She admits to working steadily and intensely when she is writing—
usually in the mornings.

Is there a recurring theme in her work?

"I have a theory that a writer is always writing the same story—like
a mosaic, a jigsaw puzzle that is put together."

"What the writer is piecing together is his view of the world."

"The stories in *Livingstone's Companions* were written over a
period of five years—there is always a connection, certain attitudes
towards people."

Is she satisfied with her work? She smiles.

"Writers are never happy with what they have done, but I never re-
read my work when it is published."

Miss Gordimer feels *A Guest of Honour* is her favourite novel.

"In *A Guest of Honour* I tried to do something I had never
done before and that I don't think many writers in Africa have
tried to do.

"I tried to write a political novel treating the political theme as
personally as a love story.

"I tried to put flesh on what have come to be known as the dry
bones of political life.

"I didn't want to brush over these things in a way which has often
irritated me about other works. It is as if the author is on uncertain
ground. Politics on the African continent are handled emotionally
and intensely."

Apart from winning the James Tait Black Memorial Prize, *A Guest
of Honour* was nominated best novel of 1971 by both the English
Sunday Telegraph and the *Observer.*

Her own personal reading tastes? Miss Gordimer smiled, thought
for a minute and said:

"I can never understand people who say they no longer read
novels—I don't say this as a novelist.

"I read novels and I constantly re-read those that have meant a great deal to me. I also read literary criticism, biography—but not as much poetry as I used to."

She spreads her hands, smiles again, and the discussion was over.

Writing in Africa: Nadine Gordimer Interviewed

Stephen Gray and Phil du Plessis/1972

From *New Nation*, September 1972, 2,3,5. Reprinted by permission of Stephen Gray and Phil du Plessis.

One of South Africa's foremost writers, Nadine Gordimer has had two substantial books published in the last year. Her outspoken views on South Africa—and more recently, her penetrating analyses of life in larger Africa—make her a key figure in the world of South African fiction. Her new novel, *A Guest of Honour,* has now won her the James Tait Black Memorial Prize for fiction. She is interviewed by *New Nation*'s literary editors, Stephen Gray and Phil du Plessis.

Gray: In your two recent books, the novel *A Guest of Honour* and the collection of stories *Livingstone's Companions,* you have expanded your fictional territory outside South Africa. How do you feel about writing about the continent at large?

Gordimer: Well, I've been travelling in Africa since 1954; the first time I ever left South Africa, instead of going to Europe as most South Africans do, I went to Egypt—it was my first country abroad. So I've always been very interested in moving around in Africa. And it's interesting that you say I've extended my territory, if by this you mean that I've now written stories and set a book in other parts of Africa, because I think that I've never regarded South Africa as something different and isolated. I have always seen it as part of the whole continent, and with so much in common with the continent. It's a curious and essentially artificial combination of circumstances that have made us somehow skip the rest of Africa and link with Europe.

Gray: How do you manage to travel so widely in Africa?

Gordimer: I've travelled on a South African passport; if I've managed at all, it has been only with difficulty, and only because I'm a writer with a name that is known, and my opinions are known as a vociferous anti-racist and anti-colonialist. This doesn't mean I then rush around like a VIP or in any capacity like that. I travel completely as a private person and see whom I like. I've not been handed around any special circuit.

Du Plessis: You don't have to keep explaining your relationship to South Africa everywhere you go?

Gordimer: Only if I've chosen to. As I have said, people who know me know my opinions. It's usually writers that I want to talk to. And there's a kind of brotherhood among writers.

Gray: You are the first of the contemporary South African writers to break the bounds and travel northward.

Gordimer: When I think of the writing that matters—I'm not talking about the odd travel and other pieces I've done, the sort of thing I've done for *Atlantic* on West Africa, and a few others—they're not of any real importance to me as pieces of writing. Apart from a few short stories, the only time I've used what one might call my experience of the rest of Africa, properly and deeply, was in *A Guest of Honour.* But I didn't choose to do this in any conscious way. I did it because whatever I wanted to say, creatively-speaking, about South Africa, I had said, and I wanted to return again to my feeling that this context that one lives in, is *Africa,* and that there are vast differences, but there are also tremendous similarities in the countries that comprise it. It's the superstructures that are different, but all the underpinnings, the earth is the same.

Gray: Do you yourself feel this new excitement of the political change in Africa?

Gordimer: Yes, intensely. I suppose it's odd to say you find the place where you live exciting, but I think we do. Those of us who are born here and who don't dislike the fact, and who don't yearn to have been European, as some people seem to do from birth almost—there are people who can't wait to get away forever and never come back for reasons quite apart from the political thing. But those of us like myself I think have always thought it was a very exciting place to live, humanly speaking.

Du Plessis: Do you find the novel by English-speakers in Africa has got away from the theme of the fear of being eaten, as in Waugh's *Black Mischief?* Your theme and development in *A Guest of*

Honour seems to me a very significant sophistication of this missionary and cannibal theme.

Gordimer: Ah, it was never only a matter of being eaten physically though, it was a matter of being eaten in other ways. The submersion of personality is the confrontation with other ethos. But I don't think writers who were born here suffered from it, do you? On the contrary, I know that when I first started to write there was a feeling that what I was writing about couldn't have been of any interest to anybody, because it was so terribly *ordinary*. Because to me what was exotic was what I'd been reading about all my life, the life and the physical background of England and America and France and Germany and Russia. So it was astonishing to find that it was the other way round, and indeed that the gold-mine community that I wrote about was extremely exotic to other people.

Gray: Was Pauline Smith a big discovery for you?

Gordimer: Yes, and I think that Katherine Mansfield's stories were. Here was a little girl living in New Zealand, and I think there were strong similarities—the whole colonial life based on an Anglo Saxon cultural tie, even if you weren't English. Reality seemed always to be across the sea. But then one felt, right, you see you can write about this—what is happening in your own backyard. Now with me it's just a bigger backyard.

Du Plessis: Does the African landscape itself have a great effect on you?

Gordimer: I think that I have a strong sense of place. Some writers have, some don't; in some it's important, in some it's not. Pauline Smith did make me think you can write about South Africa, which at the time reading Olive Schreiner wouldn't have done, because I was writing short stories. And I've often thought that when one begins as a writer, there are always one or two writers who make one realise that one can write about—in my case, the life around a gold-mine. One of the terrible things that has happened to present-day young black writers here is that with writers like Ezekiel Mphahlele and Can Themba banned, the aspirant writers have had no-one to build on, no-one to point the way to the burning realization of their own lives. That's why I think there's such a dearth of prose writers. The retrogression over the last ten years in black prose writing is startling. And I can't help thinking back to my own experience as a very young beginning writer here, and this feeling of: You want to write but is what you want to write about possible, creatively speaking? You need one or two writers speaking out of the same potential experience that you can build from; this is what tradition means to me. But the stories I've seen recently written by young Africans are built on no tradition; they show a turning away from their own life and they reproduce over and over again stories which are based on "stories" they read in their very sensational newspapers.

Du Plessis: But isn't black writing in this country very journalistically based?

Gordimer: Yes, but black writers started to break out of this journalistic mould. Then when their tiny literature was beheaded, as it were, those who came after went back to horror comic situations, cinema violence rather than that of their own lives, sob-stories, in place of expansion of genuine emotion. And, above all, every black writer should have written up on his wall: Enough About Shebeens.

Du Plessis: I think you have a theory that in these circumstances people write poetry rather than prose?

Gordimer: Let me read you something: "Poetry does indeed have a very special place in this country. It arouses people and shapes their minds. No wonder the birth of our new intelligensia is accompanied by a craving for poetry never seen before. It's the golden treasury in which our values are preserved. It brings people back to life, awakens their conscience and stirs them to thought. Why this should happen I do not know, but it's a fact." That's from *Hope Against Hope* by Nadezhda Mandelstam and she is writing of the Soviet Union. One could say this about our country, when one tries to conjecture why young blacks are writing poetry now. And one has to think then what a really marvellously tough thing the urge to write is. People find a way. I'm hardly suggesting by this let's have censorship, it's healthy, because it's going to make poets of us all. I'm simply saying that as far as black writers are concerned, nearly all their important writers were banned or went into exile, and their works are not available. This has had a terrible effect on prose writing; it has produced, subconsciously, a search for a less vulnerable form of expression. So far as prose fiction is concerned, every day I see things that are crying out to be written about by blacks; there are areas of life white writers can't enter into, even given the intuitive and imaginative powers that writers have. I hesitate to say this, because there are so many things that writers *can* write about that people could never imagine possible. But when there are certain experiences that are outside your potential, that are inconceivable and could never happen to you, then your subject matter is restricted to some extent; and it's restricted in this country with its colour bar more than in any other. White writers are cut off from the proletariat. There's no getting away from it. Even a white builder, a hard hat, doesn't have the same experience as a black man once he leaves work, so there is this vast area that you can't even make the imaginative identification with. Yet I don't see black writers now writing about the *range* of their experience; it's the good old shebeen raid, it's the black man who falls in love with a white girl—these are the cliché situations. But you've only got to go onto any farm, any factory, any mine—not one word has been written about the life there, since people like Peter Abrahams and Alex La Guma. To my mind Alex La Guma is the only black novelist that this country has produced in twenty years. He wrote about these things, but his books are not available to us; he's in exile. If black writers now were writing about the range of experience they leave untouched, I don't think that it would necessarily come under the axe; much of it would have a good chance. It seems that a certain connection has to be made again, between black writers and their material. When they want to turn again for a living tradition to people who share their own background, they find this cut off by censorship. When I say censorship I have in mind not only the censorship board, but the other legal provisions that prevent blacks from writing and being read here. If you write something which is controversial at all, even if it's not banned, if you're black you're a marked person. It's bad enough if you're white, but if you're black, because you are articulate you are suspect to begin with. Here's a potential 'troublemaker', because he's too clever by half. It's intimidation of a most subtle kind. Plus all the other things; if you're involved in politics and become banned, then even if you write a love poem it can't be published.

Gray: Are there comparable restrictions in Africa at large?

Gordimer: Well, during the colonial period they had similar difficulties, not comparable in strictness, but in kind certainly

comparable. If you had written a novel from the inside praising the
Mau Mau during the time the British were still in Kenya, or you were
writing the sort of novel James Ngugi has written since, you probably
would have got into trouble. But then when independence came,
again the question has been whether one could write a novel against
a regime. But the surprising thing is that it has been done. Chinua
Achebe has done it. I saw him in America when alas, poor chap, he
was there trying to raise funds for Biafra, during the dismal last few
months of that war. And I asked him about *A Man of the People,*
which came out just before the war. He said it was distributed in
Nigeria, and nothing happened to him and the book wasn't banned.
And the same with Wole Soyinka on the other side. But here I think
one must hand it to the African states, because they have treated
their writers better than writers have been in South Africa. I don't
think that black writers in black Africa have suffered the same kind of
pressures; I *know* they haven't; even though one would think that
with the chopping and changing of governments they might run into
trouble. And they deal with a wide range of the life of people—rural
people, city people—in the way that black writers in South Africa
haven't even touched upon yet.

Du Plessis: Do you think this is because of the air of almost
anarchic freedom which reigns in large parts of Africa?

Gordimer: There's nothing anarchic about these novels. Although, it's surprising how few strictly *political* as distinct from simply
socially-critical novels there are in Africa, considering what a
tremendously important part politics plays in black Africa, how it is
the bread of everyday life. But the novel as a social critique deals with
market life, the difficulties of people coming into the city—there you
have an analogy with our shebeen novel—but there's more variety in
it, and there are far more books about rural life, in African writing in
both French and English.

Du Plessis: Would the higher level of education have affected
this?

Gordimer: That is difficult to say. I know that in Nigeria the level
of education was high, and there's a huge population of course,
which is why they tend to have more writers than most other black
countries.

Gray: How does censorship here affect yourself? Your last two books have been embargoed shortly after publication dates.

Gordimer: You know, they do this with almost all English South African writers, I'm not the only one by any means. But naturally one speaks from one's own experience. I'm thinking of books that are published outside South Africa first. It's an extraordinary thing— you'll be able to correct me here—there's no novel banned by an Afrikaans writer.

Du Plessis: Well, some prose books and some poetry have not been published due to prepublication censorship.

Gordimer: Well, a couple of years ago I wrote that there was going to be a desk-drawer Afrikaans literature.

Du Plessis: Oh there is one.

Gray: But how does this affect the writer, for example, in hard cash?

Gordimer: Now people don't realise how this does affect you. To embargo a book for up to six weeks, specially after it's already been allowed in—if the thing was going to be banned, if the thing never comes in, there's nothing you can do, it's finished, it's still-born so far as your own country is concerned. But if, as in the case of *Living-stone's Companions,* this last book of mine, it arrives, people begin to buy it, it begins to be reviewed, and then suddenly it's embargoed, this virtually kills the popular sale of the book. The people who really want it have ordered it, and they are waiting. But what would have happened if there hadn't been an embargo? There would have been the bulk of casual sales while the reviews were out and interest was highest. I laughed to see that book of mine on a bestseller list—I hear it's difficult to buy at all, at the moment. The booksellers, understandably, are afraid to re-order while a book is under embargo, because they don't know if it's going to be banned or not. So they wait until it's been released, and then find they haven't enough copies to meet the demand, and then re-order—well, by the time the book arrives weeks after that, many people who wanted to buy a copy will have bought something else. Without embargo, a book's potential sale can be assessed early on, and the new supplies brought in in time. Every writer who has a book embargoed loses sales—and readers. What interests me is that this book was not held up when it entered the country. So what busybody, what self-appointed custodian of public morals was it who sent this book, with 25 cents or whatever the fee is, to the Censorship Board? *A Guest of Honour,* and my third novel, too, *Occasion for Loving,* were also embargoed. The position of a book that's embargoed and released can be compared with a man who's kept in custody for a crime for which he's later found not guilty.

Gray: Does the future hold more African novels?

Gordimer: Well, to me they've all been African novels.

Landmark in Fiction

Stephen Gray/1973

From *Contrast*, 30 (April 1973), 78–83. Reprinted by permission of South African Literary Journal Ltd.

In the year since its publication, Nadine Gordimer's new novel, *A Guest of Honour,* has been well-enough received in the U.S. and England. In select circles in South Africa it has generated a reinforced kind of respect for a writer who has tended to receive shadowy and even suspicious treatment. Now it has won her the prestigious James Tait Black Memorial Prize. *A Guest of Honour* is Nadine Gordimer's fifth novel (her previous *The Late Bourgeois World* is for some reason banned) and it comes to us seven years after her sprawling *Occasion for Loving.* Those same select circles are content to agree that this huge new book is a vindication of all that one expected from the early Gordimer: it is a very powerful *tour de force,* and—if one might place it in the thin context of South African English fiction for a moment—a monumental challenge to writers and readers who might wish to expand outwards. It has far more significance, and interest, than any local review of it has suggested; in fact one could go as far as saying that the half-baked flyleaf synopses that have passed for reviews of it in South Africa amount to a reception which is no less than an insult. The same insipid treatment has been given spo radically to her new short-story collection, *Livingstone's Companions.*

The guest of honour of the novel's title, Evelyn James Bray (54) returns to the independence celebrations of the new African republic he helped to negotiate out of its colonial days. He acts as confidant and discreet adviser to Adamson Mweta, the first president of the emerging nation, and runs a pacifying series of errands to the dissenting leftist, Edward Shinza. Colonel Bray is very much the welcome guest, politely but rather uselessly received by the hosts he himself cheered to power, charily remembered by the British remainders. But the party is over after one spectacular week, and he is left to readjust to the new world he can no longer hold together. His presence in the book is enormous; his predicament is balanced dramatically between all that he can only consider humane and just, and the gradual process whereby he becomes superannuated, obsolete, unwelcome. He is killed off in a violent ambush scene, a martyr to the few European liberals who see his end as ironic, and his name lives on in the narrow folder of an educational report he compiled for his host. His obituary takes up one line in a *Time* magazine report of the state of emergency and chaos with which the novel ends.

Bray is the personal thread upon which the crucial and classic feuds of post-independence African politics are strung. The story is an archetype of so much recent African history that it is not only riveting as a documentary in its own right, but hugely informative and relevant. One wonders why the press reviewers of this novel are not equipped to deal with it in a relevant manner.

A Guest of Honour is a long book, perhaps too long. In parts it bogs down in details that, while adding bulk to the texture of the world it is recording, sometimes detract from the point. One remembers the blancmange at Mweta's table and not, perhaps, what was discussed. One remembers the hairstyle of a girl Bray does no more than buy a magazine from in a news agency, instead of what the magazine contained. But that is no more than quibbling. The cast of hundreds is all physically and subtly present, playing out the complex roles of a modern state in crisis, as though the author's assignment had been to cover *everything* of a nation's transformational workings. The gain is impressive in terms of her enormous skill in authenticating by means of greater and greater nucleations of minutiae. Yet in a strange way, her handling of Bray's love affair with Rebecca, a desperately frail attempt to find confidence and humanity, is more moving than the rest, and that relationship occupies only a small proportion of the whole. These points have been made before about her writing. But in *A Guest of Honour* Nadine Gordimer comes out with a new kind of muscle and authority. The novel is a landmark in our fictional affairs. It, and her subsequent collection of sixteen stories, is the subject of this interview:

Gray: Now that you have expanded your fictional territory outside South Africa, are you finding a new stimulus in the continent at large?

Gordimer: Well, I felt that the whole theme of differences of colour had gone as far as it could go for me, and I was interested in something different—in the case of *A Guest of Honour,* a white man's commitment to a country which he happens to have lived in. He thinks he's just lived in Africa for a few years and he'll go back wherever he came from. But what happens when he finds that this was the definitive experience and he's not really alive when he goes back where his origins are? So that's why I chose an Englishman as the protagonist—Bray arriving back for the independence celebrations in a country where he was once a colonial servant. Travelling round in Africa, I've become interested in the role of white people like Bray. I think people don't realise how many there are; a very original and perhaps off-beat kind of white man who really survives in Africa. But it's never the sort of person who 'goes native', who 'loves' the African; it's somebody who's ceased to see Africans except as people whom he lives amongst, who are full of the same faults as anybody else. So often, looking at people, I see circumstances becoming choice. By that I mean they become committed. You see people taking a job just because it's a job, and out of that grows a life that they never are able to change; and then they have to realise, as Bray does, that their only reality lies there, in that life. And in order to live again, he accepts coming back to Africa and working here—he sees himself just doing some solid job, making a report on education, and he believes in this. But then he comes up against his particular liberal dilemma—how far are you to go in standing aside, in not interfering now that the people have their destiny in their own hands? When it's no longer a business of black against white, when, as in *A Guest of Honour,* there is an ideological struggle, then it would seem honest for him to make a choice, to throw in his lot with Shinza whose political vision coincides with his own, even though his personal liking is for the other man.

Gray: Hasn't Bray's violent death been misinterpreted?

Gordimer: His death doesn't matter. And I think the *manner* of his death wouldn't have mattered to him. It doesn't matter how you die. Bray's death is a stupid accident, but other Brays will carry on. So many tragedies are accidental, especially in times of turmoil. But yes, his death is tremendously misunderstood by people that read and review the book. It's sometimes taken in South Africa as a sign that that dear old kafferboetie Nadine has finally seen the light, because here she shows how 'savage' these blacks are, that the very man who's given his life helping them is brutally killed. It's a complete misunderstanding of the book. Bray is mistaken for a mercenary who's been mingling in the troubles there, that's all. It's the old business of faceless generalisations taking over. He's killed by mistake, it's gratuitous, fortuitous, it doesn't make sense to the world. But it would have made sense to him, because he'd made his moral choice there; he'd accepted the risks that it carried. He'd accepted the fact that what he thought he had to offer the country was no longer sufficient, and ineffectual. He had taken the risk, moral and physical, of *action*. Become radicalised, if you like. To risk, I think, is to live.

Gray: How did you make the jump from Joburg, which you know from your very earliest memories, into the new Africa?

Gordimer: Well, the country that I invented for *A Guest of Honour* is a synthesis of a number of African countries that I've been to again and again. Rhodesia, Zambia, Botswana I've been going to since the early '50s, and from the '60s I began to go to East Africa and other parts of Central Africa, West Africa, the Congo and so on. All this has built up—it's never been a conscious search for material; it's slowly accreted. And it's always of course had a basis on having lived here.

Gray: Did you have to research for *A Guest of Honour*?

Gordimer: I realised as soon as I got to the political core of the novel that I knew much too little. I'd become over the past decade tremendously interested in African politics, and I have kept up with current events. But I found for instance, not being engaged in practical politics, I've never been to a political congress; I had no idea how one was conducted. Well, a congress was extremely important for *A Guest of Honour*; I didn't want to gloss it over, as it was as much a part of the book as an intimate love scene. So I had to teach myself about this. I got hold of the agendas of various congresses by slipping into the United Party and Nationalist Party offices and asking for agendas, never telling them my purpose; that was very instructive. But as I knew, for a novel you may have to read ten books to get the one fact you want, and then digest it and let it find its place.

Gray: Over how long a period had you written the stories included in *Livingstone's Companions?* Two of them, 'Inkalamu's Place' and 'Abroad', appeared here in *Contrast*.

Gordimer: I think it's about seven years. I usually scribble a date on the rough copy of the manuscript and stick it away. The title story was written in '68.

Gray: In that story you have a double perspective on your material, an ironic balance between the opening up of Africa as Livingstone saw fit, and the sequel a century later.

Gordimer: Yes, I saw this essentially as an ironic thing, when reading Livingstone's *Last Journals*. First of all there is a double irony; because there is the idea that Livingstone is always presented as such a saint; Stanley is always the beater of blacks, the parvenu newspaper man and complete vulgarian. But if you read those diaries of Livingstone's carefully, I think you'll agree with me he wasn't such a saint. I found these little bits I quoted: 'Such-and-such a bearer was given forty strokes today'. But I think the whole business of Livingstone as a man is being assessed, without any spiteful denigration of him, and he's becoming a fallible human being. And the whole business of what he did unwittingly, I mean what happened after him, the horrors that have been perpetrated in his path if not in his name—well, somehow one cannot absolve him completely. For me that's the double irony; for Livingstone himself encountered some of the enraging frustrations that white men have gone crazy with, which have been Africa's revenge on them. (Thank goodness, she's had some revenge.) Then at the same time you get, a hundred years later, this bored journalist in my story meeting a lot of seedy people in the same landscape. To me titles are very important—the whole story must be in the title—and if I get a bad title, as I do sometimes, then I know the story's not going to be any good. In 'Livingstone's Companions' I knew the title was right and therefore I *knew,* in the deepest sense, exactly what the story was about—his companions are you and me, those crazy people in the hotel, the Arabs in the dhow coming down, the dead ones on the hill, the woman's husband who seems to have no place there at all.

Gray: Were you conscious again of having this irony in the story 'Rain-Queen'—this time the territory being Conrad's since *Heart of Darkness?*

Gordimer: Do you know, I didn't think of Conrad at all. To me that story's about corruption. Of a child by grown-ups. It's learning adult values the hard way, as their victim. What happens in that story?—the adults make a nymphomaniac out of that girl. And the whole story came to me from a tiny thing, a saying somebody told me of in the Congo, about eight years before I wrote that story. They told me that when it rained in the afternoons a Congolese would say: Little shower, just time for a girl. And then go off and find some little girl, and the affair lasted just for the hour the rain lasted. And it's from that germ that that story came.

Gray: You've hit a point now of five novels and five volumes of short stories. How do you feel about stories versus novels?

Gordimer: I think I used to lie about this when asked, because I had an inferiority complex about novels. I started, as you know, as a short-story writer. And so, because I felt that people thought I couldn't write a decent novel, and because I felt myself I didn't know if I'd ever write a novel that would ever come anywhere near being any good, I used to say that they were the same for me. But they weren't. Now I can say that they *really* are; there are just differences in the way I conceive of different themes. Sometimes the theme can only be a story. At others it couldn't be encompassed in a story. But with some of my stories now I have to watch out that they don't fall between two stools. 'Livingstone's Companions' just makes it as a story—another two pages, well, not only in terms of space—another variation on the theme and it would have toppled as a story.

Gray: Does the future hold more Africa novels?

Gordimer: Well, to me they've all been Africa novels.

Nadine Gordimer: The Solitude of a White Writer

Melvyn Bragg/1976

From *The Listener,* 21 October 1976, 514. Reprinted by permission of *The Listener.*

When did you start writing?

When I was about nine. I wanted to be a dancer, and I went to dancing class, like all little girls. I was an acrobatic dancer. Then I got some strange heart ailment, and had to stop dancing, and it was about then that I began to write. I time it with this illness, you see. Otherwise, I wouldn't know so precisely.

It's unusual to remember so clearly, and start so young.

Well, I had a very strange childhood, because from that age I really didn't go to school. This mysterious ailment is something that I can talk about now, because my mother's dead; as long as my mother lived, I couldn't. I realised after I grew up that it was something to do with my mother's attitude towards me, that she fostered what was probably quite a simple passing thing and made a very long-term illness out of it, in order to keep me at home, and to keep me with her.

Whereabouts were you born?

In a little town called Springs, on the string of gold mines that go to the east and west of Johannesburg. My father was originally a watchmaker who came from Lithuania, and somehow, after various wanderings, he settled in this town, which was then a coal-mining area. He settled before gold was discovered there. By the time he'd married and I was on the scene, he was no longer a watchmaker; he had a small jeweller's shop.

Your books are absolutely full of detailed descriptions of landscape. Did you do a lot of solitary walking in the landscape around?

I had a very, very narrow life for years, because this landscape was a strange one in Africa. Around Johannesburg is a very high plateau, and in the part where I lived it used to be rolling grassland, where lions roamed and great herds of game. Once the mines came, all the animals went, so you just had this great, windy, sunny plateau, with no trees, except where there are a few little hills and little ravines. So that what I became conscious of around me was a man-made landscape. The mountains were mountains of white sand, drawn up from underground—the sand that remains after the ore has been treated with cyanide. Some of them were very beautiful. They're regularly shaped, rather like the pyramids, and they're all shades of buff and yellow to rose. Then the lakes: the only lakes there were the same thing, waste water pumped out of the mine. And the only trees were either trees in gardens, or, around the mines, big plantations of eucalyptus trees, used for props underground. So it was a strange landscape concocted entirely by men, and I always had the feeling for that reason that it wasn't real—that I lived somewhere rather unreal, because, as I've told you, my life was very lonely, lived mainly through books. And the books were all set in Europe or America, and described landscapes I'd never seen and that had very little relation to my surroundings.

We lived as ordinary townspeople on the edge of a very big mine property. And between our house and the mine there were the shops, because it's amazing the amount of services that have to grow up round a mine. First of all, there's the town providing the ordinary things. But then there were also always what were called the 'concession stores'. That means that storekeepers bought a concession from the mining company and put up a general store. They would usually have a row of these on the property, so that the mineworkers, the black, migratory workers, who came from all over, who were bewildered in a small town like ours, who didn't know any English, or any Afrikaans, had stores near them where they could go and buy.

These stores along the reef, as we called it, the gold reef, were mostly run by people of the same origin as my father. Most of them were Lithuanian Jews. But most of them were—I don't know quite how to put this—well, they didn't have a trade. At least my father had a trade. So they became storekeepers of this kind.

I would walk up past these stores, and I would see the storekeepers coming out, themselves rather bewildered, immigrants who knew the

language slightly, or who'd learnt it imperfectly, both English and
Afrikaans, and who felt alien. Then their customers were, again,
people who had come to a country they didn't know—right, they
were black and this was Africa, but it was a very different part of
Africa, usually, from the part they came from. Now, these two
people, the storekeeper and his customer, understood each other
very badly. The storekeepers, feeling on a rather low level of society
themselves in this little town, tended to act out their frustrations on
their customers, to treat them roughly, and regard them as absolute
savages. And the mineworkers themselves, not knowing the language, feeling rather timid, felt a lack of proper understanding even
of the simple purchase of something. So the relationships tended to
be rough, people shouting at each other, and I noticed this as a child.
I used to go up and wander round there, and here were these men in
their blankets, the black men, some with big earrings in their ears,
necklaces, hair in a strange style, some with their hair rolled in clay,
and hanging down in strange clay locks. When I was in late
adolescence, I began to see that this was an amazing situation. I was
beginning to think about the position of whites in Africa, the
strangeness of their being there, and also beginning to look at these
black workers—there had been thousands around me all my life,
since I was born—and seeing them as people.

You know, you close your eyes, and put your hand deep down
into the world that you know around you, into your own society. And
whatever is there you come up with: this is what being a writer's
about. Your material, your themes, take hold of you from the life
around you.

*So you don't make a decision that you're going to write a story for
the betterment of a particular situation. Your own attitudes are just
simply part of your mind to start with.*

Yes. And I haven't got much faith in the power of the pen, anyway.
I don't know whether you can ever change people by what they
read. Not in the kind of situation we have in Southern Africa.

*But is there a temptation, sometimes, when—as you clearly do—
you feel strongly about circumstances and people?*

Then I write an article. If I'm really incensed about something,
then I sit down and write about it in direct factual terms.

So what you're saying is that fiction can't bear this sort of primary impact?

I think that, in a way, it's fiction that bears the primary impact. The facts are always less than what really happens. I mean the facts are just on the surface—it's what makes the fact. If you get a law, like group areas, under which various population groups are moved from one part of the country to another, uprooted from their homes and so on, well, somebody may give you the figures, how many people are moved, how many jobs were lost. But, to me, it doesn't tell you nearly as much as the story of one individual who lived through that.

It seems to outsiders such as myself that there must be a terrible battle between what you want and what you hope might happen, and what you have to put up with. I suppose this is just a daily fact of life in South Africa.

Are you talking about my life as a writer or as a woman?

Well, both really.

It's very different. Because writing is such a lonely business, and it's always such a withdrawal. One's spirit goes out, and takes in what it needs. I mean, I couldn't say that when I write, I think: 'Oh, will this be banned, what's this one going to think of it, is it going to annoy the authorities?' I don't think that at all. I'm just thinking about expressing what I've discovered, what I know, in the best way that I can.

But then as a woman, living in South Africa now?

Oh, that's a very different thing. I don't know whether writers always have this schizophrenic factor in their lives; perhaps they all do. But as I've only lived there, I can only judge by there. But maybe there it's a little more pointed, because, once you're a writer and get known a little bit, then you get regarded as someone who has a public voice, and this implies some special kind of social responsibility. Because your name is known, you feel then that you have to use it. That is the only way in which I think it's honest for a writer to use his or her position. I don't think that a writer should ever try to use the actual work for propaganda purposes. But the writer is also a human being, a citizen, with certain responsibilities towards the society that he or she lives in, and you can't simply say: 'No, I'm a writer, I have no opinion on this. I've got nothing to do with it.'

Do you feel oppressed sometimes by the world attention which is brought to bear on the South African situation? Do you feel it sometimes gets in the way of some writing that you'd like to do?

No, because I never think about it when I'm working. And in a country like South Africa there's no literary life—perhaps one should add: 'Thank God.' You're just alone with your own book that you want to write. And I think that's the way it should be.

Interview: Pat Schwartz Talks to Nadine Gordimer

Pat Schwartz/1977

From *New South African Writing* (Hillbrow, South Africa: Lorton Publications, 1977), 74–81. Reprinted by permission of Lorton Communications.

Parktown West is one of Johannesburg's more elusive suburbs. Tiny and tucked away it is a gracious reminder of a rapidly vanishing piece of the city's history. Here, in a rambling, early 20th century home with disintegrating gutters and peeling paintwork, one finds one of South Africa's most acclaimed living writers.

Dwarfed by the high ceilings of her simply-furnished house, tiny Nadine Gordimer hugs a jersey to her against the chill which is not entirely banished by the glowing electric heaters, and radiates a vibrant, no-nonsense energy.

She talks rapidly, confidently about her profession in general, her own work in particular. She is a prolific and talented phenomenon in a country in which few writers have reached international renown.

Do you make use of a specific technique in your writing?

I make use of many different techniques. I use the forms of short stories and of novels and within those separate forms I use different techniques—for example, some are narrated in the first person, others in the third person. In *The Conservationist,* the tense changes from the historic present to the past and back. It is a very delicate and complex question, the matter of technique. For me it is a matter of finding the approach that will release the most from the subject. The form is dictated by the subject. In some people's writing you are very conscious of the writer—the writer is between you and the subject all the time. My own aim is to be invisible and to make the identification for the reader with what is being written about and with the people in the work—not to distance the reader.

Is most of your work drawn from personal experience?

78

With a first novel, one has lived so little and knows so little one tends to draw on one's own background. But as time goes by, many places and situations tend to run into one. With experience comes a sense of the variety in life and the endless tunnels of possibility rolling away into other people's lives—this is where themes come from.

Do you write for a definite period every day or only when you feel inspired?
When I am working I work every day. If I start something I will work for many months at a stretch but I never have any set stint. A good day's work for me would be about 1,000 words, so roughly that is more or less my capacity at one sitting.

Physically, how do you work?
I sit at a typewriter or have one on my knee. I have never written anything by hand. I had a little typewriter when I was very young. To me, handwriting is for letters, personal things, not for work.

When you begin a novel are all the important points of the plot already established?
The theme is strongly established and certainly the main characters. The minor ones might join up en route.

Do you get very involved with your characters in that they become real people to you?
I find that as the work progresses and I go deeper and deeper into my characters they begin to take on reality and become living people to me. I can think back on old books and stories and think "Where would he be now? What would have happened to her, how would she react to this or that?" Sometimes in my books a reference will crop up to someone I have dealt with before, but only somebody who knows my work very well will recognise the allusion.

How do you hit on the names of your characters?
Names are very important. I can't really tell you how they come. For the central characters the name comes very early on. It seems to be there and the person couldn't have had any other name. At other times, I will get the first name and the surname may not come. It is a question of milieu as well as the personality of the character. In South Africa, in two names you could have a whole family history, for

instance, an Italian first name and a Dutch or German second name. Names are very important for the feeling of the person and for the physical look of the person. Physical descriptions to me must always be kept open and must suggest without describing in detail what a character looks like, his or her physical aura. The name is part of that. At other times, one sees a marvellous name somewhere—on a shop in a small town for instance—and it sticks in one's mind and suddenly, years later, there it is. It falls into place.

Do you keep a notebook recording situations and scenes you may one day use?

I keep very very few notes. If I were to show you my notes for *A Guest of Honour*—a very long book—there are perhaps six pages of jottings—names, tiny incidents. Often there will be the first sentence of the book and perhaps the last. That's all.

What about the titles of your works?

When I am writing a short story I must have the title. It is very disquieting if I don't get the title at once. Short stories are such a compressed form and the title is the distillation, so to speak. Titles either comment on or sum up the theme. For instance, *The Conservationist* is a comment on Mehring, the main character as a kind of fossil. I am always amazed when people can take titles suggested by others. The only good title I have ever heard of given a book by the publisher was Carson McCuller's *The Member of the Wedding*. I will not allow my publishers to interfere with the titles of my books.

To what extent are your characters based on real people?

It is impossible to say and every writer will lie to you. Except for journalistic writers and very young ones, no writer's characters are based on a single person. They are like a series of superimpositions of people one has known, heard about, and invented. If one were to be honest one would find that the whole creation of a character is a subconscious process. Then, of course, there is always a lot of oneself. There's always the projection of one's own possibilities—of what one might have been as well as what one is.

Is your first draft close to the final work or do you constantly revise?

Usually I rewrite very little. When I write a novel there is the one original draft where there will be changes but not major ones and never structural changes. The structure is there very strongly. One sometimes finds a weak section and that may be rewritten several times and at different stages and often one is still not satisfied when it is finished.

Which writers have had the greatest influence on your work?
Again, all writers lie about this, or simply don't remember early influences they have long sloughed off. I keep reading that I was supposed to be influenced by Katherine Mansfield. Today I find her almost unreadable in her femininity and her breathlessness. *At the Bay* perhaps influenced me as a very young writer. In a way, it opened to me the possibilities of a particular sense of place. But at that stage Lawrence was a much stronger influence on me; *Sons and Lovers*—I still think it is a very wonderful novel. It is so difficult to talk about influences—one forgets, one lies because one no longer admires someone who was influential for a while. I was definitely influenced in my attitude to what one could know and write by Proust—permanently and to a certain extent, and temporarily, by Henry James. Though James is a very bad writer for a young writer to be influenced by—too convoluted and involuted. But you must go through many influences in order to find your own means of expression. Although I don't write poetry, I was much influenced by poets—by Yeats and Lorca and Rilke. Their imagery and view of the world became my lens for a time. After a writer has forged his own style and way of seeing, he admires, but he is no longer influenced.

Do you read a great deal?
I don't read much poetry any more but I still read voluminously. I reread a lot of books that mean a great deal to me, and again these change from year to year. I have just been rereading all of Conrad. And then there are certain contemporary fiction writers I follow very carefully. Their work is important to me. I read new novels and short stories. I read non-fiction of a particular nature—literary criticism and philosophy. I don't read much biography but quite a lot of collections of letters, history and politics.

How do the censorship laws affect you? Do you cut out things you might have written in order to avoid the possibility of a book being banned?

The censorship vulture sits on everyone's shoulder. It is a most limiting thing that is only fully beginning to make itself felt now—unbelievably stultifying not only for the writer but for the reader because there is so much important work people don't get to read. An example at random: Anthony Burgess, whether one admires him or not, is one of today's important novelists. His two most recent novels have been banned. I don't tailor what I want to write. I have never tailored anything with censorship in mind but I have, as all writers must in this situation—whether in South Africa or the Soviet Union, etc—perhaps been influenced in my approach to certain explosive subjects. I have dealt with them, nevertheless. I have devised ways . . . There are certain ways of presenting themes which make them difficult for censorship to grasp and to pin down. But I work without a sense of "audience" at all and I would work like that even if I worked in a country where there was no censorship because self-consciousness is fatal in a writer. The ideal way to write is as if you were dead and will be unaffected by any repercussions. You must not look at something in the light of someone you might offend. You cannot protect yourself or worry about what you may uncover—even in yourself.

Are you affected by the critics?

There are certain critics and certain publications I respect very much so obviously I care what they say. Others are of no interest to me at all. There are private individuals whose opinions are very important to me.

Do you ever show your work to anybody before it is sent to the publisher?

As a general rule, no. There is only one book of mine that anyone has ever seen before it was printed and that was seen by only one person.

Many of your novels feature aspects of the South African apartheid system and the dilemma of the "liberal". To what extent do you hope to influence the thinking of your readers in the direction of your political and moral attitudes?

I am not a preacher or a politician. It is simply not the purpose of a novelist. I am totally opposed to apartheid and all the cruel and ugly things it stands for, and have been so all my life. But my writing does not deal with *my* personal convictions; it deals with the society I live and write in. I thrust my hand as deep as it will go, deep into the life around me, and I write about what comes up. My novels are anti-apartheid, not because of my personal abhorrence of apartheid, but because the society that is the very stuff of my work *reveals itself.* The suffering inflicted by White on Black, the ambiguities of feeling, the hypocrisy, the courage, the lies, the sham and shame—they are all there, implicit. If you write honestly about life in South Africa, apartheid damns itself.

The Writers Who Are Hardest Hit

Carol Dalglish/1978

From *Rand Daily Mail* (Johannesburg), 3 May 1978, 11. Re-printed by permission of Times Media Ltd.

Distinguished South African writer Nadine Gordimer describes art as a dung heap in which many weeds must flourish for one flower to be nourished.

Censorship, she says, is ultimately nothing less than thought control. "It's the withholding of certain images and statements that stimulate people to think."

And hardest hit are the country's black aspirant writers, of whom there has been a new wave in the aftermath of the township riots.

"Since June '76 there has been more writing than ever and the volume is growing. That period was so crucially emotional that writers perhaps previously nervous of tackling certain themes abandoned caution. All the elements had been there for a long time, but the spirit of the young people gave the adults a special kind of courage to go ahead and write.

"Of course, even the stunning, searing experience of being black doesn't make a writer of someone without talent. To be a 'real' writer is to have the ability to choose or invent the mode that will give adequate expression to your material—the life in which you are plunged.

"Doubt is very important and self-examination is the healthiest thing in the world. That's why I'm totally against censorship. If writers offend in terms of obscenity or the safety of the State, they should be subject to the due process of the law—those laws exist."

She quotes the recent banning of the Ravan Press magazine, *Staffrider*, which set out to provide an outlet for aspirant black writers as confirmation of her feeling "that the South African Government doesn't want people to know what Africans think of their own lives.

"It troubles me to think that people who appoint censors seem to suggest writers invent things that are not there. Goethe said 'a writer must thrust his hand deep into his society'."

Staffrider conveys the ideas, opinions and aspirations of 18-million black men and women.

"It doesn't matter how crudely formulated some of the writing may be. This kind of deliberately unselective publishing fertilises the ground for those with talent who will become real writers.

"The unselectiveness of *Staffrider* is very important in that it allows for wide editorial choice—the standard or quality of the writer becomes less significant and in this way aspirants are encouraged to keep writing."

She refers to Professor Ezekiel Mphahlele as an example of how the lives of black writers can be affected.

"He is a distinguished figure in world black literature. He returned to South Africa after 20 years' self-imposed exile to put his talents at the service of his own people in his own country. To do this he is prepared to accept the disadvantages under which he is now living.

"But as a 'named' or 'listed' person he cannot be quoted or speak at public or political meetings.

"Another example is Sipho Sepamla who edits a literary magazine and a small black theatre arts magazine. One of his books of poetry is widely read but a new one, dealing with Soweto '76, was published in England but banned in South Africa.

"He has applied for a passport three times with recommendations from the highest quarters here, in Britain, and America but has been repeatedly turned down.

"Apartheid can't function without censorship. The answer is to get rid of apartheid if we want to rid ourselves of censorship, if we want to know the truth about our society. The Government closes its ears to the truth writers convey, appoints a board of censors to see that the public are prevented from the self-searching that art stimulates.

"The calibre of the people on the Board? It is a criminal offence to criticise or ridicule these people. I couldn't comment on the calibre of the Minister's appointees without risk of contravening the law . . ."

"Those who direct censorship have actually suggested writers should submit manuscripts for 'approval' before publication—it's a preposterous suggestion.

"If a white writer has a book banned, an area of his professional life has been affected. But if a black writer has a book banned he comes under general suspicion as being 'subversive.' He is watched and harassed by the Special Branch simply because he is an articulate man and has the ability to express the resentments, aspirations and longings others can't formulate in words.

"Getting back to Sipho Sepamla: imagine what his future as a writer in South Africa must be! His latest book banned, and he himself denied the opportunity of seeking cultural contacts abroad, widening his experience.

"The future of any writer depends on how much freedom he has to be read. That is his form of connection with his society. But writers don't just give up; the compulsion to write cannot be killed by outside pressures and circumstances. Even if a writer comes under surveillance—a tremendous psychological burden—he will still risk writing as long as it doesn't take the bread from his family's mouth."

While the Censorship directorate and board exist, Miss Gordimer believes the future of any writer, of any colour, who strives for truth and a genuine form of expression, is a great question mark. "One would have to be a seer to answer it."

In Black and White
Nesta Wyn Ellis/1978

From *Harpers and Queen,* November 1978, 296–98. Reprinted
by permission of *Harpers and Queen.*

Every writer needs a war. To concentrate her talent on life and death
realities, force the shoot that might otherwise go to seed among
indulgent fancies. Nadine Gordimer is fortunate. Her war is a
continuous low intensity struggle. South Africa is the focus of plural
conflict—between black and white, between emergent people and
colonial culture, between democracy and timarchy, between total-
itarianism and liberalism—the crucible in which almost all the
adversary political elements of the planet seem concentrated.

South Africa's most powerful single impact is alienation. It strikes at
every level. Not just the main division of apartheid—the Ne Blankes
(Non-whites) and Blankes signs that are needles in the eye even on
arrival at Jan Smuts airport. This is a multi-apartheid society—a fact
acknowledged by the authorities who, having fractured the nation
into groups and nurtured their antagonism, have recently created a
Minister for Plural Relations. Within the crude classification of whites/
non-whites lie multiple grades of skin colour—coloured, Asian,
black—in an official descending order that inspires numerous
applications for reclassification: everyone wants to be white, at the
top of the pile.

South Africa's blacks are easily the most downtrodden in Africa;
their backwardness is a product of a system that keeps them well
below the educational standards of whites. Few of their teachers even
reach Matric (the South African O-level) standard, and they have to
pay for their own books and tuition. Only 16 Rand per head was
being spent on Bantu education as recently as 1973 compared with
350 Rand per head on whites. Few of them reach the standards
required by the jobs which they are in any case prohibited from
taking outside the Bantustans.

Bantustans are the conclusion of apartheid logic. Euphemistically
called "homelands", they have theoretically been designed as places

where each tribe can pursue its own development free of contagion from others. In reality—lacking resources, industry, investment—they will serve as a reservoir of migrant labour, at the same time keeping the majority of blacks outside white society—physically and spiritually. Conveniently placed on lands which lack the rich resources (gold, platinum, diamonds, uranium) of white South Africa, they have been populated partly by compulsion.

The first independent Bantustan, Transkei, remains unrecognised by any government, which Nadine Gordimer says is right. "To acknowledge the independent Bantustans," she confirms, "would be to recognise the Balkanisation of South Africa: and South Africa should be one country."

The worst effect of Bantustan policy has been to harden tribal divisions fostered and encouraged by apartheid and by the education system in particular. Nadine Gordimer grieves over the conflict among blacks and black consciousness leaders. "Bantustans have fostered tribal divisions which had been broken by the racial unity of the ANC [African National Congress] and other movements in the Fifties. Perhaps in the long run this is the greatest evil that has been done."

And among the whites themselves there are the subdivisions. First into Afrikaners and English; next (unofficially but nonetheless palpably) into South-African-born whites and new immigrants. Then there are the subtle implications of precedence for those from Dutch and Anglo-Saxon stock over the "inferior" olive-skinned whites from Greece, Portugal, Italy. But even the new immigrants from northern Europe find the odds stacked against them—late starters at Afrikaans, now compulsory for Matric, University and any decent job.

Beyond the institutionalised alienations of race and tongue there are the inbuilt ones of a troubled society: the divorce rate—about one in three; the crime rate, at its worst in Johannesburg's Soweto (short for South West Township), where a million blacks crowd a dismal location of prefabricated two-room rented huts and the murder rate is the highest in the world.

Multi-apartheid. A society in ruins. Loveless, unlike the rest of Africa, whose collective heart throbs with warmth, where a sense of community enwraps even a white stranger, where the traveller feels at home. South Africa carries the sickness of rejection that rots Anglo-Saxon societies to its unbearable conclusion.

And here is a society so well compartmented that whites at least can forget the existence of anyone else. Blacks are shadows, servicing comfortable lives lived well away from the crawling rattrap of townships like Soweto. Whites live in new, supermarket-studded, jacaranda-shaded islands of whiteness, where blacks never come except as servants, carrying their passbooks like visas, in the dawn; going home again at night on shabby non-white buses, a journey that takes an hour, two hours—but who cares?

At weekends, the whites retreat into these ghettos, while the city centre, emptied of the commerce that moves it at a crackle during the week, comes alive with blacks. They stroll, laugh and shop like teenagers, spending the wages the law prevents them spending on homes and businesses. (For all the fuss about wage rates, South Africa's blacks are relatively well off, when they can find work; there is now a 22 per cent unemployment rate among black youth—another time bomb waiting to explode.) White businessmen are now spreading their nets to catch this indiscriminate spending which, like the teenage market in Britain, knows no bourgeois obligations—insurance, mortgages, entertaining.

To be born white in South Africa is to be born into another world. Like Britain's upper classes before the last war, South African whites are sheltered from the realities of the mass. They are also deprived of the scope and potential of the African continent, robbed of its energies, cheated of a birthright. Blacks and whites in rural areas may play together as toddlers. But soon young whites are sent to school and taught to be superior. The education system is a most divisive factor. Christian National Education (CNE) is a system devised as a foundation for the multi-apartheid society. Each racial and tribal group is taught by its own people in their own mother tongue. So Zulus are taught by Zulus, Xhosas by Xhosas, Indians by Indians, Afrikaners by Afrikaners and English by English. They will never have an understanding of what it is like to be other—a cruel deprivation.

Many young South Africans now know and resent this. But to raise a voice, or work for change, is to precipitate a banning order—that unique form of ostracism. One is confined to one's home between

dusk and sunrise, obliged to report to police once a week, forbidden
to write, teach, broadcast, speak in public or meet more than one
person at a time. South Africa has one of the most efficient and
organised systems of subtle repression in the world. Only the
occasional brutality or death is exposed. Real leaders are whisked
into the maximum security prisons—Robben Island, or Pretoria Jail.
Liberal thorns are removed from the authorities' side by banning.

Yet the law in South Africa is an ass. So much repression on the
one hand; on the other so much bureaucracy that a blind eye
appears to be turned to frequent and widespread disregard of the
law. In employment for instance, where blacks are restricted to
certain work yet are employed to do other tasks because white labour
is short; in pornography—even a nipple is sacrosanct in South Africa,
but blue films are widespread; and in the race laws themselves. The
law does not relate to the reality of change.

Nadine Gordimer says, "There are hotels now where blacks just
march in and sit down." Africans are not supposed to be served
drinks anywhere, even in the black townships, where illicit shebeens
supply the need. Demanding a drink in a white hotel is an illegal act
which seems dependent on nothing but bravado for its accomplish-
ment. Irrespective of laws the barriers seem to be breaking down,
eroding the foundations of apartheid. It is now, she says, "radical chic
to go to certain night clubs in Johannesburg where black and white
mix illegally. It's strange—the authorities are just ignoring it. The
strangest kinds of whites go there. I was talking to a young man who
had been to one, the New Yorker, with his wife. They've been
married a year. He works in an advertising agency. You can imagine
the kind of young man he is. He said, 'You know, some of these
blacks come up and ask a white girl to dance'—I can imagine it too:
they're doing it for the sake of doing it. 'One came up and asked my
wife to dance. I didn't like it at all.' He sought the experience and
didn't want it. This is the difference between giving some report and
having the experience."

The immense curiosity of whites about experiencing blacks—
impossible on the social level—has long been satisfied by sexually
motivated trips over the borders to Swaziland and Botswana, and
more recently to South West Africa (Namibia) where the Immorality

and Mixed Marriages Acts were repealed last year. But conditioning still has a strong grip on South Africans.

Brainwashing of whites is thorough and starts at babyhood. Nadine Gordimer describes its genesis. "One is very trusting as a child . . . One accepts this [apartheid] as a sort of God-given law. Certain trees grow at certain heights on the mountainside. It is reinforced by the black nannies and maids . . . "

Blacks are always servants, nannies, workers in overalls; never bosses, smart-suited executives, glamorous secretaries. It is natural to keep a separate set of crockery in the kitchen for the servants. One fears contamination, spiritual as much as physical.

Blacks in South Africa suffer from conditioning too. Among the older ones a slave mentality exists. Many still show an exaggerated respect, even love, for the whites, which the latter have clearly done nothing to earn—another dividend from their inherited investments, which in modern industrial South Africa are an outrage.

Young blacks are now registering that outrage in an often equally exaggerated disrespect—a cultivated rejection of white society and values, a deliberate bravado. Black consciousness is rising.

Nadine Gordimer says, "Africans are very strong. It's amazing how their culture has stayed intact. The family structure has been broken tragically in the cities. People have been educated, brainwashed: but there is a tremendous return to their roots. Black education (that started a revolt that might turn out to be a revolution) has allowed blacks to escape the brainwashing of white children. They were told to go back to their roots and they have." Mother-tongue education that caused Soweto's schoolchildren to riot in 1976—they wanted to be taught in English—has been the cultural lifeline that, ironically, has nourished the present black consciousness movement.

Young blacks are now visibly in revolt against their parents, whom they blame for accepting the inferior status of apartheid. Young whites too are blaming an older generation. And Nadine Gordimer, one of that generation, feels anger against the errors of the past: "I blame my parents' generation. There was still time then. Time for my children and their children to be Africans."

Nadine Gordimer's parents were perhaps typical of their generation. "My father was uninterested. He was kind, but kindness is not the thing, is it? My mother cared about other human beings. She was—not a do-gooder exactly—she did good works. She ran a crèche. She was troubled by the conditions under which the blacks lived. But it would never have occurred to her that the answer was radical political change."

One by one the opportunities for change that would have left whites with a role and a share of their heritage have fallen into history's abyss. "My parents' generation fought the war. The biggest chance came then. There were respectable black movements. Their leaders were in love with white education, white civilisation. The blacks had served in the war. They didn't bear arms but were stretcher-bearers and they fought side by side with the whites. They came back with them and marched shoulder to shoulder through the streets of Cape Town together as comrades. Then the whites retreated. The blacks were unbelievably disillusioned. It was the second big disillusionment. The first was after the Boer War when the British sold out the blacks."

Nadine Gordimer, herself of English stock, adds angrily, "Everyone blames the Afrikaners, but the British were to blame." She is right. The evils of apartheid are directly the result of Afrikaner Nationalism and the 30-year rule of a Nationalist Party whose enshrined policy has long been Separate Development; but still English South Africans sit back passively enjoying the consequences of a system they privately deplore. And, with a few brave exceptions such as Helen Joseph and Helen Suzman, they are all by their compliance implicated in the awful guilt of which history will not acquit them.

Nor has white resistance to apartheid been exclusively English. In the Fifties, soon after the Nationalists came to power, there were mass protests and black political organisation through the ANC, the Liberal Party and the Women of the Black Sash, all of which had multiracial membership and which no longer exist since multiracial organisations are now banned. Many members of these groups suffered banning and imprisonment before and after the infamous Treason Trial that brought all open political opposition to an eventual halt.

This, says Nadine Gordimer was "the period of the Toy Telephone. It was a toy because while there were committees and groups all talking about what needed to be done for the blacks, there was no

one listening at the other end." Nadine Gordimer is hard on
liberals. In her stories they appear as superficial, chic, uncom-
mitted, opportunistic, unrealistic, never effective. Liberalism is a dirty
word in Africa. It has never delivered the goods. Too ready to
compromise, to see both sides of the question, too polite; too much
of a gesture, not enough of a commitment, not radical. Now, rougher,
ruder, more brutal attitudes have replaced that gentle ideal of
brotherly love.

Black consciousness now rejects white help and wants to go it
alone in total opposition. Africans, no longer concerned with drinking
out of the same cups (Nadine Gordimer says, "Why should they care
about these petty prejudices? They no longer want that loving cup of
Lethe"), want a power that makes no concessions to white privilege
or sensibilities. Sharing South Africa, with a genteel agreement about
white seats in the Cabinet—the multiracial approach which Miss
Gordimer says is now the liberal one—is no longer viable. She adds,
"Many young people now genuinely want majority rule. You must
accept the fact that if you want democracy, there can be no
guarantees that whites are not going to suffer."

This is the tragedy of white South Africa now. Whites born of
generations there—some go back nearly 400 years—are Africans.
Are they to be told now that they do not belong, and must find
another home?

Anguished, many are leaving. Nadine Gordimer, herself, tried it
once. "I thought of going to live in Zambia. It was a romantic idea.
But I discovered I was only a European there, just like any other
white person. I took that very hard. At least in South Africa, even if I
get my throat cut, I'm an African."

A Guest of Honour, her story of a white colonial servant who
comes back to serve a black government, was, she says, based partly
on Zambia and partly on West Africa. "It's the book that means most
to me. Maybe it expresses what I feel constitutes the post-colonial
meaning—projecting beyond my own situation—that there is something that can exist beyond it. It's about someone who tries to justify
his presence in Africa beyond the colour of his skin."

The future of whites in South Africa must be put in the hands of
those whose lives have been directed by them for so long. It will be
an act of trust. This is something the white liberals, perhaps even

more than conservatives, find hard to accept; that blacks can manage alone without their care and guidance.

Nadine Gordimer says, "There is an acceptance by a small minority of whites (much criticised by other liberals) that withdrawal of blacks from whites is necessary for their own identity, that they have to discover themselves. Whites have to accept this. It's painful to accept rejection. A contradiction in terms. But it has to be done."

The same applies to government by majority rule. "You have to accept that you are a victim of history. Here is the end of the colonial period, and what you may stand for as an individual—no matter what you do or have done—will be swamped in the general whiteness."

In South Africa one wears one's skin like a uniform. White equals guilt. Victims have hitherto been black in South Africa. Maybe there is enough forgiveness still among Rhodesian and Namibian blacks, but in South Africa, where the worst system of oppression has reigned so long, who can predict safe passage, a home, a future for any white?

"Of course, there are Africans who do understand that there are whites who want no part of neo-colonialism—who do not want to perpetuate white power in another disguise—but the average black, what does he know of it? At best he may have had a master-servant relationship."

What, then, can a writer do to blend the irreconcilable fragments of what might have been a great nation into a hopeful future? The obstacles are legion. Nadine Gordimer has had two of her books banned in South Africa, and although she successfully applied for the ban to be lifted ten years later, to lose ten years is hard when you have so much to say, and the people you most want to say it to are protected from your vision of truth. "It's the most terrible thing to write a book and that it should not appear. When it's a political thing it's worse. Perhaps only Soviet writers understand this."

Another danger is self-censorship. But Nadine Gordimer denies that her survival is due to this. Another is "the chance that your loyalties to a cause are too strong. So you can't let the side down. Those on the side of the angels must be perfect. There must be no doubts about them. Black writers in South Africa are under tremendous pressure to put their talents at the service of the Struggle.

Even as far as choice of vocabulary—they are expected to adopt certain words and phrases. The clichés are worn smooth as a bar of soap. They come from the black power struggle in the States ten years ago."

Even so, she thinks, remarkable pieces of writing will come from South African black writers. "Writers of talent are not satisfied with clichés. They hammer out their own vocabulary."

But writings by blacks about Soweto and the events of 1976 are currently being banned. "I have a black writer friend who has written a book of poems about Soweto and Rex Collings has published them. But they are banned. A magazine started by a white man—now under house arrest—has had its first number banned. It's full of personal testimony, poems, stories, fragments. These are the underground press really: but there are so many spies." South Africa has a huge system of informers, black and white. Little escapes it.

"And when a book is banned in South Africa it is banned. In Argentina or Eastern Europe the book would still be very much there. But white South Africans are afraid."

Nadine Gordimer does not politick. "I never belonged to a political party. I am not an unpolitical human being. I take issue on censorship, for instance. But as a writer I feel there is one thing I ought to do. Take Günter Grass. I've simply understood Nazi Germany from his books. But in his speeches he has made many mistakes. What he really has to give is in his books, his imaginative work. As a writer one cannot stand aside." Must not. And who but writers will testify to the future what the South Africa that is now dying was really like?

South Africa's Nadine Gordimer: Novelist with a Conscience

Diana Loercher/1979

From *The Christian Science Monitor,* 27 November 1979, B6 +.
Reprinted by permission of Diana Loercher Pazicky and *The Christian Science Monitor.*

Nadine Gordimer would probably not have become a political novelist if the "accident of birth" had not placed her in South Africa.

"I would have been a writer anywhere," mused the author of *Burger's Daughter* during a recent interview. "I'm really what is known as a natural writer. I've been writing the way people who have a voice sing, from a very young age without any self-consciousness, without saying to myself, 'I am going to be a writer.' It's just there. It's a way of life for me. So had I been born somewhere else, had the 'accident of birth' put me somewhere else, I would have written very different books, maybe. Maybe not.

"I think stylistically I probably would not have to a certain extent. . . .

"You know, I started off as a short-story writer, much in the tradition of somebody like Eudora Welty, Chekhov. In the end, for the kind of situations I've met in my life, my subject matter, I couldn't have gone on writing quite like that. It was a conscious change . . . because the vehicle was too delicate to carry what I had to say. From the point of view of finding one's voice, one's style, particularly over the last decade, my struggle has been not to lose precision and intuitiveness and a certain delicacy even though dealing with harsh themes."

Living in South Africa, more than in the United States or Europe, "imposes real questions of moral choice on our lives," she says.

In *Burger's Daughter,* her seventh and most "radical" (her word) novel, it's the "accident of birth" that burdens her young heroine, Rosa Burger, not only with a South African nationality but with the heroism of her parents—what their author calls "real revolutionaries," Communists, committed to bringing about change in South Africa's oppressive policies. Rosa grew up watching them move in and out of prison. Her father died there, still believing that "there will always be those who cannot live themselves at the expense of the fullness of life for others."

The novel focuses on Rosa's longing to "defect" from that legacy of dedication and sacrifice and to lead a free, anonymous, ordinary life. Rosa learns eventually that "no one, no one, can defect." The real tyranny of the self is not commitment but lack of commitment, and "the real definition of loneliness: to live without social responsibility."

Miss Gordimer commented, "In a sense your whole life is either swimming around happily in the situation into which you are born, or struggling to get out of it."

Miss Gordimer, it is apparent from the briefest acquaintance, is the type that struggles. A tiny woman with the carefully cultivated fierceness of the fragile found in Joan Didion and Oriana Fallaci, she is a commanding, even a theatrical, presence. Her features are sharp, her face etched with lines of humor and indignation. She speaks crisply and with a cutting candor, at no time more apparent than during our discussion of the ban on her novel:

"And when you saw the vindictiveness and the desire to smear the book, you know it's being banned for political reasons—it's smeared with charges of obscenity and crudity and offensiveness, as if it were a cheap piece of porn. This was so clear," she fulminated.

Actually the ban on the novel was lifted in a record-short time, compared with the 10 and 12 years it took to exculpate two of her earlier novels. She is surprised and delighted by this action and guardedly encouraged by other recent changes in South Africa, such as the passage of a bill allowing blacks to form trade unions.

A member of that endangered species known as the political novelist, she is a realist who invites comparison with the great Russian novelists, such as Dostoyevsky. A key scene in her latest novel, in fact, in which a man beats a donkey, is startlingly similar to the horse-beating scene in *Crime and Punishment*. Actually the scene is not an echo of that episode but is based on an incident that happened while she was writing the book.

"The ravens feed you," she says. "It's amazing, when you're writing a book, things come. I always curl my lip when I hear writers

say, 'My characters run away with me.' I wish to goodness mine
would. They don't. Life takes over."

The daughter of a Lithuanian Jewish shopkeeper and an English
mother, she grew up in a small gold-mining town.

"My family were not racist, and my mother in particular—how
shall I put it?—always felt pity for blacks that they were poor. She did
a lot of charity work, and she helped run a crèche, but it never
occurred to her that what was really wrong was that they were in a
position to be pitied. They didn't have the basic rights.

"If you had said to her, 'If they had the vote, Mother, then they
wouldn't live like this.' . . .

"My awakening really came from outside, from my reading. I had
a very strange and lonely childhood and read a great deal. Oddly
enough, I think the book that first woke me up was Upton Sinclair's
The Jungle. When I read about the meatpackers in Chicago I
suddenly realized that the blacks working in the mines lived a similar
sort of life. . . .

"These men in blankets . . . brought directly from the tribal
situation . . . wandering around in their native attire, many of them
with hair covered in clay, long clay locks and big earrings— . . .
when I began to read and think about it I realized that my sense that
they were exotic was completely false. It was the other way around. I
was the exotic element.

"But if you fall into that colonial situation you simply accept that
you are there ruling the earth. . . ."

Miss Gordimer did not suddenly decide to write political novels,
but "tremendous political influences, political entities, became the
entities of my life around me." She came to believe in heroes, men
like Bram Fischer, on whom the fictional Lionel Burger is partly based.

"Rosa's life was not mine. I was not born into a political family like
hers, but I became more and more fascinated by observing and
knowing, in some cases rather well, people who were. They became
mysterious and fascinating beings to me and still are—and also a
certain awe around them. People of such courage, a combination
almost of selflessness, gaiety, and appetite for life that you wouldn't
think would go together. One thinks of selflessness in terms of
meekness and withdrawal. . . . But these people were just the
opposite. They seemed to live life so fully. . . .

"Well, that was the contrast with Conrad [a character in the novel]. Is life a journey toward self? This is the contemplative view of life and one that many people are turning to nowadays. The other fulfillment is to extend yourself as far as possible, to move out. . . . There are people who live like this, and they regard themselves as looking for the true way. Others pity them. I think Rosa says somewhere [that] on the one hand her father is offering the opportunity through the dangers that he presents to connect with life very fully. From the point of view of others he threw his life away.

" 'He who loses his life shall save it' is really what I'm talking about. How one reconciles oneself to this, not only reconciles oneself but does it gladly. One understands why this happens from a Christian point of view because you are really believing in an afterlife. You're believing in a transcendent element. But of course there's that transcendent element among 'the faithful,' too. They're living for 'the future.' It's a humanistic transcendence."

"The faithful" and "the future" are key phrases in the novel, referring to the utopian dream that those who give their lives up to history hope one day will be realized.

Miss Gordimer elaborated: "I was also looking into the whole question, especially in this country, of this fervor for realizing yourself, for self-fulfillment. At its lowest level it's having your initial on everything you wear to show 'I am I,' and 'I am somebody.' I find this rather distasteful . . . , but I realize it's just a symbol of something deeper.

"So on the one hand you have the principle of self-fulfillment first of all through sexual fulfillment and through being loved in that way, being loved by other people—the narcissism," she said scornfully. "The other way of realizing yourself, as the modern Western-world sees it, is through your work, your 'career,' as it's called. 'Work' is such a nice honest word, and 'career' is something I don't like very much. But career, all right. The concept that it's really through work and sex that you realize yourself. But both these goals are directed toward what you do for yourself, what you achieve in terms of making yourself loved and famous," she inveighed. "But people like the Burgers have a totally different view of life, and it fascinates me, because I myself was brought up in the self-fulfillment ethic."

As for her own degree of commitment, "it's if not a day-to-day at least a month-to-month decision. Circumstances change, and you say, 'Right, I'm going to do this, that, or the other.' And then something happens, somebody asks you something, somebody demands something of you, and you're back to Square 1 in deciding what your commitment is."

Political affiliation is not the issue. Miss Gordimer is not a Communist, nor does she belong to a political party, because she is committed to the goal of "a unitary South Africa," and "I have been in the position most of my adult life of having the choice of belonging to a party which was a whites-only one. That was the crux of it."

The decisions are more subtle. "I've never feared imprisonment, but detention we've all feared from time to time even through association, you see.

"That's another decision you have to make. Are you going to restrict your human contacts? Are you going to give up certain friends who've moved into dangerous areas because guilt by association is always there, and you yourself may be 'safe,' but you may through personal friendship be drawn into the orbit where such things happen?

"I should think that at the end of my life I shall say, as Jean-Paul Sartre does, that my regret will probably be that I have not been brave enough. I know that already."

She refuses to consider that the fact she is a political novelist might be enough to take her off the hook, and while she wants "the reader to see what I see," she does not even think about whether her books will affect his consciousness.

"My eyes are not out there; my struggle is with the material. It's like a net that you keep putting down into these mysterious waters of life around you, and you are struggling to bring up what is there, what is there in the depths, and of course you're also struggling with yourself because you're also down there."

Nadine Gordimer: Interview
Johannes Riis/1979

From *Kunapipi*, 2.1 (1980), 20–26. Reprinted by permission of
Kunapipi.

Johannes Riis interviewed Nadine Gordimer when she
was in Copenhagen in October 1979.

Burger's Daughter *seems to be a further culmination of the
disillusion, not only with the South African white liberal movement,
which is to be found in your writing from around 1960, but also with
the efforts made by more radical whites for the liberation of South
Africa?*

Don't confuse the views of a large range of characters with the
view of the writer . . . *The Late Bourgeois World* from 1966 shows
the breakdown of my belief in the liberal ideals. The main character
in that book, Liz, must realize that she can get no farther on the line
she has been following; she has got as far as her liberal ideals can get
her, and her dilemma is now a new one: shall she turn radical and go
on to a more binding commitment, do something really dangerous
and give in to the black radical Luke's wish to use her bank account
to bring in money for his revolutionary movement—or should she
give up her activities completely? The book ends on an ambiguous
note: her heart repeating 'like a clock; afraid, alive, afraid, alive,
afraid, alive . . .' And what is going to happen? I wonder. Afterwards
it is always interesting to look back upon a book and consider: what
will have happened to this or that character. Liz, I think, will have
married her lover Humphrey, who is a lawyer, followed his line and
worked with him for the liberation of South Africa, but in the
'constitutional way,' within the system, using the institutions of the
stage. And she will most certainly have gone on not believing in this
way.

This book really marks the end of what I had to say about white
liberalism in South Africa, and since then I have gone further in social

101

analysis. I think that this breakdown of belief was foreshadowed already in *Occasion for Loving* with its description of an affair between a black and a white character. That book, however, ended on a note of hope. You see, during the 1950s, we believed very strongly in the personal relationship, in the possibility that in changed circumstances blacks would view us as fellow human beings—*face to face,* acknowledging all of us as individuals: the Forsterian 'only connect' lay behind what we did and believed in. But we underestimated the strength of the government, we floated in rarefied air; we did not realize the economic forces we were up against and willy-nilly represented. We were very sincere and well-meaning and naïve, but I still think that whatever the illusions and mistakes were, the attitudes from those years have had an influence, and a positive one, on the attitudes now to be found among both blacks and whites in South Africa. I think that whatever little understanding there is left now between whites and blacks may originate from the liberal era. One should not discount this psychological effect; it cannot be measured, but I am sure it is still there. Of course it is extremely sad and discouraging—if totally inevitable—to see how the blacks have turned particularly against the white liberals in recent years. But let whites remember how much pain and discouragement blacks had to suffer before they faced the necessity to liberate *themselves.* There is a conflict between good intentions and the burden of history. You have to be equal to the demands of your time and place.

Irony has always been an essential element in your narrative technique, and increasingly so. Have you ever considered why?
　　Really, irony comes to me involuntarily, unconsciously. Proust said (I paraphrase) style is born of the meeting between the writer and his situation. In a society like that of South Africa, where a decent *legal* life is impossible, a society whose very essence is false values and mutual distrust, irony lends itself to you, when you analyse what happens. Let me give an example from 'The Amateurs', my short story from *The Soft Voice of the Serpent,* which is based very much on a personal experience. I wrote it when I was very young—about 20, I had no theories about literature then.
　　It is a story about a group of amateur actors and actresses who go out to put on a performance of *The Importance of Being Earnest* for

a black audience in a black township. It was based on something that happened to me. I was one of the members of this group. I was going to play Gwendolen and was dressed up in a marvellous dress with a bustle and false bosom, all of which made me look like an hourglass. I saw myself in the mirror and really felt the cat's whiskers. Here we were, taking culture to the blacks. I had never been in a black township before, it was filthy, ghastly, all of the story's descriptions of the environment are absolutely true to what I saw. I think I suffered a sort of culture shock in my native country: what I saw was so vastly different from the white world I knew, and yet so close in distance a few miles from where I lived. And who were we, feeling superior, showing off European culture in this South African dorp, to an audience with no background for understanding what we were doing, an audience whose own culture *we* did not know at all?

When I wrote the story I was only registering and interpreting what I had actually seen. I used empathy in that story, I intended no irony, it entered on its own. The irony in this story is a by-product of my looking back on the episode, of the process of understanding it, shortly after. But as I said earlier on, irony is an appropriate way of tackling South Africa. Dan Jacobson's *A Dance in the Sun,* which I consider one of the best presentations of the South African tragedy from the white point of view, supports this view.

In your writing, irony seems to become still more pervasive, subtler and subtler, and from time to time this makes it hard for a 'new' reader with no frame of reference to your writing as a whole to grasp the meaning, for there are hardly any fixed points. I have found for example 'Africa Emergent' to be such a story.

It is true that there are more direct statements, explicit comments, and breast beating and less irony in my earliest stories (e.g. in *Face to Face*) than in the later ones. It has to do with the belief I had then in the liberal ideals, but it is just as much due to my lack of writing ability at that time. Had I written say, 'Which New Era Would That Be?'—it dates from my early thirties—earlier on, I would not have let Jake's turning up the gas and kicking the chair in the end of the story, after Jennifer Tetzel and the journalist have left, speak for itself, but would have explained, emotively, Jake's feelings, something like this: 'He was furious, who on earth did she think she was . . .' and the story would have lost its impact, which comes from the fact that the reader *himself* makes this judgement.

Here I might add that when I make selection of my short stories there is a moral problem. For how much should one revise? In revising, I feel disloyal to myself, it feels like cheating to make corrections and improvements on what one has written a long time ago. So, instead of correcting and editing, I tend to leave out stories that I don't feel are satisfactory for some reason or other.

As to 'Africa Emergent', I don't think it is a very good story, certainly not the best I can do. When I was collecting *Selected Stories* (later reissued as a paperback as *No Place Like: Selected Stories*) I was very much in doubt whether to include it or not. The problem with this story is that it is really two stories—and what is it about? Is it about the architect, or is it about the relationship between him and his black friend? Actually, it was intended as a story about one of the most terrible products of South African life, the distrust that has arisen, and has had to arise, in a state like South Africa. It was written in a state of fiery emotion. The writer and her situation didn't meet, because she wasn't equal to it.

It is true that in any group of opponents to the government one can never be sure that some of the members are not police spies, and the situation (as in the story) is becoming so absurd and perverted that the very fact that a person—and he may very well be a friend— is *not* in prison, puts him or her under suspicion: Is he or she a police spy? One can never be sure, and of course this places an enormous strain on all relationships. In order to give you an impression of the effects of this state of affairs I'll tell you about an incident from our writers' organization a short while ago.

In the organization—Southern African PEN in Johannesburg— which has both black and white members, we very often arrange poetry readings. Such readings are extemely popular at the moment, we are so to speak at the Yevtushenko stage! One reason for the popularity of this sort of arrangement is that there is a feeling that words which have only been spoken are not felt to be very dangerous, whereas the moment they have been written down they become much more politically incriminating. The quality of the poetry read out is not always very high, some of the poems are hardly more than slogans, but there is genuine feeling, real anger, real pride and determination to create a literature for the people.

One afternoon we had arranged a reading in a black township church. There were about 30 of us, 25 blacks and 4 or 5 whites. The following night, one of the black poets, a young man of less than 20, who had been one of the readers, was called upon by the police, taken to the station, and questioned all night about himself and other members of the organization.

When the rest of us got to know, it caused a great shock among the white members, and we got together in great agitation. Who is the informer? Who is a police spy? Who among us?

But the black members remained perfectly calm. I asked one how he could be so controlled, and got this answer, 'What about it? What can we do if it is found out who the informer is? Absolutely nothing. This is the way we live now.'

The informer was regarded as a victim of a system of repression, just like his victims. There is a feeling among many blacks that you have to accept the facts of the struggle. If you are not prepared or willing to live with danger like that, you can just as well lock yourself up immediately. The risk, the danger is taken so much for granted that incidents like the one I told you about don't surprise or anger any black.

Take the example of the police force. Among blacks there is a tremendous hatred of and antagonism against the white police which is only too natural. But the same hatred is not to be found against their black colleagues. Their work is the same, in fact most work done by the black police is action directed against their fellow blacks. Of course one can understand that blacks become policemen; they get a permanent job, a fixed salary, security. The white economy doesn't give blacks much choice on the matter of earning their bread.

I would like to hear which contemporary writers you read and find interesting?

I know that it is fashionable for writers to say that they don't but I readily admit that I read a lot of contemporary work. I think that Latin American writers such as Alejo Carpentier, García Márquez, Fuentes, Puig and of course Borges, form the most interesting group of writers

today. Böll's *Group Portrait with Lady,* Grass's *The Flounder,* Michel
Tournier, through whose crystal tower the winds of the world blow,
Chinua Achebe . . .

What about the English?
I think their subject matter is incredibly narrow, most of them
concentrate on more or less pathological states. Look at a writer like
Iris Murdoch. She is an immensely talented writer, but so often, what
is she doing but describing pathological states standing for metaphysical states? Angus Wilson is a very fine writer, indeed, and of the
youngest generation I think Ian McEwan is one of the most
promising, not because of his novel *The Cement Garden,* which is
mannered and contrived, but because of his short stories. I think he
has many fine works in store. Graham Greene is unique—a questing
lucidity that no other writer in the English language can come near.
Why hasn't he got the Nobel Prize? We have all learned so much
from him, as writers and readers.

*But most of the interesting news in English literature seems to
come from the Commonwealth.*
I did not mention any of the so-called Commonwealth writers
before. Do you call V. S. Naipaul an English writer? A 'Commonwealth' writer? I don't like Naipaul's *In a Free State* and *Guerrillas*
very much, I feel he 'chose' the subjects, whereas with *A House For
Mr Biswas*—a marvellous novel—and *A Bend in the River,* his
subjects chose him. He expresses a whole consciousness that has not
been expressed before. It's tremendously important.

Patrick White I admire greatly, I think he stands apart among
present day writers—think of *A Fringe of Leaves* and *The Aunt's
Story.* He has a fantastic ear for how people speak; nothing is more
deadening than when—in a novel or play—all the characters talk
alike. In White's work they never do.

Doris Lessing—always searching, always on her way to something
new and different, what a range of intelligence, her every book a
blow at artistic complacency. *The Golden Notebook* I consider her
masterpiece.

The first part of *Children of Violence, Martha Quest,* has some
very striking similarities with my first novel, *The Lying Days,* which I
wrote at the same time. Not because we influenced each other—I

don't suppose we'd heard of each other; the similarities had to
arise—there was such a similarity of development and experience
between us where and when we grew up. In another sense those
early novels complement each other. I like the idea of a literary
patchwork, novel by novel, poem by poem, by different writers,
mapping out an era, 'a continent' more and more thoroughly. No
one writer can do it.

I rank Achebe very highly, especially his *Arrow of God,* and I
consider it a tragedy that he has had to live under such disturbed
conditions and writes so little.

Among the Americans Thomas Pynchon's *Gravity's Rainbow* gives
me the strongest illumination of the American mystery. For my
personal experience of the USA doesn't expain it to me at all . . .

Bellow (what a wonderful novel *Humboldt's Gift* is), Updike and
Heller started very differently, but their own lives are octopuses
taking up more and more space in their books: their divorces etc.
Even Updike's *The Coup* which is set among blacks in Africa is a
book about John Updike. Clever, erudite, elegant, yes—but just
compare it with *A Bend in the River.* Naipaul doesn't use flashy
symbolic characters to daggle but commands the profound skill to
move deep into the end of colonial life through apparently marginal
lives.

What Mailer and Capote etc. are doing now with their writing, in
which they use factual material for their books, is in my opinion an
unfortunate failure of the imagination: sensationalism in place of
sensibility. Again, the morbid hankering after the spurious 'heightened reality' of the pathological personality.

Finally I would like to mention a writer from the American/
European borderline, Paul Theroux, whose novel *The Family Arsenal*
is one of the best about England of the last 10 or 15 years. Theroux
has passed through a remarkable development; he is one of those
writers who 'hear' what people are thinking about themselves, and
he gives expression to what goes unrealized in their society in a way
they can't do.

Nadine Gordimer: A White African Against Apartheid

Claude Servan-Schreiber/1979

From *F Magazine*, No. 21 (November 1979): 24 +. French title: Nadine Gordimer: une Africaine blanche contre l'apartheid. Reprinted with permission from Claude Servan-Schreiber. Translated by Nancy Topping Bazin.

If the French do not recognize the name Nadine Gordimer, the fault lies with the French publishing houses which, until this year, have strangely ignored one of the best living writers of the English language: six short-story collections, seven novels of which *A World of Strangers* was just recently published in France [Editions Albin-Michel] even though it was written years ago. Thus, we are speaking of a writer of considerable achievement and one very marked by the culture in which she is developing as a writer: Nadine Gordimer is South African and her country is that of apartheid.

Apartheid is a set of laws which institutionalize the supremacy of 4,400,000 white South Africans over a nonwhite population of 21,200,000 people. The "nonwhites" include mainly blacks but also Asians (mostly from India) and persons of mixed blood. At present the apartheid government, which advocates the "separate development" of racial communities, is trying to improve its image. For the past year, a new prime minister has been implementing a strategy designed, as he says, "to save South Africa from a revolution." Last month, liberalization measures were announced: interracial marriages will no longer be considered immoral despite a law forbidding them. Land set aside for the Bantustans—those tribal homelands with black leadership—will be extended. The right to unionize will be accorded to black workers. All this has occurred because, after the bloody uprising in 1976 in Soweto, a black suburb of Johannesburg, the white Nationalist government ascertained that the unrest was reaching the boiling point; at any moment violence could pose a serious threat to the social order.

Despite appearances, however, there have been no changes in the basic principles on which apartheid is founded. There has been no sharing of power between the white minority and the black majority and no racial integration. Nor has there been any revision in the way in which the mineral and industrial wealth of the country has been divided between whites and blacks. This is true despite the fact, so obvious to some observers, that the black revolution is definitely well underway.

Moreover, since the insurrection in Soweto, other very troubling events have occurred: demonstrations, strikes, boycotts, waves of violence. Just recently, 15,000 commuters using city transport designated "for blacks only" rose up to protest a big increase in fares. How can we not think of the Algerian precedent? With this difference, however—the white South African has no mother country.

In this context, Nadine Gordimer's life and her writings are of very special interest to us: those South African whites who, like Gordimer, despise racism and desire a bringing together of the two communities—what are they experiencing and what would they like to see happen? And how does one continue to write when everything seems to legislate against it?

Claude Servan-Schreiber: *Nadine Gordimer, your life's work has as its backdrop contemporary South Africa, that is to say, a society shaped, infected should one say, by the racist structures of apartheid. Twenty years separate one of your first works—which the French public is just now being introduced to—from your last novel* [Burger's Daughter], *banned in your own country but available elsewhere in English. Both of these novels demonstrate your fascination with the whites who struggle alongside the blacks against the injustices of segregation. Whether liberals or revolutionaries, the methods and the degree of involvement of these characters evolve through time, depicting what has been happening for a generation.*

Nadine Gordimer: Indeed, a great deal has changed since the first edition of *A World of Strangers* was published in 1958. In retrospect, what seems interesting to me about the period described in the book is that it was a very privileged era in the history of South Africa. In the fifties if you wanted to maintain friendly relations with blacks, work with them, discuss with them, do music or politics with them—everything was still possible. For about 12 years, the two

communities frequented each other. Naturally, the social taboo
existed. It was even very pronounced, and more than one ordinary
white citizen considered my husband and me crazy for having black
friends. But contacts were easy if you wanted them.

 During that particular era, indisputably a dream was lost because
the massive but nonviolent/pacifist movements for black liberation,
which reached their peak in the '50s, were crushed, decimated. And,
therefore, everything changed.

What happened exactly?

The blacks organized protest campaigns against apartheid which
demanded the elimination of the "passbook." This is a document
that every black must carry on his person and be able to present on
the spot anytime he is asked. These passbooks prevent blacks from
being able to move about freely within South Africa or to look for
work other than what they have already. This requirement permits a
strict and constant control over their daily lives. Hence, the blacks
rebelled, burned their passbooks in the street in front of the police
station. The police became frightened and opened fire. That
happened in Sharpeville in 1960. It is to that event that one can trace
the beginning of the end of black collaboration with white liberals,
which we had hoped and believed possible. After Sharpeville, every
white person who had felt close to blacks, who had shared their lives,
maintained with them personal relations of friendship or love, found
themselves up against the wall. We all had that experience: in a white
neighborhood, in the middle of the night, someone knocking at the
door. It was a black friend sought by the police: "Do you accept to
hide me at your place, in your garage or wherever you wish?" Well,
within the space of a few weeks, it had become extremely dangerous
to help or to support militant blacks. The African National Congress
had been banned under a law created for the suppression of
communism. Anyone helping a black was regarded as a communist,
a terrible accusation given the attitudes of that period. Therefore,
many whites were terrified. The liberals were forced to choose—
either to take risks by disobeying the laws or not to act in accordance
with their beliefs. Many were arrested or were forced later to go into
exile.

This situation was made considerably worse, wasn't it, by the

*events of June 1976, that is to say, by the uprising of the black
neighborhood of Soweto which resulted in 700 dead?*

Yes, Soweto marked the beginning of a still more difficult period.
After the banning of the major black political movements almost 20
years ago, we witnessed the collapse of those organizations and their
leaders exiled or thrown into prison. Some of them are still in exile or
in prison. Because of this repression, a new generation of blacks grew
up without the least political education.

Ten years later, at the beginning of the '70s, new ideas surged forth
from the nonwhite universities. A new movement based on these
ideas sought to restore to blacks their pride and to procure for them
an identity that owed nothing to whites—one that would be
something other than the reflection or the shadow of the white man.
The Civil Rights Movement of black Americans had a very strong
influence on this new generation.

This time it was no longer a nonviolent movement?

No, indeed, because the young, disillusioned by the failures and
the resignation of their parents, denounced the illusion that any
progress could be made in cooperation with whites. They declared:
"We must act alone. As long as we are in contact with the whites, we
will be allowing ourselves to be defeated by them. Let us find our
own way."

That is the situation still today. The white community, whether
progressive or not, must face a new generation of nationalistic and
revolutionary blacks. Ashamed of the collaboration that their parents
practiced with the whites, the young blacks reject everything about
our way of life, thus indicating that they do not intend to allow
themselves to be degraded, even by the whites who claim to desire
their well-being.

What role do women play in the black nationalist movement?

A very important one. And it is nothing new. Back when the major
mass movements (especially the African National Congress) were not
yet banned, they had within them vigorous and influential women's
organizations. We were just talking about the demonstrations against
the passbooks. The black women resisted them even before the men
did. At the time, only the men were required to have such a
document. When the government decided to extend this requirement

to women, the women protested and resisted. They even won. All
that was swept aside when the repression went into effect. However,
the women who shaped their personalities through political action
during those years remained heroines for the rest of the black
population.

What do you think of Winnie Mandela?

She is the best known. She is an admirable woman. Her husband,
one of the leaders of the African National Congress, is imprisoned for
life on our Devil's Island. As for Winnie, she never gave up the
struggle. She is put in and out of prison constantly. For example, she
was arrested after the events of Soweto because she had organized,
in collaboration with other blacks, an association of parents that
seemed, at first, insignificant but quickly became extremely important. This organization strove to eliminate the estrangement that had
developed between the young blacks, who had revolted, and the
older generation. This is one of the very serious problems facing the
black community today, this gap between the generations. The
young accuse their parents: "You allowed yourselves to become
discouraged; you were afraid to take risks. Us, we are not afraid. We
demonstrate; we confront the guns; we want to fight." And they
radicalized their elders in an extraordinary manner. By speaking out
in favor of the action of the young people, Winnie Mandela, thanks to
her eminence, certainly influenced a part of the black community that
until then had been traumatized by the acts of the young. That is the
reason she was judged and condemned.

When she is not in prison, she is placed under house arrest and
thus prevented from moving about or working. For a while after the
rebellions, the government permitted her to live in Soweto in her
house but basically forbade her to leave or to receive anyone there.
Then they did something even more horrible; they exiled her to a
small village deep in the countryside. It is there that she is living at
present. And the only news published about her appears when those
who brave the interdiction visit her and get caught.

*Are there other women who, likewise, are symbolic figures of the
resistance?*

Probably you have never heard about Deborah Mabiletza, a black
mother who is very active in religious organizations, very strong

spirited, very political. After Soweto, she did not immediately accept that the black struggle should deprive itself completely of the support of the white progressive community. She had worked too long with them not to hope that collaboration was still possible. After the uprising, she created with the whites an organization called "Women for Peace," basing it on the principle that all women, whatever their color, cannot accept to see their loved ones killed. She said to the whites: "Many black children have just been killed. Soon, white children will also be killed. The problem transcends politics. We must block this escalation." At the time, the parents of the young, imprisoned blacks did not even know where their children were being detained. The association obtained for the black families the right to locate and visit their children. But that was the end of it, because her organization had tried to function independently, without taking political ideologies into account. The white women realized this very quickly. They became afraid. And Deborah quit that organization. Today she works only with black women.

For which causes, in particular, are those black women fighting?

At this very moment, they are fighting against the municipal authorities to obtain the right to live near the cities where their men work. There is a severe housing shortage for the nonwhite population. Until very recently, in Soweto, if a man died or if he divorced his wife, she found herself immediately put out on the street. She did not have the right to be the person either owning or renting a house. A white, progressive party led by Helen Suzman won this cause for these women. This problem is now resolved, and one no longer sees these mothers thrown into the street with their children with no solution possible. But other similar problems persist which do not seem to be nearing a solution. Do you know that because of apartheid a black worker, recruited by a company which requires that he leave his village, has no right to take his wife and children with him? As a result, there is a clandestine emigration of black women towards the cities with the constant threat of expulsion weighing upon them.

You live in South Africa whereas many writers who oppose apartheid have chosen exile. Is that because they have been forced to leave?

You see, writing is not for me a political activity. Before anything else, I am a writer. But because the society in which I live is so permeated with politics, my work has become intimately connected with the translation of political events, of the way politics affect the lives of people. I imagine that the South African government considers me a political adversary—as if I were someone utilizing my profession to combat it. But I myself would not call what I do a political activity, because even if I lived elsewhere, I would still be a writer.

So you have never considered going into exile?

Yes, of course I have. But I chose to stay because my roots are there. I am often asked: "If you did not live in South Africa, where would you choose to live? In England probably?" Naturally I feel comfortable in England. I could use my own language, the one in which I work, which for a writer is of primary importance. However, I do not belong more to England than I do to France, which I love and where my daughter lives. I belong completely to my country.

Nevertheless, your work is censured there since three of your novels are or were banned. How does censorship work in South Africa?

The charges for which one can be censored are extremely numerous. For instance, my last novel [*Burger's Daughter*] was banned because they considered it to be obscene, blasphemous, pernicious in the area of race relations, offensive to certain parts of the population, and detrimental to the security of the state.

Oh, is that all? [laughter] But who decides? Who judges?

The censorship board is represented throughout the country by regional committees on which serve a total of 200 people. If only three members on a committee agree, that is sufficient for a book to be banned. Needless to say, these judges have no qualifications in the area of literary criticism. They are often retired people, appointed only because they have been loyal servants of the Nationalist Party which is in power. They are paid for their services. Unchallenged, they make their decisions sovereignly.

Are the banned books for the most part political books?

Not at all. It is interesting—and, for a writer, humiliating—to examine the list of banned books. One finds wedged between the most abject pornography and propaganda brochures marvellous contemporary novels, poems, and avant-garde literature—or to cite only one classic, Pascal's *Pensées.*

Is there any way to get around the censorship?
Yes, but only in a very circumscribed way. It's a matter of distributing the book in a foreign language. Very often a book banned in English will not be banned in other languages. It takes the censorship board a while to notice what's going on. That happened for instance with *A World of Strangers;* it was not available in English but it was for sale in translation. Also, the first edition of this novel was available for 18 months, then banned the day that the paperback was distributed. Try to figure out why—

Can just anyone put something before the censorship board?
Absolutely. Just any citizen. It's an iniquitous procedure. When someone reads a book and finds it offensive, then that person need only mail it with a little bit of money (about ten francs) and say to the censorship board: "I don't like this book; please consider banning it."

Censorship affects all writers in the opposition no matter what the color of their skin. Are there contacts between black and white writers for the purpose of collaborating or helping one another?
In contrast to what happens in political parties, the joint participation of whites and blacks is not forbidden in professional associations as long as they do not function as unions. A year ago we created a mixed professional association. Moreover, it actually functions and is useful. Most professional associations are composed exclusively of whites, but ours is 90% black. It is a branch of PEN [International Association of Poets, Playwrights, Editors, Essayists and Novelists]. Prior to that, I believed that PEN was composed of only amateur writers who got together occasionally to drink a cup of tea. Well, that's not true at all. This organization permits us to act, to aid writers in the East or in South America. We recently held our first conference in Johannesburg. We had among us some young blacks, 18 or 19 years old, who had published a few poems in a small, mimeographed journal. We were accused of not being selective enough in our

recruitment of members. But we don't care. What is essential lies elsewhere: we have a different set of goals.

In what language do the blacks write? In English?

Yes, for the most part. And they encounter exactly the same difficulties as do the black writers from the former French colonies, because their introduction to written literature—quite different from their own which is oral—occurs in the language of their conquerers. Some write in Afrikaans. However, owing to national pride, some are beginning to write in their native language. I'm thinking in particular of a woman whose name is Fatima Diké. She writes plays, doing something that no other of our writers has yet tried: she does research into the history of the black people to find episodes that have been silently passed over in histories written by whites, which begin only with the white conquest and recount everything from the white point of view. Her play has been translated into English, and it's quite remarkable.

Can plays like that one be put on? Are they not banned?

We are always kept on the edge of the razor. All the same, as I've often noticed with my own work, there are things that slip through. We always go as far as we think we can. Sometimes we fail and the work is banned. Other times, all goes well. For example, at this very moment in Johannesburg, although outsiders do not know about it, there is a racially integrated neighborhood, which, because of particular circumstances, escaped the segregation imposed upon every other area. For a while, in Johannesburg, there were even non-segregated nightclubs that were enormously popular. A friend of mine wrote a play on the topic of what this breach in the segregation created by apartheid—what this possibility to meet and to mix—meant to the black and white characters. A censorship agent came, demanded a few minor changes, but did not ban the play.

When did you begin to oppose apartheid? From the beginning? Was your family antiracist?

Not at all. I was born in South Africa in a small town known for its gold mines, and I received an education that was as colonial as any could be. We were not rich; but because we were living in South Africa, we had a black maid. She was for years the only contact I had with the black population. Therefore, I experienced the classic situation in my country in which whites who do not have a very high income still have the wherewithal to have black servants. This maid was my mother's confidante. She was very much part of the household, knew everything that went on, including all our familial crises. But she was never our equal; she never sat down with us to have a cup of tea, except in the kitchen.

In short, for a long time I regarded the specific situation of blacks to be the natural order of things. It wasn't until later, during my adolescence, thanks to the reading I was doing, that I began to see a parallel between my daily life and what I discovered in books— particularly about class struggle. Was it a natural order or, on the contrary, was it an order—which was unjust—created by people?

At the university I met, for the first time, blacks who had the same interests, the same tastes, the same level of education as I did. They wrote, painted, played and wrote music. For artists, race is not a barrier. That's how I came to see things differently from my parents.

I can't tell you if my family was truly racist. I believe that many people like them—and it continues today—do not ask themselves questions that are likely to upset them.

But you, you asked them?

Yes, and that was an extraordinary deliverance. I believe that the young, white South Africans who have their consciousness raised experience a kind of rebirth. All of a sudden, one feels whole. The only thing I can compare this with is that of a woman who suddenly becomes conscious of being a woman and all that that implies. She then sees herself differently. It's a truly freeing experience which is irreversible and makes one feel totally alive.

Did the fact that you are Jewish facilitate your awakening? In Europe during your childhood and your adolescence, millions of Jews were persecuted because of their origin and culture.

No, as a child, I didn't see the connection between anti-Semitism and the racism in South Africa because I was not raised in the Jewish tradition but rather as an agnostic. Yet my father had, during his childhood, suffered from a form of apartheid. But he never drew the parallel between the two situations. Born a Lithuanian Jew, he had nevertheless lived under Russian domination which denied Jewish

children the right to go to the same schools as the others or to attend
the university. My father arrived in South Africa at age 13 totally
uneducated. His attitude was not much different than that of the
immigrants who arrive in South Africa today—Italians, Germans,
French. They are hardly there three weeks before they adopt all the
behavior and prejudices of the white supremacists. Thereafter nothing
can change their attitude. My father quickly forgot that he had arrived
in South Africa in very humble circumstances, that he did not at first
speak English any better than the blacks. You see, even the whites
who had every reason not to feel superior did not hesitate to adopt
the biases of the South African society.

How exactly did your awakening occur?
As soon as I began to know blacks personally and interact with
them, I understood what these laws (made concrete by the "For
Whites Only" signs) meant in people's lives.
At that point, a white person goes through two different stages. At
first, the individual sees only the offense done to blacks. But then that
person perceives that it is likewise an offense done to whites—that
one's life, even if extraordinarily privileged, is diminished by the fact
that all normal contact is impossible with the majority of the people in
one's country. I realized that "my" people were not just the whites of
South Africa, but the whole population. Little by little as time went
on, I understood that I was not a European. I am a white African.
That now is totally clear for me.

*That also explains why you want to stay in your country, having
lived all your life and raised your children there. How does one
prepare the young to live in a society such as yours?*
Fighting racism in education leads to some strange things. We have
two children, a girl and a boy, both adults now. We didn't want to
send our daughter to a public school, because we wanted to avoid
exposing her to the Nationalist Christian education that was imposed
there with all that that implies. But even in private education,
although not doctrinaire like the other, the attitude of most of the
students is appallingly racist in regard to blacks, Jews, and even
Afrikaners. Thus, throughout her studies, my daughter lived with an
intense conflict between what was said at home and what was said at
school. Having learned from that experience, we wanted to do

something different for our son. We sent him to a boarding school in Swaziland [a small country (east of Johannesburg) encircled by South Africa and Mozambique]; this was an international school with no segregation. Therefore, throughout his school years, he lived, ate, slept, played, studied with blacks, as should happen in a normal, just society. But, already at the time, he was very unhappy when he returned home. His black and Indian friends also went home for the vacation, but because my son and his friends found themselves abruptly in South Africa, they could no longer drink a coke or go to the cinema together. This created a difficult situation that we had not foreseen but which became extremely clear as soon as the studies were over and he came home. Also, he had to do his military service in the South African army and, as you can imagine, that was a horrible ordeal for him. In wanting to help him adopt a just way of behaving in life, we had prepared him for a world that did not exist. Now he has left to study in the United States. I don't know whether he will ever return to South Africa. That is for him to decide.

Is the white fear of blacks visible today in South Africa? Statistics indicate that it is one of the most armed populations in the world, with more than 1,500,000 individuals owning guns—not counting all those which have not been declared or additional arms in white families owning more than one gun.

No doubt there is an inherent justice because these overarmed people spend their time firing on one another. They get what they deserve. A young man sees his girlfriend go out with someone else, he drinks and—kills her. I appear to make light of this situation but really take it very seriously. Children find guns in their parents' homes and kill each other or kill someone else while the adults are watching television. People are continually killing one another by mistake.

Do you have any guns in your house?

No. [Smile] But most people do because of the major panic that gripped them after 1976. Peaceful people, sometimes not racist at all—people who would never have thought of arming themselves— bought a revolver because they thought the blacks were going to attack the white neighborhoods.

Do you have the feeling that a civil war is inevitable?

You know, the revolution is already in progress. True revolutions do not occur between clear time lines. What we have at home is a situation where there are sporadic uprisings, incidents of all sorts, a kind of civil war. Then, is a larger civil war, a still more dramatic one, going to break out? I do not see any way to answer such a difficult question. The present government is announcing some reforms yet continues the division of the country into a powerful white state on the one hand and a miserable black state on the other. What does that mean in practice? It means that, in an extremely rich country, the resources remain in the same hands—in those of whites.

When one thinks as you do that apartheid is unbearable, how do you continue to live in South Africa? One cannot avoid adopting as one's own the most unjust practices. You take buses reserved for whites; you go to a cinema for whites, you go to a beach open only to whites. How does one deal with that?
One has an immense sense of shame. But one ends by forgetting it. When you take a bus, you direct yourself automatically towards the stops reserved for whites. It is human nature to allow oneself to be conditioned without even noticing it is happening.

What happens, for example, if you board a bus reserved for blacks?
The conductor will say to you politely: "This is not a bus for whites," and he will not permit you to board. It's rather comic to watch whites coming from another country, full of good intentions, saying: "I don't care; I refuse to acquiesce." What courage that person has when one knows very well that a week later he or she will peacefully go back home having created a small incident that has served no purpose at all! Indeed the blacks dislike that kind of protest. That kind is of no interest to them.

Are there nevertheless some whites who do resist and conduct themselves with an authentic heroism?
Yes. There still exists in my country a feeling that there can be something greater than one's own life, than the satisfaction of one's own desires or needs. One sees this in South Africa among the whites as well as among the blacks.

Do they succeed in not being immediately arrested?

They don't care if they are arrested. These authentic heroes do not look upon their lives as you and I do. I can cite you a case which is very close to me. There is a young, white writer, Jeremy Cronin; he is currently in prison for 12 years for having thrown virulent pamphlets into a street in Cape Town at a moment when there was heavy traffic. The reason for his conviction was that he was trying to overthrow the state! Unlike others, during his trial he did not apologize. Nor did he promise never to do it again. He even stated during his trial: "If it had to be done again, I would start doing it tomorrow. I do not accept to live in this country as it is, and I believe that what I did should have been done." I have never met this man, but I read in the newspaper the account of his trial. A short time ago, he wrote to me (he is authorized to receive two letters a month of 500 words each), asking me if I would accept to correspond with him because, as a specialist in English literature, he wanted to deepen his knowledge of my work. Since then, we have corresponded, and his letters astonish me. He is not at all in despair. He believes in the utility of what he has done; he sees the end of the tunnel; he is there for 12 years and he waits.

Twelve years is an interminable length of time. Many things may happen in the meantime.
Who knows?

Nadine Gordimer on BBC's "Arts and Africa"

Alex Tetteh-Lartey/1979

Transcription of "Arts and Africa" program #283 printed by permission of Alex Tetteh-Lartey and BBC's African Service.

AT-L: Born in 1923, Nadine Gordimer, who has published five collections of short stories and seven novels, has established herself as South Africa's leading lady novelist and short story writer, although two of her novels have been banned in the Republic. Nadine Gordimer has won three major British literary awards for her work and also shown herself to be a perceptive critic of African literature in her book *The Black Interpreters: Notes on African Writing.*

Nadine, I would like to start this discussion by defining what African writing is and I'll take a quotation from your book written in 1973, *The Black Interpreters.* Now you say there that, to you, African writing is "done in any language by Africans themselves and by others of whatever skin colour who share with Africans the experience of having been shaped, mentally and spiritually, by Africa rather than anywhere else in the world." People like you who have a sense of humanity and try to understand the black man's point of view—that's all right, we can understand if *you* write about Africa. But how about the conservative white in South Africa who claims he's an African or the conservative white in Zimbabwe-Rhodesia who claims he is an African and at the same time traces his ancestry to Europe? What would writing by such a person be?

NG: I wouldn't consider that African writing. I think the claim would be invalid. It's not African writing. I think that you have to be steeped in the African consciousness, even if you are white. You have to have a deep interest that will lead you to an understanding of it. There's a reason why, as I remember it, that I phrased the definition as I did—I thought a long time about it: what about in South Africa? There are half a million Indians who've been there for a couple of generations, and there are some writers among them who are very politically committed to the black cause. A writer like a friend of mine who has just published a book there—what should he be regarded as? He's an Indian, but he was born there and politically he's at one with the black cause. We must allow him to be an African writer of some kind.

AT-L: Now you put a great premium on politics as a worthy theme for the novel and you say in *The Black Interpreters* that not enough has been made of the political situation in Africa in its novels and that in Africa, "politics is fate"?

NG: Yes, and I believe that. Because for the last two or three generations or more, let us say since the beginning of the colonial period and now in the postcolonial period, politics enter so closely into everybody's life. In every country in Africa, I think this present generation is deeply conscious of how much their lives are manipulated by politics, so naturally, writers take their material from the life around them—if they are honest writers; they don't suck it out of their thumbs or bring it down from the clouds. Therefore, intrinsically and implicitly, many novels—and many of the best—are likely to have political themes.

AT-L: Well, many African novels have been based on politics. Ayi Kwei Armah of Ghana has written *The Beautyful Ones Are Not Yet Born*. Kofi Awoonor has written about politics in *This Earth, My Brother*. Peter Abrahams has written *A Wreath for Udomo,* which is about politics.

NG: Yes, one of the early ones.

AT-L: You also say that although they've written about political themes and criticised the existing political situation, they have not replaced it with any ideology—anything to replace what they condemn.

NG: You know I'm not sure that it's the writer's function to do so. Because the writer—the novelist—reflects upon what the people in the society he is writing about are doing and if they are uncertain of what ideology they want to replace the former colonial government by, it's not for the novelist to invent it. And in Africa, I think you'll agree, we've only got to look at present-day history, contemporary history, with one regime toppling another. It's a time of trial and experiment when a new social order has not really emerged— whether it's a socialist one or a capitalist one. It's still so much in an experimental stage.

AT-L: Do you think one should write about politics when the thing is actually happening? When I read *A Wreath for Udomo,* I could see at once Nkrumah as the hero of the book. Although you can say that it was a little prophetic about what was going to happen in other parts of Africa, even then I could recognise the character of Nkrumah. It gave me a rather uncomfortable feeling that this was too near to the bone.

NG: Too close. But you must remember that we are talking about a novel that was written, how long ago? Twenty years ago! But think of a novel like Chinua Achebe's *A Man of the People.* That corrupt politician there, perhaps it's based on some particular person, but the fact is it could now be based on many. Achebe, in that novel, deals with things so brilliantly, he makes him a universal type. We can recognise him among us in many countries.

AT-L: It's interesting that you have raised the theme of universality. I interviewed Achebe recently, and he seemed to think that this idea of universality is a sort of thorn in his flesh. He disagrees with the likes of Wole Soyinka, Ayi Kwei Armah, in that they tend to create characters who can be recognised as "universal."

NG: I understand.

AT-L: And you feel that the African writer should not bother about whether or not a character is universal? He should concern himself with an African problem?

NG: Absolutely right in my opinion. When I say that in *A Man of the People* Achebe has created a character who is universal, this has happened after he did it. In other words, he chooses to create an individual, not a type, and when this has been done as well as it has been done in that novel, it creates its own universality afterwards. It's for us to recognise the universality. But I know exactly what he means when he criticises writers who try to use a man who is Everyman, so to speak. Then he loses his humaness, his individuality, loses his flesh and blood quality when you write like that. I agree entirely that what one should do as a writer is to strive to plumb the mystery of the individual. Let the critic say whether he's a type or not and let the reader say this, but not the writer himself. Achebe, while we're talking about him, has done something else. He has begun to resuscitate and reinstate the past, the precolonial era. I'm thinking of *Arrow of God,* which to my mind is perhaps the best novel to come out of Africa. I think it is an absolutely wonderful novel. And if you look at that novel, it really has almost nothing to do with the impact of the white man. It is about black life, black civilization, before the period of conquest. The period of conquest is just on the horizon, so to speak. But there are not many people who have tackled that kind of theme. There are not many black writers who have done it yet.

AT-L: You have said that the great political novel is yet to come out of Africa and that when it does come eventually, it will come out of South Africa. Do you still hold to this?

NG: Yes. Maybe I'm a little prejudiced in favour of South African black writers! But in the rest of Africa what is the theme now? The theme is the crisis of expectation after independence, isn't that so?

AT-L: Yes.

NG: And the inevitable theme of corruption when people get into power and power corrupts. This is *the* theme. But in South Africa, there are still many others. Take, for example, contemporary events. You were saying you feel there has to be a little period between the actual event and the time when the writer digests it, goes through an imaginative process, and transforms the real figures. They become something imagined. They become something bigger than themselves. Take Soweto '76. This is a tremendous psychological experience for blacks, really enormous, and one of such subtlety and so wide and deep that it's very difficult to explain it to anybody quickly. It's difficult to understand from outside. You can understand the events—that so many people were killed, that this happened, that that happened. You can read the newspaper reports, but the psychological process within people, how it changes them, how they examine themselves and their own position vis-à-vis their own people as well as the white man, this is stuff for the novelist, not for the journalist. That hasn't yet been touched. A few poets have written about it, and people are beginning to write stories. It's coming out piecemeal, but I think literature is made like that. It's made out of patches or pieces in a jigsaw put together by a different number of writers. Then the society gets a full expression of what has formed it.

AT-L: You make the point, which I think is very genuine, that because of the banning orders and Acts passed by the South African Government, creative writing inside South Africa in the novel is stifled. Now what you have is novels by people in exile who probably,

having lived abroad for a number of years, have lost touch with the
common man inside South Africa. Now those inside tend to use the
fable or the allegory in poetry as a way of escape!

NG: Well, it's interesting. Since *The Black Interpreters* was
published in the early seventies, things have changed quite a bit, and
they have changed encouragingly. I'm glad to have the opportunity
to tell you a bit about it. First of all, there have been quite a number
of small publishing houses, two or three, which have decided to take
the risk. These are publishing houses run by whites, progressive
whites, who really care about writing and who take the risk of
publishing the works of black writers that are unlikely to see the light
of day otherwise. And if the book is banned, too bad, they've got
very little money anyway and they've lost the little that they had. If,
as sometimes happens, a book that you expect is going to be axed
isn't, it's a triumph because it gets a readership that it could never
have had if the writer had only been writing in little magazines. A
good example was a poet, whom you probably know, Oswald
Mtshali. Unfortunately he's also in voluntary exile at the moment, but
we hope that he will come back. One of these little publishing firms
published a book of his poems and that book sold fifteen thousand
copies! For a book of poems, that's a pretty good distribution
anywhere. That was the beginning; and now every month there are
small books by new writers, some of them very young, some of them
young people who were seventeen, eighteen years old and in the
higher classes at school in Soweto '76, who went through that whole
thing, who were detained, who were imprisoned. They've gone
through this tremendous experience, and they are grappling with it.
They are looking for means to express it in poetry and prose.

AT-L: Nadine Gordimer, South Africa's leading lady novelist and
short story writer. Should you wish to read her works, you couldn't
find a better introduction than the paperback collection of some of
her short stories, published in the Heinemann African Writers Series,
entitled *Some Monday for Sure.*

The Art of Fiction LXXVII: Nadine Gordimer

Jannika Hurwitt/1979 and 1980

From *Paris Review,* 88 (Summer 1983), 82–127. Interview with Nadine Gordimer reprinted in *Writers at Work: The Paris Review Interviews, Sixth Series,* Ed. George Plimpton. © 1984 by The Paris Review, Inc. Reprinted by permission of Viking Penguin, Inc.

This interview with South African writer, Nadine Gordimer, took place in two parts—in the fall of 1979, when she was in America on a publicity tour for her most recent novel, *Burger's Daughter*, and in the spring of 1980, when she was here to see her son graduate from college.

Our first meeting was in a room set aside for us by her publisher, Viking Press—one of those conference rooms made cozy by lots of books and claustrophobic by its lack of windows. The hotel room where our second meeting took place was slightly more conducive to amiable conversation. But Gordimer does not waste words in conversation any more than she does in her prose. On both occasions she was ready to begin our interview the moment I walked in the door and ready to end it the moment the hour she had suggested for our meeting was up. Her clarity and mental focus allow her to express a great deal in a short amount of time.

A petite, bird-like, soft-spoken woman, Gordimer manages to combine a fluidity and gentleness with the seemingly restrained and highly structured workings of her mind. It was as if the thirty-five odd years that she had devoted to writing at the time we met had trained her to distill passion—and as a South African writer she is necessarily aware of being surrounded by passion on all sides— into form, whether of the written or spoken word. At the same time, she conveyed a sense of profound caring about the subject matter of her writing; those subjects natural to any writer concerned with the human condition, but set, in her case, in the heightened context of South African life. Her manner seemed to say, "Yes, these are important subjects we're discussing. Now let's get through talking about them so I can get back to the business of writing about them."

Nadine Gordimer was born nearly sixty years ago in a small gold-mining town near Johannesburg. Her first short stories were published in 1939, when she was fifteen. In the United States, during the '50s, her fiction appeared in the *New Yorker,* among other magazines. Her first novel, *The Lying Days,* was published in 1953, after which she produced seven novels, including *Burger's Daughter* which was published to world-wide acclaim. Since then Gordimer has published her eighth novel, *July's People,* and her seventh collection of short stories, *A Soldier's Embrace.* Among the awards she has received for her work are the Booker Prize for Fiction, the James Tait Black Prize, the W.H. Smith Award and the international Grand Aigle d'Or in France.

Interviewer: Do you have seasons in South Africa, or is it hot all year round?

Gordimer: Oh no, we have seasons. Near the equator, there's very little difference in the seasons. But right down where we are, at the end of the continent, and also high up where I live in Johannesburg—6000 feet up—you have very different seasons. We have a sharp cold winter. No snow—it's rather like your late fall or early spring—sunny, fresh, cold at night. We have a very definite rainy season. But you don't see rain for about half the year. You forget that rain exists. So it's a wonderful feeling when you wake up one day, and you smell the rain in the air. Many of the old houses, like ours, have galvanized iron or tin roofs. It's very noisy when there's a heavy rain—it just gallops down on the roof. The house that I was brought up in had a tin roof, so it's one of my earliest memories, lying in bed and listening to the rain . . . and hail, which, of course, on a tin roof is deafening.

Interviewer: When was your first trip out of South Africa?

Gordimer: My first trip out was to what was then called Rhodesia—Zimbabwe. That might seem very much the same thing as South Africa to you, but it isn't. Zimbabwe is Central Africa, sub-tropical, shading into tropical. But my first real trip out was much later. I had already published two books—I was thirty years old. I went to Egypt, on my way to England, and America. Perhaps it was a good transition. In London, I felt at home, but in an unreal way—I realized when I got there that my picture of London came entirely from books. Particularly Dickens and Virginia Woolf. The writers who, I'd thought, had impressed me with the features of English life, like Orwell, did not have this evocation when I was actually in the place; they were not writers with a strong sense of place. Woolf and Dickens obviously were. So that when I walked around in Chelsea, I felt that this was definitely Mrs. Dalloway's country. I remember I stayed in a hotel near Victoria Station. And at night, these dark, sooty buildings, the dampness when one leant against a wall—absolutely decayed buildings . . .

Interviewer: Were you as unprepared for this first trip off the African continent, and as awed by it as Rebecca in your novel, *A Guest of Honour?*

Gordimer: No, my mother, who hadn't been back to England for about twenty years, prepared me. She provided me with woolly underwear and whatnot, which I threw away after I arrived. But Rebecca's trip to Switzerland . . . I think descriptions of impressions from the air are something that writers nowadays have to be careful of. Like train journeys in mid-nineteenth century literature . . . they made such a change in people's lives. They produced a . . . leap in consciousness, especially so far as time was concerned. I can imagine what it must have been, the thought of taking a train that was to go rushing through the countryside. There were so many descriptions of trains in the literature of the day. But I think writers must be careful now not to overdo the use of travel as a metaphor for tremendous internal changes. "The journey" now is by air, and think of how many writers use this—in my own books it appears in *The Conservationist* and in *A Guest of Honour.* And indeed, in *Burger's Daughter*, Rosa Burger takes her first trip out of South Africa; I had to resist the temptation to talk about the journey—I describe only the landing, because that particular piece of the landscape could be useful later on.

Interviewer: Was this trip to England a sort of "back to the roots" expedition?

Gordimer: No. But it brought an understanding of what I was, and helped me to shed the last vestiges of colonialism. I didn't know I

was a colonial, but then I had to realize that I was. Even though my
mother was only six when she came to South Africa from England,
she still would talk about people "going home." But after my first trip
out, I realized that "home" was certainly and exclusively—Africa. It
could never be anywhere else.

Interviewer: What brought your parents to South Africa?

Gordimer: The same thing brought them both. They were part of
the whole colonial expansion. My maternal grandfather came out in
the 1890s with a couple of brothers. South Africa was regarded as a
land of opportunity for Europeans. And indeed, he went prospecting
for diamonds in Kimberley. I don't think he found very much—
maybe some small stones. After that, his entire life was the stock
exchange. He was what we call a "tickey-snatcher." A tickey was a
tiny coin like a dime—alas, we don't have it anymore. It was equal to
three English pence. "Tickey" is a lovely word, don't you think? Well,
my grandfather was a tickey-snatcher on the stock exchange, which
meant that he sat there all day, and that he bought and sold stocks—
making a quick buck.

My father's story is really not such a happy one. He was born
in Lithuania, and he went through the whole Jewish pogrom
syndrome, you know. He had hardly any schooling. There wasn't
any high school for Jewish kids in his village. His father was a
shipping clerk and there were twelve children. I'm sure they must
have been very poor. Their mother was a seamstress. As soon
as my father was twelve or thirteen the idea was that he would
just go—*somewhere*, either to America or wherever—it was
the time of the great expansion, you know, the early 1900s. So
his was the classic Ellis Island story—thirteen years old, not
speaking a word of English, traveling in the hold of a ship, but
all the way to Africa instead of America—it must have been
extraordinary. He was a very unadventurous man; he didn't have a
strong personality—he was timid. He still is a mystery to me. I
wonder if he didn't burn himself out in this tremendous initial
adventure, whether it wasn't really too much for him, and once
having found a niche for himself somewhere, he just didn't have the
guts to become much of a personality. There was something *arrested*
about my father.

Interviewer: What did he do once he got to Africa?

Gordimer: Like many poor Jews—one either became a shoe-maker, a tailor or a watchmaker. He had learned watchmaking. All he had was a little bag with his watchmaking tools. He went to the Transvaal, to the goldfields. He took his little suitcase and went around the mines and asked the miners if anybody wanted a watch fixed. And he would take the watches away to a little room he had somewhere: he would just sit there and mend watches. Then he bought a bicycle and he'd go back 'round the mines. But by the time I came on the scene he had a little jeweller's shop and he was no longer a watchmaker—he employed one. Indeed, he imported his brother-in-law from Russia to do it. By now my father was the tycoon of the family. He brought *nine* sisters out of Lithuania—the poor man—saving up to bring one after the other. I found out later that he hated them all—we didn't ever have family gatherings. I don't know why he hated them so much.

Interviewer: Where exactly was this jeweller's shop?

Gordimer: In a little town called Springs, which was thirty miles from Johannesburg. I grew up in a small, gold-mining town of about 20,000 people.

Interviewer: What were the schools like there?

Gordimer: Well, I've had little formal education, really. I had a very curious childhood. There were two of us—I have an elder sister—and I was the baby, the spoiled one, the darling. I was awful—brash, a show-off, a dreadful child. But maybe that had something to do with having a lot of energy that didn't find any outlet. I wanted to be a dancer—this was my passion, from the age of about four to ten. I absolutely adored dancing. And I can still remember the pleasure, the release, of using the body in this way. There was no question but that I was to be a dancer, and I suppose maybe I would have been. But at the age of ten, I suddenly went into a dead faint one day, having been a very skinny but very healthy child. Nobody took much notice. But then it happened again. So I was taken to the family doctor, and it was discovered that I had an incredibly rapid heartbeat. Nobody had noticed this; it was, I suppose, part of my excitability and liveliness. It was discovered that I had an enlarged thyroid gland, which causes a fast heartbeat and makes one hyperactive. Well, I've since discovered that this isn't a serious malady at all. It happens to hundreds of people—usually at puberty. But my mother got very alarmed. This rapid pulse should have been ignored. But my mother was quite sure that it meant that I had a "bad heart." So she went immediately to the convent where I attended school and told the nuns, "This child mustn't have any physical training, she mustn't play tennis, she mustn't even swim." At ten, you know, you don't argue with your mother—she tells you you're sick, you believe her. When I would be about to climb stairs, she would say, "Now, take it slowly, *remember your heart*." And then of course the tragedy was that I was told I mustn't dance anymore. So the dancing stopped like that, which was a terrible deprivation for me.

It's really only in the last decade of my life that I've been able to face all this. When I realized what my mother had done to me, I went through, at the age of twenty, such resentment—this happens to many of us, but I *really* had reason. When I was thirty, I began to understand why she did it, and thus to pity her. By the time she died in '76 we were reconciled. But it was an extraordinary story.

In brief, my mother was unhappily married. It was a dreadful marriage. I suspect she was sometimes in love with other men; but my mother would never have dreamt of having an affair. Because her marriage was unhappy, she concentrated on her children. The chief person she was attracted to was our family doctor. There's no question. I'm sure it was *quite* unconscious, but the fact that she had this "delicate" daughter, about whom she could be constantly calling the doctor—in those days doctors made house calls, and there would be tea and cookies and long chats—made her keep my "illness" going in this way. Probably I was being wrongly treated anyway, so that what medication should have cleared up, it didn't, and symptoms persisted. Of course, I began to feel terribly important. By that time I was reading all sorts of books that led me to believe my affliction made me very interesting. I was growing up with this legend that I was very delicate, that I had something wrong with my heart.

When I was eleven—I don't know how my mother did this—she took me out of school completely. For a year I had no education at all. But I read tremendously. And I retreated into myself, I became very introspective. She changed my whole character. Then she arranged for me to go to a tutor for three hours a day. She took me there at ten in the morning and picked me up at one. It was such incredible loneliness—it's a terrible thing to do to a child. There I was, all on my own, doing my work; a glass of milk was brought to me by this woman—she was very nice but I had no contact with other children. I spent my whole life, from eleven to sixteen, with older people, with people of my mother's generation. She carted me around to tea parties—I simply lived her life. When she and my father went out at night to dinner she took me along . . . I got to the stage where I could really hardly talk to other children. I was a little old woman.

Interviewer: What about your sister's relationship to you during this time?

Gordimer: My sister is four years older than I am. She went away to university; she wasn't really a companion to me. I stopped going to the tutor when I was fifteen or sixteen. So that was the extent of my formal education.

When I was twenty-one, or twenty-two, already a published writer, I wanted to go to university to get a little more formal education. But since I hadn't matriculated, I could only do occasional courses at the University of the Witwatersrand—that's Afrikaans for "ridge of white waters." There was something called "general studies"—this was just after the war, and there were lots of veterans who had interrupted their education, and so it was very nice for me—there were people my own age mixed up with the others. A few years ago I gave a graduation address at that same university.

Interviewer: Are you one of these writers to whom they're always trying to give honorary degrees?

Gordimer: I don't accept them in South Africa. I've taken one—in Belgium in 1981, from the University of Leuwen. It turned out to be quite extraordinary, because the man who got an honorary degree with me, Monsignor Oscar Romero, was assassinated two weeks later in El Salvador. In Belgium he had given the most marvelous address. He was such a striking man. He received a standing ovation for about eight minutes from the students. And two weeks later he was lying on the floor of a church, dead.

Interviewer: How long did you go to university?

Gordimer: One year. This was the first time in my life I'd mixed with blacks, and was more or less the beginning of my political consciousness. Perhaps the good thing about being carted around

with my parents was that they would sit playing gin rummy or
something while I wandered around the host's house seeing what I
could find to read. I discovered everybody from Henry Miller to
Upton Sinclair. It was Sinclair's *The Jungle* that really started me
thinking about politics: I thought, good God, these people who are
exploited in a meat-packing factory—they're just like blacks here.
And the whole idea that people came to America, not knowing the
language, having to struggle in sweat shops . . . I didn't relate this to
my own father, because my father was bourgeois by then . . . but I
related it to the blacks. Again, what a paradox that South Africa was
the blacks' *own country*, but they were recruited just as if they had
been migrant workers for the mines. So I saw the analogy. And that
was the beginning of my thinking about my position vis-à-vis blacks.
But though I didn't know anything—I was twelve or thirteen, and
leading the odd kind of life I did, living in books—I began to think
about these things before, perhaps, I was ready for them. When I got
to university, it was through mixing with other people who were
writing or painting that I got to know black people as equals. In a
general and inclusive, non-racial way, I met people who lived in the
world of ideas, in the world that interested me passionately.

    In the town where I lived, there was no mental food of this kind at
all. I'm often amazed to think how they live, those people, and what
an oppressed life it must be, because human beings *must* live in the
world of ideas. This dimension in the human psyche is very important. It was there, but they didn't know how to express it.
Conversation consisted of trivialities. For women, household matters,
problems with children. The men would talk about golf or business or
horseracing or whatever their practical interests were. Nobody ever
talked about, or even around, the big things—life and death. The
whole existential aspect of life was never discussed. I, of course,
approached it through books. Thought about it on my own. It was as
secret as it would have been to discuss my parents' sex life. It was
something so private, because I felt that there was nobody with whom
I could talk about these things, just *nobody*. But then, of course,
when I was moving around at university, my life changed. From
Europe—it was just after the war—came Existentialism, and at home
in South Africa there was great interest in movements of the Left, and
black national movements. At that time, the Communist Party, and

various other leftist movements were not banned. So there were all
sorts of Marxist discussion groups. This was an area of thought and
conviction I simply never had heard mentioned before. I'd only read
about it. And there, of course, were people who were mixing with
blacks. So it was through people who were writing, painting, or
acting that I started mixing with blacks.

Interviewer: What did you do after that year at university? Did
you begin any political activity?

Gordimer: No, you see I was writing then—a lot. I was
concentrating tremendously on writing. I wasn't really interested in
politics. My approach to living as a white supremacist, perforce,
among blacks, was, I see now, the humanist approach, the
individualistic approach. I felt that all I needed, in my own behavior,
was to ignore and defy the color bar. In other words my own attitude
toward blacks seemed to be sufficient action. I didn't see that it was
pretty meaningless until much later.

Interviewer: Were you living on your own then?

Gordimer: No, I wasn't. In that way I was extremely backward.
But you have to look at the kind of dependency that had been
induced in me at the crucial age of ten. When other kids were going
off to the equivalent of what's known as "summer camp"—"Nadine
can't go camping, she's got a *bad heart*! If people go on a hike, she
can't go. She's got to stay with mama." A child like that becomes
very corrupt, a kind of jester, an entertainer for grown-ups. Especially
at the age of fifteen and sixteen. Adults find you charming. You flirt
with other people's husbands instead of with boys your own age. It's
a very corrupting thing. I was rather a good mimic. Perhaps it was the
beginning of having an ear for dialogue? So I would take off people.
Grown-ups would sit around at drink parties, getting a little tight, and
there was Nadine prancing around, rather cruelly imitating people
whom they knew. It didn't occur to them that the moment their backs
were turned I was doing it to them as well.

At any rate, I was still living at home when I went to university, and
I used to commute by train into Johannesburg. Then my sister got
married and lived in Johannesburg, so that when I didn't want to go
home I would go to her, which was very nice for me, to have a base
there. But I still didn't have the guts, I don't know why, to move out
of home, the mining town of Springs. And you see I wasn't earning

enough by my writing, heaven knows, to live on. I was doing something that no kid does nowadays—I was living off my father. On the other hand, my needs were so modest. It never occurred to me that one would want a car—now every kid has a jalopy—this was just not the kind of thing that I would have dreamt of. All I wanted was to buy books. I earned enough with my writing here and there to do this, and of course I also used the library tremendously, which, again, people don't seem to do so much anymore. When I talk to young writers, and I say, "Have you read this or that?"—"Well no, but books are so expensive . . ."—I say, "Well for God's sake! The central library is a wonderful library. For heaven's sake, use it! You're never going to be able to write if you don't read!"

Interviewer: Perhaps the isolation of your childhood helped you to become a writer—because of all the time it left you for reading—lonely though it must have been.

Gordimer: Yes . . . perhaps I would have become a writer anyway. I was doing a bit of writing before I got "ill." I wanted to be a journalist as well as a dancer. You know what made me want to become a journalist? Reading Evelyn Waugh's *Scoop* when I was about eleven. Enough to make anybody want to be a journalist! I absolutely adored it. I was already reading a lot, obviously, but of course I was reading without any discrimination. I would go to the library and wander around, and one book led to another. But I think that's the best way. An Oxford student who is doing a thesis on my writing came to visit me in Johannesburg the other day. I did something I've not done before. I told him, "Right, here are boxes of my papers, just do what you like." I liked him so much—he was so very intelligent and lively. I would meet him at lunch. He would emerge, and so would I, from our separate labors. Suddenly he brought out a kid's exercise book—a list, that I'd kept for about six months when I was twelve, of books that I'd read, and I'd written little book reviews. There was a review of *Gone With the Wind.* Do you know what was underneath it? My "review" of Pepys's *Diary.* And I was still reading kid's books at the time, devouring those, and I didn't see that there was any difference between these and *Gone With the Wind* or Pepys's *Diary.*

Interviewer: Were you publishing stories in the *New Yorker* before you published your first book?

Gordimer: No. I published a book of stories in South Africa, in 1949. I must have started publishing stories in the *New Yorker* when I was twenty-six. I had one story in the *New Yorker,* and several in journals like *Virginia Quarterly Review,* the *Yale Review*—the traditional places where young writers in the Fifties submitted their work. Then my first book was published abroad—a book of short stories.

Interviewer: You sent your manuscripts around to these magazines?

Gordimer: No, no, by that time I had an agent. It came about that I had an agent in New York. I never sent anything on impulse to those magazines, because I wasn't familiar at all with American publications. The publications I was familiar with were the English ones. Of course, publishers in those days usually watched magazines. And my first publisher, Simon and Schuster, became interested in me through reading that first story of mine in the *New Yorker.* Katharine White became my editor and friend at the *New Yorker.* She told me, years after, that all those other stories which were in my first book had already been submitted to the *New Yorker* via my agent. But they had been read by the slush-pile people. She had never seen them, and she regretted very much that she hadn't. But of course these things happen. And I don't quite know how that *one* story surfaced.

Interviewer: Who was your agent?

Gordimer: My agent was an extraordinary man called Sidney Satenstein. He was an extremely rich man who loved writers. He had no children, and I think writers were his children. He had very few writers really, because he wasn't principally an agent. I came to him through somebody who knew him and knew my work and said, "It's ridiculous—you should have an agent abroad." He was such an incredible man—a sort of John O'Hara character, or even coarser, really. He spent half his time flying to Las Vegas to gamble, or to Florida to play golf. He was a kind of caricature rich American. He always had a cigar in his mouth. He was big, and wore the most ghastly clothes—checked trousers and things like that. He was an absolute darling. Of course he gave me a completely false idea of what an agent was. When I met him I was exactly thirty—though he had taken me on in my mid-twenties—and he was in his mid-sixties.

He established a sort of fatherly relationship with me, very fond. Strangely enough, he really liked my writing, which surprised me. One wouldn't have thought that my writing—especially my stories— would have interested *him*. But they did. He was incredible. He knew the circumstances of my life. I was newly divorced; I had a small child—a baby, indeed, eighteen months old—and I had no money. And he really fought for me. If somebody bought something of mine—and after all I was totally unknown—he insisted that I was a hot property. He got sufficient money for me to live on. When Simon and Schuster bought my first book of stories, they wanted to know if I was writing a novel, and indeed I was. And again he pushed them to give me, what would now be considered a *teeny* advance, the amount someone would get to write a line today; but then publishers were not so generous, nor writers so demanding. But at least they gave me a modest sum that I could live on. And once the book was well along, and they saw part of it, Satenstein said to them, you've just *got* to give her more, she's got nothing. So they gave me another advance—all due to him. He used to send me enormous bottles of French perfume. The times I came here—twice—while he was alive, he threw parties for me at the 21-Club, with caviar and sturgeon . . . he had a big heart, and style.

Unfortunately, he died—of a heart attack—just when I began to get known and make a success. He deserved better, because it would have been terribly exciting for him. At least he was able to be thrilled with the response to my first novel. Though not a best-seller—I've never been that—it was a big critical success here . . . a completely unknown writer with a front page review in the *New York Times*.

Interviewer: What role do you feel politics and the constant conflict it evokes in South Africa have played in your development as a writer?

Gordimer: Well, it has turned out to have played a very important role. I would have been a writer anyway; I was writing before politics impinged itself upon my consciousness. In my writing, politics comes through in a didactic fashion very rarely. The kind of conversations and polemical arguments you get in *Burger's Daughter* and in some of my other books—these really play a very minor part. For various reasons to do with the story, they had to be there. But the real influence of politics on my writing is the influence of politics on

people. Their lives, and I believe their very personalities, are changed
by the extreme political circumstances one lives under in South
Africa. I am dealing with people; here are people who are shaped
and changed by politics. In that way my material is profoundly
influenced by politics.

Interviewer: Do you see that as an advantage for a writer?

Gordimer: Not really. Life is so apparently amorphous. But as
soon as you burrow down this way or that . . . you know Goethe's
maxim? "Thrust your hand deep into life, and whatever you bring up
in it, that is you, that is your subject." I think that's what writers do.

Interviewer: If you had grown up in a country that was not
politically oppressed, might you have become a more abstract writer?

Gordimer: Maybe. Take a writer whom I admire tremendously,
the greatest American short-story writer ever, Eudora Welty. In a
strange way, if she had lived where I've lived, she might have turned
these incredible gifts of hers more outward—she might have written
more, she might have tackled wider subjects. I hesitate to say this,
because what she's done she's done wonderfully. But the fact is that
she hasn't written very much; I don't think she ever developed fully
her gifts as a novelist. She was not forced by circumstance to come to
grips with something different. And I don't believe it's just a matter of
temperament, because my early writing had qualities similar to hers. I
got to hate that word about my work—"sensitive." I was constantly
being compared to Katherine Mansfield. I am *not* by nature a political
creature, and even now, there is so much I don't like in politics, and
in political people—though I admire tremendously people who are
politically active—there's so much lying to oneself, self-deception,
there has to be—you don't make a good political fighter unless you
can pretend the warts aren't there.

Interviewer: Do you have the same complaint about Virginia
Woolf's novels as you do with Eudora Welty's?

Gordimer: No, because Virginia Woolf extended herself the other
way. I mean she really concentrated totally on that transparent
envelope that she'd find for herself. There are two ways to knit
experience, which is what writing is about. Writing is making sense of
life. You work your whole life and perhaps you've made sense of one
small area. Virginia Woolf did this incomparably. And the complexity
of her human relationships, the economy with which she managed to

portray them . . . staggering. But you can't write a novel like *Burger's Daughter* with the sensibility of a Virginia Woolf. You have to find some other way. You're always trying to find some other way. I'm interested in both ways of writing. I started off by being interested in that transparent envelope.

Interviewer: Was Woolf a big influence when you began writing?

Gordimer: Midway, I think—after I'd been writing for about five years. She can be a very dangerous influence on a young writer. It's easy to fall into the cadence. But the content isn't there. The same could be said for a completely different kind of writer like Dos Passos, or Hemingway. You've got to be very careful, or you do if you are a writer like me, starting out with an acute sensibility and a poor narrative gift. My narrative gift was weak in my early novels—they tend to fall into beautiful set pieces. It was only with *The Late Bourgeois World,* which was published in 1966, that I began to develop narrative muscle. From then on, my struggle has been not to lose the acute sensitivity—I mean the acuteness of catching nuance in behavior (not in description, because as you get more mature that falls into place) and to marry it successfully to a narrative gift. Because the kind of subjects that are around me, that draw me, that I see motivating me, require a strong narrative ability.

Interviewer: Do you feel that your political situation—the political situation in South Africa—gave you a particular incentive as a writer?

Gordimer: No. For instance, in *Burger's Daughter*, you could say on the face of it that it's a book about white communists in South Africa. But to me, it's something else. It's a book about commitment. Commitment is not merely a political thing. It's part of the whole ontological problem in life. It's part of my feeling that what a writer does is to try to make sense of life. I think that's what writing is, I think that's what painting is. It's seeking that thread of order and logic in the disorder, and the incredible waste and marvelous profligate character of life. What all artists are trying to do is to make sense of life. So, you see, I would have found my themes had I been an American or an English writer. They are there if one knows where to look . . . if one is pushed from within.

Interviewer: How do you feel that fiction from relatively non-oppressed countries compares with that produced in countries where the political situation necessitates a certain amount of political consciousness?

Gordimer: To me, it's all a matter of the quality of the writing. To me, that is everything. I can appreciate a tremendously subjective and apolitical piece of writing. If you're a writer, you can make the death of a canary stand for the whole mystery of death. That's the challenge. But, of course, in a sense you are "lucky" if you have great themes. One could say that about the Russians in the nineteenth century. Would they have been the wonderful writers they are if they hadn't had that challenge? They also had the restrictions that we chafe against in South Africa—censorship, and so on. And yet it seems on the face of it to have had only a good effect on writing. Then I think it depends. It can have a deleterious effect. In South Africa, among young blacks who are writing—it's difficult for them to admit it, but they know this—they have to submit to an absolute orthodoxy within black consciousness. The poem or the story or the novel must follow a certain line—it's a kind of party line even though what is in question is not a political party, but it *is*, in the true sense of the word, a party line. For example, nobleness of character in blacks must be shown. It's pretty much frowned upon if there's a white character who is human. It's easy enough to understand this and it's important as a form of consciousness-raising for young blacks to *feel* their own identity, to recite poems which simply exalt blackness and decry everything else, and often to exalt it in crude terms, in crude images, clichés. That's fine as a weapon of propaganda in the struggle, which is what such writing is, primarily. But the *real* writers are victims of this, because as soon as they stray from one or two clearly defined story lines, they're regarded as . . .

Interviewer: Traitors. Are there many blacks writing and publishing in South Africa?

Gordimer: There are a lot and there's a fairly good relationship between black and white writers. Literature is one of the few areas left where black and white feel some identity of purpose; we all struggle under censorship, and most white writers feel a strong sense of responsibility to promote, defend and help black writers where possible.

Interviewer: *Burger's Daughter* was banned three weeks after it was published, wasn't it?

Gordimer: Yes, and it remained banned for several months. Then it was unbanned. I was pleased, as you can imagine. Not only for myself, but because it established something of a precedent for other writers, since there are in that book blatant contraventions of certain Acts. In that book I published a document that was a real document, distributed by the students in the 1976 riots in Soweto, and banned by the government. It's in the book with all the misspellings and grammatical mistakes . . . everything exactly as it was; and indeed that's important because, as Rosa points out, these kids rioted because they felt their education wasn't good enough. And when you read the text of that pathetic little pamphlet you can see what the young blacks meant, because that's as well as they could write at the age of sixteen or seventeen, when they were ready to matriculate. So here is one example where, indeed, I flagrantly crossed the line to illegality. Now that the book has been unbanned, it's going to be a difficult thing for the censors to ban other books on evidence of such transgressions.

Interviewer: Why was the book unbanned?

Gordimer: If I hadn't been a writer who's known abroad and if this hadn't been a book that happened to receive serious attention at a high level abroad—it obviously made the censors feel rather foolish—the book would not have been released. So there we are.

Interviewer: Is it common for a book to be unbanned?

Gordimer: Well, not so quickly. Of my two previous books, one, *A World of Strangers,* was banned for twelve years, and the other, entitled *The Late Bourgeois World,* for ten; after that length of time most books are pretty well dead.

Interviewer: How does a book get banned?

Gordimer: First of all, if the book is imported, the authorities embargo it. In other words, it's just like any other cargo arriving at the docks. It is embargoed at Customs and the customs officer sends the book off to the Censorship Board. He's got a list of suspects. For instance, a South African writer like myself would be on it, you see, because they know the kind of subjects I've chosen, and, in any case, I've had three books banned previously. So would somebody like James Baldwin; several of his books were banned. Then there's another way that books get embargoed with the possible outcome of a ban. After normal distribution, somebody, some Mother Grundy, old busybody, reads a book that's already in the bookshops, objects to it, and sends it off to the Censorship Board with a complaint. On the recommendation of just one person, a committee will read the book to see if it's "objectionable." But while it's being read by the censors, it's under embargo, which means that although there are copies in the bookshops the bookseller can't sell them; he's got to put them away, take them off the shelves. Sometimes the book is then released. It happened to my novel, *A Guest of Honour;* it happened to *The Conservationist. The Conservationist,* I think, was held by the censors for ten weeks, which is iniquitous because the first ten weeks in a book's life are crucial from the point of view of sales. Then it was released by the Director of the Board. The members of the censor's committee—there are a number of those, usually with three people comprising a committee—read the book, each writes an independent report, and if these concur that the book should be banned or released, right, it's done. If they don't concur, then a fourth person has to be brought in. If they concur that the book is undesirable, then it is banned. The author isn't told. The decision is published in the *Government Gazette* which is published once a week. And that's the end of the book.

Interviewer: What happens then? Is it like what happened with *Ulysses?* Do people scrounge around frantically trying to get hold of it and hide it when policemen walk by?

Gordimer: People do, people do. Books are usually banned only for sale and distribution but not for *possession,* so that if you've already bought the book you may keep it; but you may not lend it to me or the person across the road and you may not sell it.

Interviewer: You can't lend it?

Gordimer: No. This, of course, is perfectly ridiculous. Everybody lends banned books all the time. But people are very nervous, for instance, about buying them abroad or having them sent. They're rather too timid about that. They don't like to have to smuggle them in.

Interviewer: So there isn't much smuggling going on?

Gordimer: Some people don't, some do. But with some of us, it's a point of honor always to do this.

Interviewer: To smuggle?

Gordimer: Yes, of course. It's a legitimate form of protest. But, unfortunately, when a book is banned, very few copies get around.

Interviewer: Getting back to the idea that oppressed societies produce better writers . . .

Gordimer: Well, I don't know. I think in the case of Latin American countries, they seem to have experienced so many forms of oppression and for so long that it's become a normal state. But notice that they all write about the same thing . . . the themes are as obsessive as the African ones. *The* theme among the remarkable Latin American writers is the corrupt dictator. Nevertheless, despite the sameness of theme, I regard this as the most exciting fiction in the world being written today anywhere.

Interviewer: Which Latin American novelists?

Gordimer: García Márquez, of course. Hardly necessary even to name Borges. Borges is the only living successor to Franz Kafka. Alejo Carpentier was absolutely wonderful. *The Kingdom of the Earth* is an exquisite little novel—it's brilliant. Then there's Carlos Fuentes, a magnificent writer. Mario Vargas Llosa. And Manuel Puig. These just roll off my tongue quickly; there are others. But always there's this obsessive theme—the corrupt dictator. They all write about it; they're obsessed by it.

Interviewer: I suppose that an oppressed culture such as South Africa's creates the possibility for heroes to exist, and that this is why some of your novels, such as *A Guest of Honour* and *Burger's Daughter,* have heroes as their motivating force.

Gordimer: Well, you know, it amazes me . . . I come to America, I go to England, I go to France . . . nobody's at risk. They're afraid of getting cancer, losing a lover, losing their jobs, being insecure. It's either something that you have no control over, like death—the atom bomb—or it's something with which you'd be able to cope anyway, and that is not the end of the world; you'll get another job or you'll go on state relief or something of this nature. It's only in my own country that I find people who voluntarily choose to put everything at risk—in their personal life. I mean to most of us, the whole business of falling in love is so totally absorbing; nothing else matters. It's happened to me. There have been times in my life when I have put the person I was in love with far ahead of my work. I would lose interest, I wouldn't even care if the book was coming out. I'd forget when it was being published and I wouldn't worry about the reception it got because I was in such a state of anguish over some man. And yet the people I know who are committed to a *political* cause never allow themselves to be deflected by this sort of personal consideration or ambition.

Interviewer: How do you think romantic love manifests itself in families such as Rosa's, where people's passions lie in politics?

Gordimer: This is what interested me so much, and this is what I partly tried to explore in the relationship between that girl and her family, who loved her, exploited her, but at the same time felt that they were doing this not for each other or to each other but because the *cause* demanded it.

Interviewer: We get only very brief glimpses of the love affair between Burger and his wife. In fact, the reader hardly gets any picture either of their relationship or of Rosa's mother at all.

Gordimer: That was one of the points that's fascinated me about such people: you could know them very well, and yet even in their intimate relations with one another they remained intensely secretive; it's part of the discipline that you have to have. I have a very, very close friend—no character in the book is modeled on her, I might add—but much that I know or have discovered intuitively about such people started with my fascination with her. She has been my closest friend for many years—she's a political exile now—and we've talked nights and days. She's one of the few people for whom I suppose I'd put myself physically at risk if there were to be cause. That's long ago. There are so many things I don't know about her that normally would come out in confidences between people who are as close as we are, and it's because of her political commitment that I can't ask her and she won't tell me. I think that this could extend even to family relationships. It's part of the discipline that the more you know, the more dangerous you are to the people around you. If you and I are working together in an underground movement, the less I know about you the better.

Interviewer: We've talked about the South American writers you admire. What about other writers?

Gordimer: Lots of novelists say they don't read other novelists, contemporary ones. If this is true, it's a great pity. Imagine, if you had lived in the nineteenth century and not read the writers that we now turn back to so lovingly, or even if you had lived in the twentieth century and hadn't read Lawrence or Hemingway, Virginia Woolf

and so on. At different times in my life I've—liked is not the word—
I've been psychologically *dependent* upon different writers. Some
have remained influential in my life and some haven't, and some I
suppose I've forgotten and do them an injustice by not mentioning.
When I first began to write, I wrote short stories, and of course I still
do; I've written a great many. It's a form that I love to write and to
read. I was very influenced by American, Southern, short-story
writers. Eudora Welty was a great influence on me. Years later, when
I met Eudora, visited her in Jackson, there were such parallels between the way she was living, even then, and my life: a black man
was mowing the lawn! There was a kind of understanding. Of course,
this really had nothing to do with the fact that I thought she was a
superb short-story writer. Katherine Anne Porter was an influence on
me. Faulkner. Yes. But, again, you see, one lies, because I'm sure that
when we were doing the five-finger exercises of short-story writing,
Hemingway must have influenced *everybody* who began to write in
the late Forties, as I did. Proust has been an influence on me, all my
life—an influence so deep it frightens me . . . not only in my writing,
but in my attitudes to life. Then later came Camus, who was quite a
strong influence, and Thomas Mann, whom I've come to admire
more and more. E.M. Forster, when I was a young girl; when I was in
my twenties—he was very important to me. And I still think *A
Passage to India* is an absolutely wonderful book that cannot be killed
by being taught in the universities.

Interviewer: In what way did Hemingway influence you?

Gordimer: Oh, through his short stories. The reduction, you
know, and also the use of dialogue. Now I think a great failure in
Hemingway's short stories is the omnipresence of Hemingway's
voice. People do not speak for themselves, in their own thought
patterns; they speak as Hemingway does. The "he said," "she said"
of Hemingway's work. I've cut these attributions out of my novels,
long ago. Some people complain that this makes my novels difficult
to read. But I don't care. I simply cannot stand he-said/she-said any
more. And if I can't make readers *know* who's speaking from the
tone of voice, the turns of phrase, well, then I've failed. And there's
nothing anyone can do about it.

Interviewer: It certainly enforces concentration when one is
reading your novels.

Gordimer: Yes.

Interviewer: The dashes are very effective.

Gordimer: Oh, that's very old. It started with Sterne's *Tristram Shandy.*

Interviewer: What technique did you use that was the same?

Gordimer: A kind of interior monologue that jumps about from different points of view. In *The Conservationist,* sometimes it's Mehring speaking from inside himself, observing, and sometimes it's a totally dispassionate view from outside.

Interviewer: It's a much more standard narrative technique than that of *Burger's Daughter.*

Gordimer: Well, no, it isn't you know. In *The Conservationist* you've got interior monologue and you have a real narrator. It's not always Mehring speaking. But the line between when he is and when he isn't is very vague, my theory being that the central personality is there, whether it's being observed from outside or whether from inside—it's the same entity.

Interviewer: You mentioned that the way in which you came up with the structure of *Burger's Daughter,* in which Rosa is always speaking to somebody, was from the idea that when one is writing one always has a listener in mind.

Gordimer: Oh, no, not in your writing, in your *life.* I believe that in your life, in your thoughts when you are alone, you are always addressing yourself to somebody.

Interviewer: And you are not doing this when you write?

Gordimer: No, because you're no longer yourself when you're writing; you're projecting into other people. But I think in your life, and sometimes even in the conduct of your life, you're imagining that some particular person is seeing your actions. And you're turning away, sometimes, from others.

Interviewer: How has Faulkner influenced you? Do you see any similarities in the structure of *Burger's Daughter* and, say, *As I Lay Dying?*

Gordimer: No, none at all, and I don't think there could be any influence there. I think the big time when people influence you is when you're very young and you start to write; after that you slough off what you don't need and you painfully hammer out your own style.

Interviewer: There's a similarity between the way your method of narration in *Burger's Daughter* and some of Faulkner's books address themselves to the relative nature of "truth."

Gordimer: Yes. Well, of course it is a method that points out the relativity of truth. The point I'm trying to make is about the relationship between style and point of view; in a sense, style is the point of view, or the point of view is the style.

Interviewer: Right, and that's why you choose to structure your narratives in the way that you do.

Gordimer: And then it was Proust who said that style is the moment of identification between the writer and his situation. Ideally that is what it should be—one allows the situation to dictate the style.

Interviewer: So that you are expressing a point of view, with the style that you choose, about the way life is in South Africa.

Gordimer: Yes. I'm expressing a point of view of the way life is for that particular person and the people around her (in the case of *Burger's Daughter*), and, by extension, a view of life itself.

Interviewer: In Conor Cruise O'Brien's review of *Burger's Daughter,* which appeared in *The New York Review of Books,* he says that your novel is constructed with a "properly deceptive art." He talks about how the construction makes the book seem as if it were a book in which nothing happens, and then several cataclysmic things do, in fact, happen. I was wondering if you have any response.

Gordimer: For me again, so little of the construction is objectively conceived. It's organic and instinctive and subconscious. I can't tell you how I arrive at it. Though, with each book, I go through a long time when I know what I want to do and I'm held back and puzzled and appalled because I don't know before I begin to write how I'm going to do it, and I always fear that I can't do it. You see, in *A Guest of Honour,* I wrote a political book, a book that needed certain objective entities relating to and acting upon the character's life in particular. And I wrote that book as a conventional narrative so that at the point where there was indeed a big party congress there was no difficulty then in presenting it almost like a play. Then I wrote *The Conservationist,* where I chose to ignore that one had to explain anything at all. I decided that if the reader didn't make the leap in his mind, if the allusions were puzzling to him—too bad. But the narrative would have to carry the book in the sense of what is going on in the characters' minds and going on in their bodies; the way they believed things that they did *really were*. Either the reader would make the leap or not, and if the reader was puzzled now and then— too bad. In other words, the novel was full of private references between the characters. Of course, you take a tremendous risk with such a narrative style, and when you do succeed, I think it's the ideal. When you don't, of course, you irritate the reader or you leave him puzzled. Personally, as a reader, I don't mind being puzzled. Perhaps the writer doesn't know the consequences implied in his/her books, because there's a choice of explanations; and, as a reader, I enjoy that. To me, it's an important part of the exciting business of reading a book, of being stirred, and of having a mind of your own. And so, as a writer, I take the liberty of doing this.

Interviewer: You don't consciously create a complete structure before you begin writing a novel?

Gordimer: No. For *Burger's Daughter*, perhaps four or five pages of very scrappy notes for the whole book. But, for me, those half-sentences or little snatches of dialogue are tremendously important; they are the core of something. And I've only got to look at them, and know that that's the next stage in the book that I'm coming to.

Interviewer: Is this the way you usually write your novels?

Gordimer: Yes. With me it's really a very natural process once I get started. An organic process.

Interviewer: How long do you prepare before you get started?

Gordimer: It's so difficult for me to say because, looking back at *Burger's Daughter*, for example, I know that I've been fascinated by the kind of person Rosa is for many years. It's as if the secret of a life is there, and slowly I'm circling, coming closer and closer to it. Perhaps there are other themes that present themselves but finally spin off instead of drawing me to them. I suppose one's ready for different things at different times in one's life. And also, in a country where so much is changing, the quality of life around one is changing; so that perhaps I wouldn't be attracted now to write the book that I wrote ten years ago and vice versa.

Interviewer: So you feel that the way your books are written is more an inevitable phenomenon than a conscious choice.

Gordimer: I don't think any writer can say why he chooses this or that or how a theme impinges itself. It may have been around for a long time and then a stage comes in your life when your imagination is ready for it and you can deal with it.

Interviewer: I wanted to ask you about *The Conservationist,* in which death is almost an obsessive theme. There are certain sections where it is continually brought up in ritualized ways: the man hopping up from his grave in different people's minds throughout the book, and the ritual of killing the goat to get back at Solomon's injury . . .

Gordimer: In *The Conservationist* there's a resurrection theme, and that is also a political theme. At the end of the book there's a disguised message. The slogan of the biggest banned liberation movement, a kind of battle-cry widely adopted, is the African word, "mayibuye." This means, "Africa, come back." You can see the whole idea of resurrection is there. And if you look at the end of *The Conservationist* you'll see that this thought is reworded, but it is actually what is said when the unknown man is re-buried: that although he is nameless and childless, he has all the children of other people around him; in other words, the future. He has people around him who are not his blood brothers and sisters but who stand for them. And that he has now been put with proper ceremony into his own earth. He has taken possession of it. There's a suggestion of something that has been planted, that is going to grow again.

Interviewer: This theme is repeated in one of your short stories— "Six Feet of the Country."

Gordimer: Yes. But the repetition is in reverse: "Six Feet" was written years before *The Conservationist.* Oddly enough, that early story is based on a true incident.

Interviewer: Do you have a fascination with death?

Gordimer: Not consciously, but then . . . how can any thinking person not have? Death is really the mystery of life, isn't it? If you ask, "What happens when we die? Why do we die?" you are asking, "Why do we live?" Unless one has a religion . . . . Without a religious explanation, one has only the Mount Everest argument: "I climb it because it's there. I live because there is the gift of life." It's not an answer, really, it's an evasion. Or, "I think my purpose on this earth is to make life better." Progress is the business of making life more safe and more enjoyable . . . fuller, generally. But that justification, it stops short of death, doesn't it? The only transcendent principle is that you are then seeking to improve the human lot for future generations. But we still don't get past the fact that it's a turnabout business; it's your turn and then it's mine, and life is taken up by somebody else. Human beings are never reconciled to this. In my own life I am made puzzled and uneasy by my attitude and that of others to death. If somebody dies young it's so terrible, it's such a tragedy, and the sense of waste is so strong; you think of all the promise that was there. And then if people live into old age, there's the horror of decay, especially—it's awful to say—but especially with exceptional people; when you see their minds going and their bodies falling to pieces, and they want to die and you want them to die, then that's equally terrible. So it's the mere fact of death that we can't accept? We say it's terrible if people die young, and we say it's terrible if they go on living too long.

Interviewer: Are you a religious or mystical person?

Gordimer: I'm an atheist. I wouldn't even call myself an agnostic. I am an atheist. But I think I have a basically religious temperament, perhaps even a profoundly religious one. I went through a stage in my life when I was thirty-two or thirty-three years old—when I was very fascinated by the writings of Simone Weil. In the end, her religious philosophy left me where I was. But I felt that there was something there that answered to a need that I felt, *my* "need for roots" that she wrote about so marvelously. I couldn't find the same solution.

Interviewer: How do you feel about Conor Cruise O'Brien's idea about there being Christian overtones in *Burger's Daughter?*

Gordimer: Well, I'm thinking of that. I'm sure that many of my friends, people who know me well, laughed because they know that, as I say, I'm an atheist. But he hit on something that is there in me, a certain inclination—more than that—a pull. Perhaps, brought up differently in a different milieu, in a different way, I might have been a religious person.

Interviewer: Then there is the resurrection of the black man in *The Conservationist.*

Gordimer: But of course the idea of resurrection comes from the Greeks, from the Egyptians. You can begin to believe in a collective unconscious without having religious beliefs.

Interviewer: I've noticed that sensual elements play a key role in your writing: smells, textures, sexuality, bodily functions. You don't

write about the so-called "beautiful people," the leisured class of
South Africa, and the beautiful environment in which they must live.
In fact, I noticed that almost all of the white women in your *Selected
Stories* are physically and mentally both highly unattractive and
middle-class. Does this reflect the way in which you view white
colonialists in your country?

Gordimer: I don't make such judgments about people. After all,
I'm a white colonial woman myself, of colonial descent. Perhaps I
know us too well through myself. But if somebody is partly frivolous
or superficial, has moments of cruelty or self-doubt, I don't write
them off, because I think that absolutely everybody has what are
known as human failings. My black characters are not angels either.
All this role-playing that is done in a society like ours—it's done in
many societies, but it's more noticeable in ours—sometimes the role
is forced upon you. You fall into it. It's a kind of song-and-dance
routine, and you find yourself, and my characters find themselves,
acting out these preconceived, ready-made roles. But, of course,
there are a large number of white women of a certain kind in the kind
of society that I come from who . . . well, the best one can say of
them is that one can excuse them because of their ignorance of what
they have allowed themselves to become. I see the same kind of
women here in the U.S. You go into one of the big stores here and
you can see these extremely well-dressed, often rather dissatisfied-
looking, even sad-looking middle-aged women, rich, sitting trying on
a dozen pairs of shoes; and you can see they're sitting there for the
morning. And it's a terribly agonizing decision, but maybe the heel
should be a little higher or maybe . . . should I get two pairs? And a
few blocks away it's appalling to see in what poverty and misery
other people are living in this city, New York. Why is it that one
doesn't criticize that American woman the same way one does her
counterpart in South Africa? For me, the difference is that the rich
American represents class difference and injustice, while in South
Africa the injustice is based on both class *and* race prejudice.

Interviewer: What about the "beautiful people" of South Africa?

Gordimer: They're featured very prominently in an early book of
mine called *A World of Strangers* but very rarely since then, until the
character of Mehring in *The Conservationist.* They are not the most

interesting people in South Africa, believe me . . . although they may regard themselves as such.

Interviewer: Is it intentional that so often the physical details of characters are not brought home strongly in your work? One gets a very strong sense of the mind's workings in major characters, but often a very limited sense of what they actually look like.

Gordimer: I think that physical descriptions of people should be minimal. There are exceptions—take Isaac Bashevis Singer. He very often starts off a story by giving you a full physical description. If you look very closely at the description, of course it's extremely good. He stamps character on a twist of the nose or a tuft of red beard. My own preference is for physical description to come piecemeal at times when it furthers other elements in the text. For instance, you might describe a character's eyes when another character is looking straight into them so it would be natural . . . a feature of that particular moment in the narrative. There might be another scene later, where the character whose eyes you've described is under tension, and is showing it by tapping her foot or picking at a hangnail—so if there was something particular about her hands, that would be the time to talk about them. I'm telling you this as if it were something to be planned. It isn't. It comes at the appropriate moment.

Interviewer: In the introduction to your *Selected Stories,* you say that: "My femininity has never constituted any special kind of solitude, for me. In fact, my only genuine connection with the social life of the town (when I was growing up) was through my femaleness. As an adolescent, at least, I felt and followed sexual attraction in common with others; that was a form of communion I could share. Rapunzel's hair is the right metaphor for this femininity: by means of it I was able to let myself out and live in the body, with others, as well as—alone—in the mind." You go on to say you "question the existence of the specific solitude of woman-as-intellectual when that woman is a writer, because when it comes to their essential faculty as writers, all writers are androgynous beings."

What about the process of becoming a writer, of becoming an androgynous being? Isn't that a struggle for women?

Gordimer: I hesitate to generalize from my own experience. I would consider it an arrogance to state my own experience as true for all women. I really haven't suffered at all from being a woman. It's inconceivable, for example, that I could ever have become interested in a man who regarded women as non-beings. It's never happened. There would be a kind of war between us. I just take it for granted, and it has always happened, that the men in my life have been people who treated me as an equal. There was never any question of fighting for this. I'm somebody who has lived a life as a woman. In other words, I've been twice married, I've brought up children, I've done all the things that women do. I haven't avoided or escaped this, supposing that I should have wished to, and I don't wish to and never wished to. But, as I say, I don't generalize, because I see all around me women who are gifted and intelligent who *do* have these struggles and who indeed *infuriate* me by allowing themselves to be used by men. It's the mental abuse that I think of, really, women who give up their development as human beings because they're willing to subordinate this to some man. As for my attitude to feminism . . . I always have become indignant over the fact that women in professions don't have the same working conditions or salaries as men. In my own country—I don't know how it is here—as soon as a woman is married, if she's a schoolteacher, for example, she's paid less because she's regarded as a poor risk: she's probably going to have a baby and interrupt her career. And if she comes back to teaching when she's older, she is still paid on a lower grade because she's married. This I think is disgusting. I see it as part of the whole question of human rights and disaffected groups in various societies.

Interviewer: Certainly it must appear even more clearly in that light from the perspective of someone living in South Africa.

Gordimer: Black women have so many terrible disabilities that they share in common with men—the oppression of racism—that the whole feminist movement means something quite different there. Unless feminism is seen as merely part of the general struggle for black liberation, and the struggle of all, white and black, against racial oppression, it has no validity in South Africa, in any view. So as far as writing is concerned, I cannot help generalizing from my own experience that, in writing, sex doesn't matter; it's the writing that matters. I can't see why any publisher should care whether you're a man or a woman if you've written a good book. Or if you've written a bad book that he thinks he can make a commercial success of . . . there are plenty of those.

Interviewer: You also say in the introduction to *Selected Stories:* "I know that writers need solitude and seek alienation of a kind every day of their lives." How do you gain your own solitude, and maintain it within your family? Where do you write?

Gordimer: Of course now my family's grown up and it's easier. But I did manage to maintain it when my children were young, I suppose, by being rather ruthless. I think writers, artists, are very ruthless, and they have to be. It's unpleasant for other people but I don't know how else we can manage. Because the world will never make a place for you. My own family came to understand and respect this. Really, when my children were quite small they knew that in my working hours they must leave me alone; if they came home from school and my door was closed, they left and they didn't turn on the radio full blast. I was criticized for this by other people. But my own children don't hold it against me. I still had time that I spent with them. What I have also sacrificed, and it hasn't been a sacrifice for me, is a social life; and as I've got older, I'm less and less interested in that. When I was young I did go through some years when I enjoyed party-going very much and stayed out all night. But in the end, the loss next day, the fact that I had a hangover and that I couldn't work, quickly outweighed the pleasure; and, as time has gone by, I've kept more and more to myself. Because a writer doesn't only need the time when he's actually writing—he or she has got to have time to think and time just to let things work out. Nothing is worse for this than society. Nothing is worse for this than the abrasive, if enjoyable, effect of other people.

Interviewer: What conditions do you find to be most conducive to writing?

Gordimer: Well, nowhere very special, no great, splendid desk and cork-lined room. There have been times in my life, my God, when I was a young divorced woman with a small child living in a small apartment with thin walls when other people's radios would drive me absolutely mad. And that's still the thing that bothers me tremendously—*that* kind of noise. I don't mind people's voices. But Muzak or the constant clack-clack of a radio or television coming through the door . . . well, I live in a suburban house where I have a small room where I work. I have a door with direct access to the garden—a great luxury for me—so that I can get in and out without anybody bothering me or knowing where I am. Before I begin to work I pull out the phone and it stays out until I'm ready to plug it in again. If people really want you, they'll find you some other time. And it's as simple as that, really.

Interviewer: How long do you usually work every day? Or do you work every day?

Gordimer: When I'm working on a book I work every day. I work about four hours nonstop, and then I'll be very tired and nothing comes anymore, and then I will do other things. I can't understand writers who feel they shouldn't have to do any of the ordinary things of life, because I think that this is necessary; one has got to keep in touch with that. The solitude of writing is also quite frightening. It's quite close sometimes to madness, one just disappears for a day and loses touch. The ordinary action of taking a dress down to the dry cleaner's or spraying some plants infected with greenfly is a very sane and good thing to do. It brings one back, so to speak. It also brings the world back. I have formed the habit, over the last two books I've written, of spending half an hour or so reading over what I'd written during the day just before I go to bed at night. Then, of course, you get tempted to fix it up, fuss with it, at night. But I find that's good. But if I've been with friends or gone out somewhere, then I won't do that. The fact is that I lead a rather solitary life when I'm writing.

Interviewer: Is there a time of day that's best?

Gordimer: I work in the morning. That's best for me.

Interviewer: How long does it usually take you to write a book?

Gordimer: It depends. The shortest has been about 18 months. *Burger's Daughter* took me four years.

Interviewer: Four years of steady writing?

Gordimer: I wrote one or two other things, small things. Sometimes when I'm writing I get a block, and so I stop and write a short story, and that seems to set me going. Sometimes when I'm writing a book I get ideas for stories, and they're just tucked away. But alas, as I get older, I get fewer ideas for short stories. I used to be teeming with them. And I'm sorry about that because I like short stories.

Interviewer: What about writer's block? Is that a problem for you?

Gordimer: No. And I say so, as you see, with hesitation and fear and trembling because you always feel that that demon is waiting behind the back of your brain.

Interviewer: You have the short story to loosen you up?

Gordimer: Yes, and occasionally I do some nonfiction piece, usually something involving travel. For me, this is a kind of relaxation. During the time I was writing *Burger's Daughter* I did two such pieces.

Interviewer: You don't even have minor fits of procrastination, endless cups of tea or things like that?

Gordimer: No, no. Though I do have, not blocks but . . . problems moving on from one stage to the next; particularly when I've got something done with and it's worked well. For instance, I finished that chapter with Brandt Vermeulen, you know, the nationalist in *Burger's Daughter,* which went unexpectedly well. I simply wrote it just like that and it all came right. I had been dreading it. I had been dreading getting the tone of voice and everything right. And then, knowing where I was going on from there, there was suddenly an inability to get out of that mood and into another; and so there were perhaps a few awful days; because when that happens, I don't stop and do something else. I sit in front of that paper for the normal time that I would be writing. And, then, well, I break through.

Interviewer: There's no specific routine that gets you from the bedroom or the living room into the writing room, bridging that terrifying gap between not writing and writing?

Gordimer: No—that's the advantage if you're free to choose the time you're going to write. That's the advantage of writing in the morning. Because then one gets up and in one's subconscious mind one knows: I am going to write. Whatever small thing you have to do, such as talking to other people at breakfast, it's only done with one part of you, so to speak; just done on the surface. The person with whom I live, my husband, understands this and has for a very long time. And he knows that to say to me at breakfast, "What shall we do about so-and-so?" or, "Would you read this letter?"—he knows that isn't the time to ask. I get irritable, and irritated, I don't want to be asked to do things then. And I don't want to phone an order to the grocer at that time. I just want to be left alone to eat my breakfast. Ideally, I like to walk around a bit outside, which you can do, of course, with a garden. But I often think that even that becomes a kind of procrastination because it's so easy then to see a weed that one has to stop and pull up and then one sees some ants and wonders, where are they going? So the best thing to do is to go into the room and close the door and sit down.

Interviewer: Do you go through much revision of your work?

Gordimer: As time goes by, less and less. I used to. When I was young, I used to write three times as much as the work one finally reads. If I wrote a story, it would be three times the final length of that story. But that was in the very early times of my writing. Short stories are a wonderful discipline against overwriting. You get so used to cutting out what is extraneous.

Interviewer: Do you ever find critics useful?

Gordimer: Yes, but you must remember they're always after the event, aren't they? Because then the work's already done. And the time you find you agree with them is when they come to the same conclusions you do. In other words, if a critic objects to something that I know by my lights is right, that I did the best I could and that it's well done, I'm not affected by the fact that somebody didn't like it. But if I have doubts about a character or something that I've done, and these doubts are confirmed by a critic, then I feel my doubts confirmed and I'm glad to respect that critic's objections.

Interviewer: Frequently writers say they don't read reviews because even one bad review among ten shining ones can be devastating.

Gordimer: Of course, it depends very much on the reviewer. There are people who are not reviewers, one or two, to whom I give my books to read, perhaps even in manuscript. I am sick with apprehension while they are reading them. And certainly there are certain reviewers I would be very wounded by if they were to say, "Well, this one's rotten."

Interviewer: But this hasn't happened yet.

Gordimer: Not yet. With *Burger's Daughter* I've had, out of perhaps fifty or sixty reviews, two bad ones.

Interviewer: You say that writers are androgynous. Do you recognize any difference between masculine and feminine writing, such as say, Woolf's vs. Hemingway's writing?

Gordimer: Hemingway is such an extreme example, and his writing is really an instance of machismo, isn't it? Henry James could have been a woman. E.M. Forster could have been. George Eliot could have been a man. I used to be too insistent on this point that there's no sex in the brain; I'm less insistent now— perhaps I'm being influenced by the changing attitude of women toward themselves in general? I don't think there's anything that women writers don't know. But it may be that there are certain aspects of life that they can deal with a shade better, just as I wonder whether any woman writer, however great, could have written the marvelous war scenes in *War and Peace*. By and large, I don't think it matters a damn what sex a writer is, so long as the work is that of a real *writer*. I think there *is* such a thing as "ladies' writing," for instance, feminine writing; there are "authoresses" and "poetesses." And there are men, like Hemingway, whose excessive "manliness" is a concomitant part of their writing. But with so many of the male writers whom I admire, it doesn't matter too much. There doesn't seem to be anything *they* don't know, either. After all, look at Molly Bloom's soliloquy. To me, that's the ultimate proof of the ability of either sex to understand and convey the inner workings of the other. No woman was ever "written" better by a woman writer. How did Joyce know? God knows how and it doesn't matter. When I was a young woman, a young girl, I wrote a story about a man who had lost his leg. He couldn't accept this, the reality of it, until he was sitting recuperating in the garden and saw a locust that had its leg off; he saw the locust struggling because it felt its leg was still there. I don't know how I wrote that story, somehow I just imagined myself into it. A psychiatrist once told me it was a perfect example of penis envy.

Interviewer: Is there anything, new or otherwise, that you hope to do with your writing in the future?

Gordimer: I would always hope to find the one right way to tackle whatever subject I'm dealing with. To me, that's the real problem, and the challenge of writing. There's no such feeling as a general achievement. You cannot say that because I have managed to say what I wanted to say in one book, that it is now inside me for the next, because the next one is going to have a different demand. And until I find out how to write it, I can't tackle it.

Interviewer: In other words, you don't know the question until you have the answer?

Gordimer: Yes. I would like to say something about how I feel in general about what a novel, or any story, ought to be. It's a quotation from Kafka. He said, "A book ought to be an icepick to break up the frozen sea within us."

"A Story for This Place and Time": An Interview with Nadine Gordimer about *Burger's Daughter*

Susan Gardner/1980

From *Kunapipi*, 3.2 (1981), 99–112. Reprinted by permission of *Kunapipi*.

In July 1980 Susan Gardner sought an interview in Johannesburg with Nadine Gordimer to discuss her 1979 novel, *Burger's Daughter.* This was banned for import and distribution in South Africa one month after its London publication on a range of grounds specified in the Publications Act, 1974, including propagating Communist opinions; indecency and offensiveness to public morals and religious feelings or convictions of some inhabitants of South Africa; being prejudicial to the safety of the State, the general welfare, peace and good order; creating 'a psychosis of revolution and rebellion'; making 'several unbridled attacks against the authority entrusted with the maintenance of law and order and the safety of the state.'

Could you tell me how and when you decided that Burger's Daughter *was a story that* had *to be told about this particular place and time?*

Well, I was fascinated by the *idea* of the story for a long time. I can't tell you exactly when because these things always begin very much in the subconscious. I can't say which came first, the general idea or the story. Maybe first of all there was the idea: the role of white hard-core Leftists. But that would be a kind of theoretical approach, an historical or a socio-political approach, and I'm an imaginative writer, I don't write that kind of thing. One could have written a factual book about that: it has been done, I think, very thoroughly. But that is approaching it as a phenomenon—a sociological/political phenomenon. So perhaps it occurred to me originally in that form.

But then something—as an imaginative writer—really took hold of me, and that was the idea of what it would have been like—what it would be like—to be the son or daughter of one of those families. I became fascinated to see how, as time went by, in my own life, for instance, my own generation, we moved away from our parents' lives and our parents' political beliefs (or lack of them): we changed our whole attitude. But—the children of Communists, of white Communists, and of hard-core Leftists generally, but particularly of Communists, did *not*: they simply took up the torch. It was a relay race of generations, so to speak, and they did not seem to question the way of life that these political beliefs dictated. It wasn't just simply a matter of saying I think this or I think that, and voting, and going to a political meeting. It was putting your whole *life* on the line. Your political beliefs as a Communist completely dominated your whole way of life in a country like this, even before the Communist Party was banned. And you must remember, the Communist Party was formed in 1921, here. So the children of these Communists—and perhaps even their grandchildren—were Communists during a much more trying period: because in 1950 the Communist Party was banned.

Now, what happened to these young people? The amazing thing was that it was quite clear—since they got arrested, since they went to prison, since they took part in all sorts of activities *after* the Party was banned—that they had *not* thrown off, or abandoned, their parents' beliefs or their parents' incredibly disciplined way of life. I became fascinated by this long ago, I should think—perhaps as long ago as 1949, the first big Treason Trial . . . I had never been to a large political trial before; I don't think I had ever been to a political trial at all. This trial—the preliminary examination part of it—went on for nine months; then, indeed, that was the trial, because everybody was dismissed. But it was the beginning of a series of political trials where, alas, this didn't happen. After that they came thick and fast, and I went to quite a lot of them. And looked at some of these very young people—children or teenagers, left with the responsibility of the whole household and younger children. It must have affected their lives tremendously; it must have been a great intrusion on the kind of secret treaties that you have when you're an adolescent: you know, the time that you spend with your buddies, and don't want to be involved in grown-up responsibilities. That's how I became fascinated with these young people, and I suppose the character Rosa gradually began to take shape. Since I'm a woman myself, it was in the form of one of the young women, or one of the girls, that I saw the story.

Why was it Rosa rather than her brother Tony who was given the job, in the novel, of critically inheriting the political task?

It may be that women were particularly prominent; and also because I knew a number of women in this position, either as children, or in the position of Rosa's mother. And their relationship fascinated me.

But why is Rosa's relationship to her ideological inheritance patriarchically presented? It is after all her mother Cathy who is in prison when the book starts, and who is identified as 'the real revolutionary' both by Ivy Terblanche (who admired her and worked with her) and by Katya Bagnelli, whom Cathy supplanted as Lionel Burger's wife and comrade.

Yes, but you see again, the incredible layers of meaning in the lives of people like this. The question of who was the more important person in Party work would very often be covered up, in the eyes of the world, with the facade of the marriage. So that one would conveniently make use—particularly in this country, particularly because the Burgers are an Afrikaner family—of the convention that Papa is the master; meantime, probably, it was the woman who was the more important member.

Who, perhaps, by capitalising on sexual double standards, could be getting away with some political manoeuvres?

Yes, yes, in the end this was no protection; but it had to be tested, perhaps, to see whether it was. And, of course, a woman could be treated more leniently in court, when it came to bail: if a woman and her husband were arrested, their application for bail might also be on compassionate grounds, that her children were young and were left at home without anybody to care for them. The court was much more likely to let the woman out on bail than the man; yet that woman might be the brains of the whole organization. This kind of layer after layer of meaning in people's lives was so different from the lives of the sort of people that I grew up with, whose lives were simpler, whose *loyalties* were so much simpler . . .

*Might your presentation of Rosa as a dissident Afrikaner woman
who is betraying her racial heritage account for some of the
Publication Control Board's hostility?*

I don't think so. It might, perhaps, on a certain deep-psychological
level, have influenced one of the censors who read the book originally and banned it. Rosa certainly would not seem to be a nice
Boere meisie, (but) the whole idea of the *Boere meisie,* this good,
quiet, church-going girl, has clearly become outdated. It's a concept
not equal to the realities of the present life here. And I think one can
draw an interesting parallel with the Voortrekker period. Think of the
kind of role that women played then. When necessary they picked up
a gun, and they gave birth to their children in the middle of the *veld,*
without any medical help, without the proverbial kettle of hot water
boiling. So they stepped out of this idealistic role of the woman in
the background, the submissive woman, and now you have your
Rosas and, indeed—what was her name?—Marie, her cousin, who
in a different way went out into the big world to advertise South
African oranges in Paris and ended up sheltering an international
terrorist.

*C.J. van der Merwe, the 'expert on security matters' consulted by
the Publications Appeal Board, concluded that the book's readership
would be limited to 'literary critics and . . . people with a specific
interest in subversive movements in South Africa.' Did you have an
implied or envisaged audience in mind while you were writing the
book?*

I don't write that way. I never have anybody in mind; I think that's
death to any writer. You can't get anywhere near the truth as you
know it if you have any idea—if you're wondering what this one's
going to think of it, what that one's going to think of it. I've said
before, and for me it's a truth that must be repeated—I think the best
way to write is as if you were already dead. This is sometimes
misunderstood. I don't mean that you *ignore* the reality around us.
Far from it. My idea is that, in order to come to grips properly with
that reality, you must have no fears for yourself, for the embarrassment that it's going to cause your family, for the embarrassment that
it's going to cause *you.* One can refuse to answer questions, but
when one is sitting down and writing something, one mustn't refuse

any truth that comes to mind, one mustn't censor oneself from following any line of thought. I'm analysing this now, but it's to me absolutely natural. I simply *don't* think about it. When I first began to write, and was not politically aware (when, indeed, there was no political danger as there is now), again, I didn't think at all about whether I was going to offend when I wrote my first novel (*The Lying Days,* 1953), which obviously, like most first novels, has elements of my own childhood. My mother was alive. Afterwards, when it was published, I thought, Oh my God, what's she going to think when she reads it? But had I begun to think about this while I was writing it, I should never have written it. That's the answer, I think. For me.

Burger's Daughter is *an appealing book for feminists because it explores that movement's basic contention that 'the personal is political'. And I'm intrigued by the attraction for Rosa of other women: Marisa Kgosana, the wife of an imprisoned black political leader, and Katya, her father's first wife. They seem to be very important, emotionally and as models, and although Rosa is said to be trying to understand and relate to her dead father, Lionel, she could also be regarded as* searching for her mother. *And I think the novel relevant to feminists not least because the 'women's liberation meeting' (if that is what one could call it), described as a 'harmless liberal activity' and organised by the fellow-traveller Flora Donaldson, may be too pessimistic and dismissively presented. Do you think there* are *any South African women's organisations that could be effective in the struggle against South Africa's racial capitalism?*

There are, and there have been. *But*—and it's a big but—as soon as they say, 'We are completely apolitical,' they might as well shut up shop. Because there's no issue in this country—I defy anybody to bring up an issue, except perhaps the very personal one of the love relationship between men and women . . . But all the other issues— can you have a bank account in your name, the ownership of property, the rights over your children, what happens when you get divorced, all these things, not to mention of course the most important of all, equal pay for equal work, and other conditions, maternity benefits and so on—as soon as you touch any of the real feminist issues you are going right into the heart of the racial problem.

But I think Flora represents a facile, and rather biological, notion of sisterhood, and she's too optimistic and sentimental about it; perhaps very generation-bound as well. She doesn't realise that any solidarity between black and white women would have to be constructed and fought for, and always changing.

It's also curious because Flora is the kind of woman who has been—well, all right, she's been on the fringe of real political action, but then she's moved into the typically feminine position of being warned by her husband. And this happens so much here. After Sharpeville—but it was always there, it must have been quite a source of conflict within the bourgeois marriage here (white marriage I'm talking about, of course), that the husband said, Right—I admire you for your courage, I admire you for your views, I share them of course, but I don't want you going to prison, what benefit is it going to bring to anybody? It was then that somebody like Flora, with the very genuine feelings that she had about liberation, would look around for another outlet. It's interesting, too, because it relates to a little theory I have about the basis of this society still being so colonial, especially in personal relationships, and how this affects one's effectiveness in the outside world. Women in our frontier society (the ordinary women, not politicised women) were the first really to begin to have uneasy feelings about blacks, and about the conditions under which blacks lived. And, for example, the problems that black women have with their children; there were few if any nursery schools for blacks, so this kind of thing began to interest public-spirited women. Again, of course, it was not 'political'; no, it was not even reform; it was charity. So that kind of activity, along with fringe artistic activity . . . I can remember as a child in a mining town where I was born and brought up, the choirs, the amateur theatricals—right, there would be men in the cast of these amateur plays, but the audiences were likely to be predominantly female. When a musician came from abroad, or a ballet company, perhaps, came from Johannesburg to this mining town—again, the audience would be 90% female. So that culture and charity, with a slapdash kind of social reform, were a woman's domain. A social conscience was a leisure-time activity, because the man was busy earning a living; he was the breadwinner and protector. This was a real frontier society conceptualising of the roles, the 'ordained' roles. . . . And I think this lingers, and it has lingered to the extent that it has produced Floras. Highly intelligent, well-educated women who are still in that kind of relationship to the husband.

The Black Sash organization, which I admire very much, is a most interesting example of this. I've often said to people, 'Why is there no Black Sash for men?' The Black Sash is now open to men, and I have one or two friends (I think Sydney Kentridge, the Biko lawyer, is one, who belongs), but this is obviously just a nominal thing. The fact is—who are the husbands of these women? Why are the women so much more enlightened? Why are the women defiant of public opinion, defiant of the police, and certainly *not* apolitical? The Black Sash is a women's organization that is trying to bring about real social reform, that is opposing this government, that is opposing National Party policy, and is now going radically further than the Progressive-Reform Party policy and all the white political parties. And these *women* have the guts to do this. Now what happens when they go home, I wonder? What are the discussions at home? I know of two cases where the man has been politicised by the wife, to a very interesting extent. So far, insofar as it has affected the children (again influenced by the mother)—the children, having started off with some sort of liberal teaching from the mother, move on and become more and more radical. I know of one who is indeed in exile now, having had to flee on an exit permit. When this girl was detained—in prison without trial—her father, a conventional and conservative man until then, made a stand on principle, which is so rare. He had been politicised by his wife and by his children. Yet there is no men's Black Sash. Men do *not* go and stand in protest outside the university or John Vorster Square. And there is no feminist lobby at all in the Parliament. But it would be by proxy, because there would be a couple of white women talking about the disabilities of black women. And as far as black women are concerned, their concern is the oppression under which all blacks live. The feminist battle must come afterwards.

I think it must come simultaneously, but it's very difficult for black women to admit that, especially if under pressure in their own communities.

Yes, it's very difficult. My view is a different one. I feel that if the real battle for human rights is won, the kingdom of . . . feminine liberation follows. Because if we are all free individuals, that's all we need, we don't have to have any special feeling because we are women. But I know this view is not shared by feminists.

About relations with blacks as they are experienced and recounted by white characters, Anthony Sampson in The New York Times *said that no one had better described certain aspects of township, in this case Soweto, life. Yet one of the co-publishers at Ravan Press, Mothobi Mutloatse, as reported in* The Star *(Johannesburg), has stated (12 July 1980):*

> I feel that whites writing about blacks is just nothing but an academic exercise. It is not authentic. It lacks that feeling of the people. Good writing should have emotions and a purpose. . . . whites, be they writers or politicians, experience only the life of the privileged. All they can do is just imagine the Black Experience. (p. 12)

What are the prices that whites must pay for acceptance by, and collaboration with, blacks? To what extent are these still possible?

There are really two questions here, because the point you're getting from Mothobi's argument is a political one, it's about political action, and the other question is its reflection in literature. My comment about that statement is that it ignores completely the very large areas of contact between black and white, here, *all our lives.* This, indeed, is the failure and lie of apartheid; it has *not* succeeded.

But Mothobi's statement seems to uphold or echo apartheid, in fact.

In some ways apartheid has succeeded only too well. I've said this before; there are areas of black experience that no white writer can write about. But there are vast areas of actual experience—rubbing shoulders with blacks, having all kinds of relationships with blacks. . . . It's not as simple as it sounds . . . all kinds of conflicts, of a very special nature, that arise between black and white. . . . And this leads whites to know quite a lot about blacks. And it leads blacks to know quite a lot about whites. The author of that statement cast no opinion on white characters in black books. Are we to say then that no black person can possibly create a white character? Of course, this is nonsense. I do believe that when we have got beyond the apartheid situation—there's a tremendous problem for whites, because unless you put down cultural roots, unless whites are allowed in by blacks, and unless we can make out a case for our being accepted and we can forge a common culture together, whites are going to be marginal, because we will be outside the central entities of life here. To a large extent we are now. But there's still that area of conflict which is from an artistic point of view fruitful. But when that is gone, if we are not integrated, if we have not cut loose from the colonial culture . . . . And make no mistake about it, blacks are hampered by it, too. The very fact that the black writer, Mothobi Mutloatse, who gave that interview, edits a magazine, or the fact that he is inter- viewed—these are all the tools of white culture that he has taken over, and why not? Why not use them? They are there. I object to the attempt to convince people that blacks do not want to use any of these tools at all. The fact is, you cannot have a literature without them. And you can't have a modern culture without them. And all blacks want a modern culture. Why on earth not? This is a heritage that belongs to all of us.

But there are areas where I know there are things I cannot write. For instance, if I were to want to write a novel about a black child growing up between 1976 and now—not so much in Soweto, because all my life I have had contacts with city blacks and all my life I've been in and out of townships, I may not have lived there, but I know something about it . . .—But a black child, say, living in a country area, who perhaps doesn't even speak a word of English— there are many like that—and perhaps a few broken words of Afrikaans—I think that the concept of reality, the relation to the entities in the life of that child would be something beyond my imaginative powers as a writer, even though writers are extraordinary people. They're monsters in a way, they can enter other people's lives. Imagination is a mysterious thing.

Is there anything about the style of Burger's Daughter—*or any of your other work, for that matter—that you regard for whatever social or genetic reasons as most likely to have been written by a woman?*

No. I don't think so. It's difficult to judge. And of course, I have written one book in the first person as a man, and I've written two or three from a male point of view. Perhaps some man will say, as some black may say, how can she possibly know. But I don't really feel we're all that different. I have this feeling that there's this overriding . . . humanity—not in a 'humanitarian' sense, but just what it is to be a human being: to know hurt, pain, fear, discouragement, frustration, this is common to both sexes—

And sexuality. Your 'inside' descriptions of male sexuality astonish me.

Yes, but I've often been astonished by the 'inside' descriptions of female sexuality written by men. So perhaps we know each other on these levels. Below our consciousness. And when you come to write, that's what you tap.

Would you regard the style of Burger's Daughter *as different, or a development from, your previous work? How would you compare it vis-à-vis stories in* A Soldier's Embrace *(1980), for instance?*

For me it's very, very simple. For each idea, there's never been anything but one right way to say it. Perhaps that way is going to be in the first person, perhaps it's going to be in the past tense, perhaps it's going to be a monologue, perhaps it's going to be a free association, perhaps it's going to be . . . classical. If I don't find it, I can't write. In *A Soldier's Embrace,* there's a story called "Oral History," where the title is the key to the right style for the story. I wanted to tell it the way you tell something that has actually happened (an episode in the chronicle of a village, a people). Then it has to have these echoing *tones,* like a bell tolling, that you've heard many times before, but the sounds mean something, you can retell a hundred times. That was for me the right way to tell that story; I had to find it. Then there is the story about the unborn child. Well, there's no way to 'tell' that in a direct narrative fashion. Because it is a mystery. It's surrounded by strange waters in a womb; it's projecting yourself into a journey we've all taken, and God knows what it is like, it's like going into space. So the style has to be something that suggests an apprehension of the world much removed from normal senses.

But—with *Burger's Daughter*—here again there's this slippery fish, Rosa, who is herself a girl like any other girl; she has roles imposed upon her by her mother and father; underneath those roles there's her own. For instance, she's sent to visit the young man in prison: there is a role imposed upon her, but she's playing another role, and the young man is playing yet another. So there are three roles somehow to be conveyed by the same character. It came to me, when I was pondering about writing that book, since she was someone who had so much imposed upon her from the outside; since these were people who lived with layers of protective colouring in order to carry out what they thought was their purpose in life; since it has been my own experience, knowing people like that, that there are infinite gradations of intimacy. . . . I had somebody, a woman friend, whom I've known all my life, and terribly intimately, who lived in this house—but there are areas of her life I've known nothing about. I would, almost certainly, if she'd not been a devout Communist, but there were things she didn't tell me and there were probably other things she didn't tell other people. Life lived in compartments, well, how do you approach somebody like that? And so the idea came to me of Rosa questioning herself as others see her and whether what they see is what she really is. And that developed into another stylistic question—if you're going to tell a book in the first person, to whom are you talking? You asked me earlier when I write, what is my audience. And I told you I have none, and that is the truth. But if a character of mine is speaking in the first person there's an audience assumed, which is one person or the whole world. It's always there. And that is why Joseph Conrad uses the device of Marlow—because then Marlow is speaking to him. Conrad [the character in *Burger's Daughter*] is somebody who's living the individual life that she's never tried, she's testing his word against hers all the time. This hippie son of a scrap dealer, brought up with a completely different idea about what's meaningful in life, in her life. And when she's talking to him, she's indeed appealing to him: this is how it was for me, how is it for you? Then—it's obvious, but the thing is, it only really came to me afterwards—if she goes to Europe, to whom would she go? She must go to Katya, to her father's first wife.

That wasn't originally planned?
No. When I began to write the book, I knew she would go to Europe, and under very strange circumstances (guilty over having compromised herself for a passport). She doesn't know her father's first wife, and she has a certain curiosity about her; and Katya lives at a remove from the active political exiles whom Rosa has more or less undertaken to avoid. She goes to Katya, it seems, because there is

nowhere else to go . . . And then, as so often in life, the unconscious motive appears: Rosa thought to learn from Katya, how to defect? Because Katya has 'defected' from Lionel Burger.

To turn to the question of the different people whom Rosa addresses. Inevitably, in the end, she does talk to her father, but perhaps only after he's dead. So you can see how for me style really grew out of content. I couldn't have told that story the way I did *The Conservationist,* which was without any concessions explaining anything to anybody. If you didn't catch on—who was who and what was missing and what was assumed, then you were just left in doubt. But, in *Burger's Daughter,* you see there was too much—take for instance the whole question of what the Communist Party *was,* here. I couldn't *not* explain that, so I had to find a way to do it, and fortunately for me the device of the biographer of Lionel Burger enabled me to fill some of that in.

You have called Burger's Daughter *a political novel, and a novel of ideas. And you've also distinguished contemporary white South African writing by saying that it's predominantly critical, analytical, 'protestant in mood', while black writings are 'inspirational', 'and that is why the government fears them.' You've claimed that the inspirational presently predominates over satire in Black writing, for instance, because satire requires 'a licence for self-criticism that loyalty to the Black struggle for a spiritual identity does not grant at present.'[1] But would you further claim that* Burger's Daughter *is not inspirational—in intention or in effect?*

Burger's Daughter is—much more, I think, than my other books. My method has so often been irony. I find irony very attractive in other writers, and I find life full of irony, my own life and everybody else's; somehow one of the secret locks of the personality lies in what is ironic in us. In *Burger's Daughter* irony is like a kind of corrective, a rein. It comes from Rosa, she has that in her confrontation with Clare (a contemporary of hers, also the daughter of Communist parents), but very often the inspirational took over. Because there are things— it comes from what is here, if you look at what happened in Soweto in '76 and what has happened again now (school and meat workers'

[1]Nadine Gordimer, 'New Forms of Strategy—No Change of Heart,' *Critical Arts: A Journal for Media Studies* 1, No 2 (June 1980), pp. 27–33.

boycotts; municipal workers' strikes in Johannesburg), there's so much inspiration in it: a reaching out, a bursting forth . . . the very recklessness comes from that. The very courage to risk, with your stone in your hand, being shot down. You know, if you look at the history of Africa or any other country—let's confine it to here—the famous time when the Xhosas burnt their crops and said 'the white man is going to be pushed into the sea'; 'on a certain day the sun will come up twice, two blood-red suns will rise', and they feared nothing. There was the same thing in Madagascar, there were bloody riots against the French and they believed that bullets would turn to water (that same legend really comes from Africa, it has been inspirational here before, too). There was something of that in these school kids in '76—something that suddenly took fear away.

If, voluntarily like Joyce or forced like Solzhenitsyn you had to leave South Africa, what then would be your available source and substance?
I've lived here for 56 years, all my life. I've still got a great deal inside me and don't know if now, at this stage of my life, I have it worked out. It would depend, too, on how I got involved in the society I went to live in. This theory that you lose your roots—I know that this is very true, and there are very few writers who have the strength, and the character, and the talent, to overcome it. If you look at what happens to black writers in exile, you don't know. It's very bad. But—if you look at Doris Lessing, if you look at Dan Jacobson, particularly with Lessing, it's possible for some writers to transplant and grow.

Have any critics missed what you regard as especially important aspects of Burger's Daughter?
I think some critics discovered things in it I didn't know about. Two reviewers pointed out that it is also the story of a daughter-father relationship and of a child-parent relationship. And I hadn't thought about it in that way, but of course it is. And then Conor Cruise O'Brien says that it's a profoundly religious book. Which, of course, is written by an atheist. But that could happen, most certainly.

Well, Conor Cruise O'Brien once editorialised in The Observer *that*

E.P. Thompson is not a Marxist, and neither is Cristopher Hill—so he's twisting his own definitions.

But I think he had a profound point in that in the book was the idea of redemption being entered into through suffering. Taking it on in one way or another, politically- or religiously-motivated, that is the only choice you have. You can't opt out of it. One thing I think lots of people have missed—the reason why Rosa goes back to South Africa and, ultimately, to prison. It's not just because she has that terrible midnight telephone call with her former black step-brother, Baasie, and that really brings her nose to nose with reality. It started long before, it started in France, in that village, when she met that woman in the street in her dressing gown, who doesn't know where she is. And it really hits Rosa that you get old, lonely, dotty. That you suffer. That Katya, running from political suffering, has simply post-poned what is coming. And Didier is also very important, because he shows Rosa what the alternatives are. The alternatives have some horrible sides to them, too. That young man is living for pay with a woman much older than he, a kind of prisoner who thinks he's free.

I wonder if the terminology of redemption and suffering—which gives history a metaphysical cast—isn't too fatalistic and amorphous a formulation for what is really systematic, structural exploitation and oppression in South Africa—which can be transformed.

Oh, quite, and that's why Rosa comes back. If you sit around on a Greek island and . . . I don't know, take a purely feminine example, have a face lift and tint your hair, what's happening is staving off the suffering that will come to you. It's a fact of life, that kind of animal suffering. But there's *another* kind of suffering that you *can* fight and that human beings have been fighting generation after generation, for thousands of years. And I think Rosa's overcome by disgust; this passivity, this submission. And wants to become embattled with suffering.

Do you think that the sensuous-redemptive appeal of blacks is romanticised in the book, especially through the character of Marisa?

I think the sensuous-redemptive thing is dangerous. But I've seen it even among my—my Burger-type friends. It's very strong, you know. And it's powerful. It also sounds so sentimental, but it's true that when we whites go away we miss that certain warmth. Even now, I find when I'm in New York I just can't believe that the vibrations that come from the blacks I see are what they are. Because I'm used to a different relationship with blacks. It's just incredible that this endures, has endured. With all the awful resentments that there are between us, and all the troubles, there still is this strong bond.

An Interview with Nadine Gordimer

Stephen Gray/1980

From *Contemporary Literature*, 22.3 (1981), 263–71. © 1981 by
the Board of Regents of the University of Wisconsin System.
Reprinted by permission of the University of Wisconsin Press.

This interview took place on the mellow afternoon of 8 April 1980,
during the South African autumn, at Nadine Gordimer's home of
many years in Parktown, a lush, old residential suburb of Johannesburg. The setting is familiar to many South African writers, for,
although Gordimer avoids coverage of her very private life, her house
is always open to those blacks and whites who have a little magazine
to launch, a new manuscript to prepare for print, a practitioner's
problem to solve. Gordimer is the *doyenne* of South African English
letters. Her concern has always been that the literature should
flourish despite the climate of repression that has created a daily
struggle with censorship, bannings of books and people, police
intervention, and financial hardships.

For three decades, now, her firm support of the notion of freedom
of expression in literature, a notion alien to the apartheid society, has
been an inspirational touchstone to many. Although to her coun-
trymen at large she might seem a remote figure—an intellectual
stylist who has accumulated an international reputation, one who
brings back home the big prizes no South African has won before—
to the few peers she has within the country of her birth, she is reliably
at the center of the tender and beleaguered literary scene, on call,
ready with a strategy or a statement.

A slight and elegant person, a grandmother at 57, Gordimer has in
recent years had her inscrutable privacy invaded by the publicity
following her joint winning of the Booker Prize for *The Conservationist* (1974) and the promotional hype attendant on the
appearance of her *Burger's Daughter* in 1979. After a promotional
tour for Jonathan Cape and for Viking—she appeared even on the
Tonight Show—she was off again, this time to Belgium, to receive an
honorary doctorate at Leuven (Louvain), alongside El Salvador's

176

Archbishop Romero, assassinated shortly thereafter. Awarded an honorary doctorate in South Africa, she had refused it as a gesture of nonacceptance of the segregated nature of the university in question. Her growing success has caused far more public appearances than one imagines she would like to make.

With her new collection of short stories (*A Soldier's Embrace,* 1980), the first since her *Selected Stories* (1975), in preparation in London, she was, during the week of this interview, once again fighting another round of the old, protracted, and gruesome battle with the South African controllers of publications. This time it was the fate of the imported copies of *Burger's Daughter,* which had precipitated the publication of her pamphlet, *What Happened to Burger's Daughter,* or *How South African Censorship Works*—a semi-clandestinely published collection that describes in full the bureaucratic labyrinth of checks that had had *Burger's Daughter* embargoed, banned from sale within the Republic, and—curiously— unbanned, from within, as *"bona fide* literature."

Since the novel describes among other things the inner workings of the revolution in South Africa, the dynamics of subversion on the part of liberation groups, Gordimer was fortunate: many works, particularly and predictably by black writers, not necessarily as frontal in their approaches to such contentious and, in fact, illegal matters, are neither sprung nor cleared. Currently all her work is available in her own country.

But compulsory involvement with the crisis situation of all other South African writers in a restricting situation like this has been Gordimer's platform at home for an unendurably long time—and her answer has consistently been a refusal to collaborate with, or participate in, the controls that drastically reshape the flow of information and opinion about literature and politics between the outside world and South Africa.

Yet, and this came out in the hours we talked, the everyday urgency of having to make a stand proves wearying, eroding. I had asked her if she would talk, for once, about herself—if she would drop, for once, the role of defender and champion, and let her attitudes to her own work be the subject. With that conceded, we began, almost with relief, to discuss what in other societies is a writer's privilege, taken for granted—his or her own right to a private world

of ideas—but which, in the context of the society around us, felt like
a rare luxury.

Q. With the publication in 1974 of *The Conservationist,* and now
with *Burger's Daughter,* it seems that your novels are showing a
marked turning inward. Do you feel you have entered a new phase?

A. I don't see it as definitively as that; I don't see a break. I see it
as part of learning your craft, entering a new phase with every book.

Q. What is your aesthetic motivation for this increasing exploration
of the internal landscapes of character?

A. Insofar as it's aesthetic, it has to do with finding the right means
to express what I am discovering. Perhaps it's got more to do with the
degree to which we conceal ourselves here. It's part of living in South
Africa, having these incredible layers of concealment, and I suppose
I've become more and more conscious of them in relation to other
people, and even to myself. I've always said, and I still feel, that style
is something that is dictated by the subject; it comes about through
looking for the right way to deal with a particular subject, or an
aspect of a subject. This inner-directed style comes about from the
feeling that what we say and do—well, it's always only half of what
we mean, but in South Africa it's less than half. And this constant
shifting of foothold is both in terms of our society—in terms of
relations to other people around you—and in terms of your own self-
respect and your own self-esteem. I want to convey this constant
shifting along, on very uncertain and uneven ground.

Q. Both these novels use an alternating method of narration,
between an exterior, impersonalized narrator and an interior monologue, juxtaposed. Is your intention to strip off exteriors more
effectively by this means?

A. It's to get increasingly at what is really there. I suppose it comes
about through finding that if you are drilling straight ahead, so to
speak, you are constantly slipping and glancing off what is in the
person, off the true center of their motivation and the conglomeration
of circumstances and inherited attitudes that make up the inner
personality. I think the method is almost spelled out and becomes
part of the actual book at the beginning of *Burger's Daughter*, where
Rosa says to herself, in a natural kind of way, because she doubts
what she is, what is it that they saw when they saw me standing

outside the prison? That sums up the method that I've come to use. In order to grasp a subject, you need to use all the means at your disposal: the inner narrative, the outer, the reflection on an individual from other people, even the different possibilities of language, the syntax itself, which take hold of different parts of reality. So in the beginning of *Burger's Daughter* the high-toned, brave-sounding political prose of the faithful—all the clichés strung together, the set of half-truths along with the truths that go there—is contrasted with the very personal, allusive style of the old interior monologue.

Q. Do you feel that this method is ultimately more liberating for your reader in South Africa, given our contemporary situation?

A. Yes, I think so. It should be. That's what one is trying for.

Q. Do you take the South African reader much into account?

A. Well, I hope this doesn't sound patronizing, but no. The South African public, normally speaking, doesn't read much modern fiction, never mind contemporary fiction that breaks with the mode of direct narrative. In *The Conservationist* I completely ignored the difficulties of the reader. I've had some complaints. But people who have difficulty with a book like that one of mine have probably never read Faulkner, nor Virginia Woolf, never mind the *nouvelle vague*. I'm a little bit embarrassed by their difficulty. But the fact is that I made a tremendous effort to let the context spring its meaning upon the reader—I wasn't lazy or self-indulgent, I think. The success or failure of the book is the degree to which I have succeeded in doing that. But I felt in that book, writing about somebody, Mehring, who so lacked self-knowledge—not through lack of intelligence, but out of fear—it was absolutely necessary to let him reveal himself, through the gaps, through the slightest allusions. In *Burger's Daughter* there are two things going—Rosa's conscious analysis, her reasoning approach to her life and to this country, and then there is my exploration as a writer of what she doesn't know even when she *thinks* she's finding out.

Q. The method is very similar in both novels, yet the characters are poles apart. How do you relate them to their society?

A. The same method, but it's being used *on* Mehring in *The Conservationist,* whereas for Rosa it's being used much more subjectively. Mehring is hidden in a different way from the way that Rosa is hidden, in terms of the South African scene. And it's quite a shock even for me to think of it—Rosa Burgers and Mehrings are probably living within a few miles of one another. Right, there are tremendous differences between individuals in other parts of the world, particularly economic differences, but this instance is, somehow, particularly striking to me. Mehring is living a consciously restricted life, and he's doing it successfully so far as he's concerned. What this is doing to him, he really doesn't see. There's a glimmering of it only when his son comes to visit him. The terms of his relationship to society, I think, are worked out in his conversation with the woman with whom he has a love affair. From my point of view, that is the most successful part of the book, in achieving what I wanted to do; in the two people they are, in the pretenses that both of them have, I think very much comes out and conveys itself to the reader, even if the reader does not know the surrounding factual circumstances of their lives and doesn't understand every reference that is there. But in the case of somebody like Rosa—she belongs to a segment of society whose prime motivation is their relationship to society; it's the touchstone of their lives. So that, I suppose, sums up how I see it: that you can't opt out altogether. You are either running away from your inevitable place, or you are taking it on. By place I don't mean a predetermined place; your place depends on the role you take in society. But the fact is that you *have* a role; there's no such thing as an ivory tower—that's a place in itself. You are consciously or unconsciously creating a position in your society.

Q. The common theme is the pursuit of happiness for the individual in conflict with his or her duties to society. Is this more densely true of *The Conservationist* and *Burger's Daughter* than of your previous works?

A. It's densely and deeply true of these two, and if I've moved in a certain direction in the second half of the seventies, it has been in this direction. But I don't think that you can draw any moral about the happiness or unhappiness of the individual life. It would be very nice to say that if you live only for yourself, you're miserable. But I'm afraid it's not true. That's one of the truths that I've tried to air in *The Conservationist.* You can live Mehring's way, and probably get more fun, more immediate satisfaction out of life on many levels, than living the kind of life the Burger family did. Then again, it depends on what being alive means to you.

Q. Do you consciously rely on common givens between yourself and your readers?

A. There are givens that are understood only in South Africa, that perhaps people in England and America simply don't understand. But it's happened to me again and again, since I've traveled after my books have been written and have talked to people or perhaps been interviewed, that these blanks obviously do exist. But this is something that happens *after the event,* after the book has been written, and I could put my head on a block—I'm not lying to you when I say that I never think about them when I'm writing. Perhaps it's because in my own life, and in my own experiences, I feel that I'm living proof of the patronage and falsity of deciding that there is a reader who will understand this or that, a specific being to whom you are speaking, and a reader who will understand or will not. If I look back at my childhood and early adolescence, and remember what I was reading—without any preconceived notions of what I *ought* to be reading as an intelligent girl—then I can see that you simply never know what will light a spark of understanding in a reader who has never thought along that line before. To me that is what writing is about. So, the business of in-jokes, never mind in-inferences—if they come up naturally among my characters, then they are there. But it's not something that I would seek consciously. I think I've only done it once, and that's at the end of *The Conservationist,* where the body that has been buried and "comes back" refers to Mayibuye, the black political slogan that means "Come back Africa"—back after the years of internal exile and white domination. It's the only beautiful, poetically valid slogan I've ever heard. That I put in, really, for myself, hoping perhaps that somebody would take note of my affirmation; as far as I know, nobody has . . .

Q. In reviews of *Burger's Daughter,* when you are compared to any other writers, it is quite frequently to the Russian novelists of the nineteenth century. Do you feel that parallel is there? Were they and are you both writing about pre-revolutionary societies?

A. Yes, there is a basic similarity of historical stages. Because of this, overseas reviewers sometimes recognize things that people over here very often miss. For example, we are in a revolutionary stage; we are in that stage *now.* A revolution doesn't happen overnight. The Russian Revolution started in 1905, and it went on through the century. And if you look at the pattern, our revolution is happening; our revolution started a long time ago, at least in the sixties, if not the fifties, and we go from phase to phase inexorably. I'm not talking about revolution in classic Marxist terms, obviously; when black majority rule comes, it will not necessarily be the dictatorship of the proletariat . . . it may be black capitalism, though I doubt it.

Q. In *Burger's Daughter* Rosa's consciousness dawns with the Sharpeville Massacre and the novel really closes with the riots of Soweto in 1976. Her life is drastically bracketed by these events. Is the novel an historical critique of this period, then?

A. I think it is an historical critique. But you must remember that Soweto overtook me while writing that book. This is what I think is so interesting about writing—how closely connected you are, not in a journalistic way, but inescapably connected with events.

Q. So the events weren't part of your structuring from the very beginning?

A. No, but Rosa would have come back to South Africa; that was inevitable. There would have been a different ending, though, without the Soweto riots. But that shows how there is a logical pattern to what is happening here. And when Rosa begins to talk to her father, at the end—I paraphrase—"You knew what the children have discovered, you knew that it would come from the people, as Lenin predicted." Well, here it came, indeed, not from the fathers of the people but from their children. Which is also, of course, a kind of reversal of what has happened to her; it's a turning over of predestination. She struggles against what she inherited from the father, embraces and struggles; and here you have a generation that turns the tables and takes the initiative.

Q. Do you regard your work as extremely personal?

A. Well, there is always this constant interplay of factors in a writer's life. This is what often distresses me, or very often distresses me, when I have an interview in America or in England—because the interest there tends often to be only in my life vis-à-vis the apartheid society in which I live. The other side—what happens to you as an individual, as a woman, as a writer—nobody is very interested in that. And I think that this kind of journalistic approach is tremendously one-sided, because the one couldn't be without the others.

Q. You've said elsewhere that Africa needs an "articulated consciousness" and that it's the novelist's job to provide it. Do you stick with that?

A. Yes, and I think that is what changes all the time in my own writing. My own consciousness has changed. I can certainly see that if I look at my early work. And, no doubt, if I keep my wits about me for a few more years, it'll keep on changing.

Q. Reaction to your work here is severely polarized between awards of the highest literary honors and reliable official execration, bannings, embargoes, and so on. How do you handle this invariably bizarre reception?

A. Well, I suppose I've never really thought about it, because I suppose I know it is going to happen. I have been protected all my life, and still am—after all this time and all these books and this middle age of mine—by such a fascination with what I'm trying to do, while I'm writing it, that I honestly don't think till afterwards, and sometimes in quite personal ways, of the consequences. I'm reckless when I write, and I always have the feeling that, oh well, it doesn't really matter, I'm *going* to do it. It's got to be done completely, or not at all.

Q. But when the book's out, published, then embargoed, next thing wins some prize, it's banned, it's unbanned—do you just take it? I know that as a public spokesperson you are powerfully against this censorship process. But I mean, how are you personally affected? Water off a duck's back?

A. Yes, because if you look at what happens to writers here, there's nothing unusual, really, about what happens to me.

Q. Has this recurring humiliation worn you down over the years?

A. No; but it depresses me. There's always this feeling about the book's life here, where it is so important to me. It's a platitude, but it's true; here you are among your own people, and you want to be read by them, and there's this grey area, this fog, that you struggle through to reach them. Indeed, you can't struggle through it, because there's nothing you can do—what *can* you do?—sell the damn thing on the street-corner? And be arrested for doing so?

Q. What has your general attitude to your work become in the seventies?

A. Well, speaking for myself as a woman and a citizen, I've become in the seventies much more radical in my outlook. This doesn't mean to say that I have suddenly taken on a new faith; I haven't. My way of coming to certain convictions, and accepting my convictions, is with eyes open; I can't do it any other way—I haven't in me that element of faith; it's missing. I mean "radical" in both senses. Politically I've become socialist in my general outlook, philosophically speaking, despite the fact that these are the years where one has seen the greatest failures of socialist experiments. But still, it's not in my nature to be totally cynical. I think that to be alive is an expression of belief in something, of an unkillable element in human advancement. I don't believe in perfection; I believe in limited goals, Camus' limited goals. So I'm ready to accept a tremendous element of failure that can't be eliminated, that one's never going to see the millenium—it probably doesn't exist. But this doesn't mean that one can live saying, right, let chaos come. I will still, in my life and in my work, seek for some principle of transcendental order, which implies progression in human terms. I still believe in that. But I would also say that the only thing that I'm one hundred percent sure of—and I have been since before I could formulate what was wrong with our life here, with this country—I just know that any form of racism is wrong. I don't see how one can see both sides of this ugly question; there aren't two sides—there are people who have the right to be human. That's the only thing I can say that I'm sure of. Nothing else.

A Conversation with Nadine Gordimer

Robert Boyers, Clark Blaise, Terence Diggory,
and Jordan Elgrably/1982

Reprinted by permission of the editors from the quarterly *Salmagundi*, issue #62 (1984), 3–31; special issue on Nadine Gordimer.

This is an edited transcript of two interviews. The first (Part One) was conducted in October 1982 at Skidmore College before a large audience. The second (Part Two) was conducted by Jordan Elgrably in Paris in July 1982. Our special thanks go to Martha Callahan and Sarah Strickler for preparing this transcript in its early stages.

Part I

R.B.: Would you argue that ideas, and by this I mean really *abstract* ideas, are indispensable to a serious novel of high ambition, not merely as motive, but as texture? It's often thought that ideas fatally endanger novels in the way that ideas are often said to endanger lyric poems, for example. I think of this in connection with Henry James' famous notion of a mind so fine that it couldn't be violated, even by its own ideas. I often remember that when I read your fiction. Though there are a great many ideas in the work one doesn't feel that the mind has ever been violated by any of them because they're always converted into sensuous texture. Do you agree that ideas are important in a novel of high ambition?

N.G.: I can't imagine how there could be a novel of high ambition without ideas; to me, ideas become themes. They are the thematic and the transcendent aspect of any imaginative work, novels and poems alike. When I write a novel, there are usually two or three themes running concurrently. I see them as layers. I don't consciously seek that, it just seems to happen, perhaps because life is so complex. Human beings are complex, and we writers strive for the ultimate expression of the section of life that we dredge out from time and

185

from place. So I think that ideas are of supreme importance, but the word "ideas," to me, comes afterwards. You analyze the themes of a novel, and often there are themes that one person would find that another would not. There are themes that come in without the right of being there. I think they may come from some kind of collective consciousness. Often they appear, not by the writer's intention, but from the society which acts upon, influences him or her.

I'll give you an example. To my astonishment and that of those who know me, one critic, writing of *Burger's Daughter,* said that it was a profoundly religious book. Yet when I really think about the book, I can see that it could be interpreted that way. At one point in the book, Rosa, who is starting out from under a political interpretation of the meaning of life, finds that this interpretation is not quite adequate to the mystery of life. Yet, in the end, she comes to accept her father's attitude towards life and his ideological political stand because she realizes that political commitment is not only *about* suffering but that it is actually an attempt to *end* suffering. When I think about the people in *Burger's Daughter,* I find that what they're trying to do is reorder society in such a way as to do away with as much suffering as possible. The idea of putting your life on the line, and risking suffering, is not only a political but a traditionally Christian idea: first comes suffering, then redemption.

R.B.: And the fact that these characters, themselves, don't think of it in religious terms, but have translated it into secular terms, doesn't make it less religious.

N.G.: Yes, the central idea of *Burger's Daughter* is transcendence. And though the characters act on behalf of secular goals, one could certainly see their belief in the cause and their ability to transcend immediate difficulties as *religious* in nature.

R.B.: Have you ever paid deliberate attention to the danger, represented vividly by the writings of Camus, that strenuous moral analysis in fiction may turn, as I think it sometimes does in Camus, to a kind of sententiousness? I thought about this recently when I read an interesting statement you had made some years ago, namely that "the only dictum I always remember is André Gide's 'salvation for the writer lies in being sincere, even against one's better judgment.'" I thought that was a remarkable statement. I wondered if you'd say something about it.

N.G.: I think that the decision to be sincere is an artistic one. It's the kind of decision I often face when I'm writing because I have strong political convictions in the country where I live. I am partisan, yes. Sometimes when I'm writing, there will be a character who belongs to "my" side, the side of radical opposition to apartheid, but who is devious, perhaps exhibitionistic, and represents certain lies that are told on "my" side, too, for expedience. If I were Lionel Burger I would no doubt say, "Well, what does this artistic sincerity and integrity matter? What matters is the cause." But I don't accept that. As a writer I feel that my first duty is integrity as an artist. I have a superstitious notion that if I lie, my characters will be damaged, somehow; their verity will be destroyed. I'm making that kind of decision all the time, while knowing that I'm writing something that would be criticized and regarded as disloyal by the people on whose side I am. Lately, I've written a couple of stories where this decision has become a minor obsession with me because in a society like that of South Africa there are so many people, and so many sides. There are people whom one trusts absolutely who turn out to be police agents. I've talked to people like Kundera who know that too well. It's a very extraordinary thing to take someone into your confidence only to discover that all along he's an agent who's been paid to spy on you.

R.B.: While we're on the subject of the role sincerity plays in the writing of fiction, I'd like to discuss a very minor though perhaps an important criticism I've heard levelled at *Burger's Daughter*; it focuses upon the section of the novel in which Rosa Burger goes to France. The criticisms are basically levelled in terms of the incoherence this introduces into a book which is otherwise unified in place, and in terms of the human types that are used. The notion is that, in France, Rosa meets up with people who are altogether different. Not only does the setting change, but the tone of the book changes. It has always struck me as one of the most wonderful things about that book that it can accommodate that kind of seeming incoherence. I think about that in connection with what you've just said, as a decision that has more to do with sincerity than with the careful or the correct aesthetic choice. It seems to me, if you wanted to be absolutely safe and correct, you might not have included that section of the book. Am I misreading?

N.G.: No. I don't *ever* want to be safe and correct. I want to say what I think, what I see, and what I think needs to be said. First of all, looking back on it, I think that that section of the book is too long. It should have been shorter. I could have said what I wanted to say less expansively. Now I'd have to say also that there was too much about Rosa getting out of South Africa. But—I stress—the section which takes place in France cannot be looked upon as self-indulgent or as something that is not germane to the book. It was necessary to have Rosa leave South Africa in order to show *how impossible it was for her to stay away.* It was not just the frivolity of those people in France, their political irresponsibility and inability to understand Rosa's concrete South African experience. For Rosa, these people seem as if they're from another planet. Yet the attitudes of Europe are a large dimension of that which threatens life in South Africa.

T.D.: We've been talking for a while about *Burger's Daughter,* but I'd like to ask you about something which struck me while reading *The Conservationist.* Earlier, you mentioned your concern with the landscape in that book. It's occurred to me, in the little reading I've done of novels coming out of Africa, that there seems to be a distinction in the approach taken by white writers as opposed to blacks. Alan Paton, for example, refers to the land a great deal in *Cry, the Beloved Country.* With black writers, it seems the identity is with the people as opposed to the land. Does that jibe with your knowledge of such writers?

N.G.: Yes. I think there's something very interesting there. I think that whites are always having to assert their claim to the land because it's based, as Mehring's mistress points out, on a piece of paper—a deed of sale. And what is a deed of sale when people have first of all taken a country by conquest? Tenure is a very interesting concept, morally speaking. When you come to think of it, what is tenure? What is "legal" tenure? Blacks take the land for granted, it's simply there. It's theirs, although they've been conquered; they were always there. They don't have this necessity to say, "Well I love this land *because* it's beautiful, *because* it's this, that, and the other."

T.D.: Does the anxiety for whites, then, become not only the need to establish that tenure of the land, but to compensate for a lack of interpersonal identity? Or is there a genuine sense of identity with the people in the way that blacks can respond to a community rather than to a landscape?

N.G.: No, the whites identify themselves as a racial community too. I should have mentioned that the farmers, who are mainly Afrikaners, have much more of a relationship with the land than other whites have because they've tilled it for so long and are very close to it. The pity is that this is used as a justification on the part of the white powerstructure, for owning it exclusively.

T.D.: I wonder if I could ask a journalistic question, in connection with your own interest in other African writers. You've done a lot, not only to make your own contribution to the novel, but to bring attention to what else was going on in the literature of that region. What writers, currently, do you especially admire, in South Africa, or on the continent as a whole?

N.G.: There are quite a number of black writers in South Africa that one wishes were better known. A white writer whom I admire very much is somebody who was unknown here until very recently. Five years ago I tried to interest my own publishers in an earlier book of his, and they were stupid enough not to take it up. Last year Coetzee's *Waiting for the Barbarians* was published here. I'm sure many of you have read it or seen it. I think he's a wonderful writer and marvelous things are going to come from him. Among black writers, there is one who is particularly well-known, Es'kia Mphahlele. He has written very fine essays and short stories which are being reprinted here and there. He's also a novelist. He was a professor at the University of Pennsylvania. He was in exile from South Africa in various parts of the world for nineteen years, and now I'm glad to say that he's back. He's written a wonderful autobiographical book called *Down Second Avenue* that I'm sure is available in paperback here; and a critical work (I don't think critical works can ever really be outdated) called *The African Image*. A wonderful black novelist in exile is Alex La Guma.

There are very talented younger people coming up who've been published locally in South Africa, including some good playwrights, but they haven't published much and you can't get their books here. There's also a South African Indian writer who is very good, and I'm trying to get somebody interested in him here. His name is Ahmed

Essop. He's written a short, very strange, ironic novel called *The Visitation* and also a book of stories. He writes with a special feeling for details of people's lives and for strange lives hidden behind walls.

R.B.: Are there regular contacts between black and white writers in South Africa? Is it, for example, considered legitimate for serious white writers to comment publicly upon works produced by blacks?

N.G.: Well, the contact is invariably politically charged. When a white writer includes black characters in his work, he expects to come in for a lot of criticism—which is more political than literary in nature. During the seventies, when the black consciousness movement was particularly strong, there was a withdrawal on the part of black writers, painters, and actors from contacts with whites, and from any kind of professional association or professional loyalty and interest. In other words, it's the old division, again, based on the idea that a black non-writer and writer have more in common than a black writer and a white writer—which on the professional level, of course, isn't true. There is now in South Africa some informal contact between black and white writers. There's much more contact in the theatre. Indeed, we writers sometimes look with an envious eye on the way black and white seem to work together in theatre. The actors don't concern themselves with the criticism that they are working in a non-racial organization when it is "correct" to work only with blacks. They ignore their differences and go on because they feel that they're doing good work, they're enriching their range. The trouble with writers is that we theorize much more and do our work alone. The people associated with the theater belong to a community; their work requires that.

In 1976, we started a writers' organization that lasted for two years. As you know, 1976 was the year of the Soweto uprising, which spread all over the country and exacerbated the feeling between blacks and whites during that time. We didn't have many white members, because we decided that this couldn't be, so to speak, a "corporate" organization. We couldn't worry about strictly literary matters. What we had to worry about were writers who went to prison, writers whose books were banned, and writers who, themselves, were banned—meaning that they couldn't move around freely or work and publish freely. We raised money to help support their families while they were in jail. This sort of thing, of course, didn't make us very popular with the government. And on the other hand, if you were in that organization, you had to be committed to the idea of black liberation. So we lost a lot of white writers because of this. They would argue that they were writers, not political activists. For two years we were useful, but then the black journalists' organization began to pressure the black members of our group to form an all-black writers' organization. Our fellow black writers were put in a difficult position; many of them resisted for a long time, although they were also being harrassed by the police and advised not to mix with these troublemaker "white leftists." They were being pulled from both sides, so eventually we had an extraordinary meeting where we decided we would have to dissolve our organization, which we sadly did, but without hard feelings. I still have black writer friends who were in that organization.

R.B.: Is there a substantial community of readers in South Africa itself? Or do you essentially feel that you write for readers outside of South Africa?

N.G.: Well, that's really two questions. First of all, I, myself, don't write for any audience. I simply write for anybody who is there to read me. Unlike Rosa Burger, I never have any idea of whom I'm addressing. She had to because she was trying to see herself, to put herself together out of other people's ideas of her. I often say that the best way to write would be as if you were already dead. That way, you don't have to worry whether you're going to offend your grandmother or your lover or child; more particularly, the people whose political views you share. You have to take that freedom for yourself. I often find when I've finished a book or a story that it really may have awful consequences for me personally. But it's done, and there it is. While I'm writing it I have this crazy illusion that it's only for me, and that I don't need to worry about who's going to read it.

You ask about the community of readers in South Africa. Until a few years ago, the figures were quite high, considering the size of the country and of the literate population. Because of political reasons, we only got television four years ago. The officials were worried that it was too risky. I don't know why, because it's entirely government-owned and everything is highly censored. They don't let anything out over any of the channels that could possibly harm them. But since there has been television, apparently there has been a significant

drop in the readership figures. Perhaps our readers will return to
books once they get sick of the government-controlled box.

C.B.: You've written, in various autobiographical sketches, of the
rather typical Commonwealth upbringing you experienced: the
colonial schools, the repressive and imitative social rituals, the
slighting of the indigenous culture and history that surrounded you in
South Africa. As a Canadian, my immediate reaction is to place you
in the Commonwealth tradition, in the company of such authors as
Joyce, Naipaul, Katherine Mansfield, Doris Lessing, and Patrick
White. Others might link you with the Russian and English authors of
the nineteenth century or, understandably, with the literary tradition
of the African continent.

Could you help us by placing yourself within a tradition and
perhaps talk about your formation as a contemporary South African
writer? What did you have to overcome? What writers influenced you
most early on and with whom do you now feel most closely
identified?

N.G.: I'm going to start off with an objection. It's always easy to
start off that way. I think that Patrick White and I have a completely
different basic identity from the other writers that you mentioned,
because we are *still there*. But, to answer your question, I think I was
very lucky when I began to write at the early age of fifteen, because I
was able to write in a very unselfconscious and natural way. I enjoyed
a strange kind of freedom, living as I did, in such a cultural backwater
from the point of view of the rest of the world, a place which totally
ignored what was on its own doorstep and instead was always looking toward the main cultural streams abroad. There was the local
public library in the small gold-mining town in which I lived, and I
was like a calf in clover there; nobody guided or advised me; nobody
told me which books I ought to read if I wanted to become a writer. I
read a lot of French and Russian nineteenth-century novels, in translation of course, and I drew, completely unselfconsciously, from
whatever there was for me to feed on there.

But, at the same time, as I was beginning to write, I felt that
nobody would be interested in the world that I knew, that indeed I
wasn't living in the world, that the world I knew about in books was
something to aspire to, perhaps to see one day; to walk in Virginia
Woolf's and Dickens' London, to come to Nathaniel Hawthorne's

and Ernest Hemingway's America. Faulkner I read later: I might have found some parallels with my own life if I'd read Faulkner in my teens, but I didn't—at least not until my late teens.

Then I read Katherine Mansfield's stories, which rang a bell because she was somebody *also* living at the end of the world, knowing that she did, and writing about simple things in her own life. This made me feel that this gold-mining town in which I lived, the people around me there, the little dramas in the street—that these were things one could write about, and which, perhaps, somebody might even be interested in reading about.

Growing up as a white colonial in South Africa, I spoke, read and wrote in English because, at that time, we were part of the British Commonwealth. Naturally, these political realities caused me to identify with English literature and culture, rather than with American or other Anglo-Saxon cultures, and in spite of the fact that the province in which I was born in 1923 had been a Boer republic. I remember as a little girl celebrating the twenty-fifth anniversary of the ascension to the throne of King George VI: it was autumn and I went out into the garden and cut off branches of leaves to decorate the house, and felt very patriotic. It was *our* king and queen. So I would have to admit that at the beginning, if I could claim any tradition, I claimed the British tradition.

But more precisely, when I began to write I chose as a model, from the point of view of attitude (I'm not talking about a stylistic model but an approach to the world), that of British liberal writers, and in particular, the Bloomsbury people, such as E.M. Forster. Forster's *A Passage to India* was another book that spoke to me in a way that I didn't quite understand, yet it represented the only British liberal tradition of that era and, at the same time, it referred to a foreign country in the way that my own country was a foreign country. D.H. Lawrence, De Maupassant, Chekhov, and Hemingway were also a great influence on me when I first began to write short stories, very different as they all are. But, then who is there, what modern writer of short stories has not been influenced by those four? They created the modern short story. So in a way, I suppose my influences were the same as anybody else's writing in the English language.

What came later was a kind of analysis of my own work, of the attitudes that it implied and, in some cases, of the inappropriateness of following those foreign, imported attitudes. I'm telling you this now in an analytical fashion. It didn't happen to me that way. I simply felt my way out of aping the way British liberals thought because it was inappropriate to the life that I was living and to what was around me. I had to find a way to express what *I* had to say because it was coming out of my own life and that society in which I lived. So I had to break with that English liberal tradition and range further.

C.B.: How does one break with the English liberal tradition and still remain an English-speaking liberal?

N.G.: Well I don't think *that* kind of English-speaking liberal exists any more in South Africa. If this person does exist, he or she is an anachronism and the work is likely to be anachronistic.

C.B.: Could Alan Paton have been that at one time?

N.G.: No, not really, because if you look at *Cry, the Beloved Country,* which was such an important book in political terms—it made the rest of the world wake up to South Africa in a way that it hadn't before—you'll find the thinking was a British, Christian, liberal tradition with a strong emphasis on *Christian.* Whereas the liberals I'm talking about in literature were indeed agnostics, if not atheists. Certainly the whole Bloomsbury crowd were; Forster was the ultimate humanist writer, surely? So Paton, I think, was linked more to the missionary tradition. This attitude didn't have any meaning for me at all, because I didn't have any religion. I'm Jewish, but have never had any kind of Jewish upbringing; I have never been to a synagogue except for a wedding, et cetera. In fact, I read the Bible as literature, when I was growing up. The lack of a religious upbringing had made my approach to literature different from Paton's. Our respective motivation for writing was not the same: Paton wrote *Cry, the Beloved Country* at forty out of social indignation. Whereas, I started to write at fifteen the way other kids dance or sing: because they just have some drive to do so.

T.D.: In looking back over the development of your career, you recall your concern about people not being interested in the world that you had to write about. In a review of Wole Soyinka's autobiography published last year in *The New York Review of Books,* you praise especially the precise, concrete detail that Soyinka brings into the work which, you say, enables us to make contact with the world he writes about. Your own work has been both praised and faulted for its accumulation of precise detail. Do you feel this density of detail is what makes the strange world you write about more accessible to people elsewhere?

N.G.: No, I don't think so. It's *significant* detail that brings any imaginative work alive, whatever the medium. If you can't see things freshly, if you can't build up through significant detail, then I think you fall into cliché, not only in the use of words and phrases, but even in form. That fresh eye is the most valuable thing in the world for any writer. When I look at my early stories, there's a freshness about them, there's a sensuous sensibility that I think you only have when you're very young; after that you go on to analyzing your characters, you go on to narrative strength. But first, you've got to have that fresh eye with which to see the world.

What I sensed in Soyinka is that, for the most part, as a middle-aged man he is able to look back on his childhood and still see his early life with that fresh eye. However, I see in myself the tendency to lose it as one gets older. I don't think that in my later work I've got that vividness quite to the extent that I had it, though I may have gained other strengths. I have lost that freshness because I've seen everything too often.

T.D.: What other strengths would you say you have gained?

N.G.: Well first of all, I think that narrative was often weak in my early work. I've always been interested in literature that was held together by what I think of as invisible stitches or invisible connections. But when attempting a complex novel, like *A Guest of Honour* or *Burger's Daughter*, one can't depend solely on that kind of intuitive observation. So in order to develop complex themes you have to develop narrative strength. Perhaps that's a compensation then: a little of the one went and I gained with the other.

T.D.: I'd like to pursue the issue of detail one step further. In *The Conservationist,* the protagonist, Mehring, is endowed with the kind of consciousness that causes him to sometimes focus very closely on precise detail, and in one passage of the book, speaking through Mehring's consciousness, you say: "distress is a compulsion to examine minutely." Is your compulsion to examine minutely any sign of distress, or, are your examinations simply a matter of artistic intuition?

N.G.: No, I was referring purely to times of stress when you feel that in order to hang onto your nerve you've got to look at that paper cup on the table because that cup is *there*. It's made of paper and it's full of water and you can touch it: it's real. I was thinking of those moments in life when there seems to be no solid ground underfoot; when you cling to some apparent sanity, as evinced in a concrete object.

C.B.: . . . the very cupness . . .

N.G.: Yes—indeed. However, the criticism that you mention about the accumulation of detail, I think, comes from comparison with my earlier books, where there is much less descriptive detail. But in *The Conservationist,* the landscape is the most important character. So therefore, it had to be allowed to speak and the land could only speak and come alive for the reader through my finding its significant details.

R.B.: In *July's People* you describe a South Africa in the throes of political revolution. Though it's not possible to say what exactly will occur in the later stages of that revolution, it does seem likely that white people will not want to stay around to see it through. Do you think there will inevitably be a time, in the near future of South Africa, when sensible whites, whatever their political convictions, will have to get out in order for blacks to consolidate their gains?

N.G.: I would hope (and there are some signs) that "sensible whites" are busy trying to find ways to stay, not to go. Nevertheless, this may be difficult, because we whites have been brought up on so many lies; we've been led up the garden path or sold down the river by our ancestors in South Africa. In other words, whites have developed a totally unreal idea of how they ought to live, of their right to go on living in that country. Consequently, they must undergo a long process of shedding illusions in order fully to understand the basis for staying in South Africa. Unfortunately, there aren't enough people who have the will to attempt this. It's very hard to peel yourself like an onion, without producing a lot of tears in the process. Yet, it is absolutely necessary for anybody who wants to stay. People say to me: "Isn't it a terribly depressing place to live?" Well in some ways it is and one gets filled with self-disgust for being there. But, at other times, it's completely the other way, because there are people there who are so remarkable. The wonderful thing is, that every time you think now it's all finished—this one's gone off to jail, or that one has emigrated, that one is forced into exile, and you allow yourself to think there are not going to be any more people of that caliber— you're proved wrong. Because with each generation there are more people who grow up and rise to the occasion, and this gives you back your faith in the human spirit.

It's just over a year ago that, at last, black trade unions were recognized. I say that to you in one sentence, but it's very complex because there are all kinds of conditions that hedge about this new right that has finally been given after three hundred and fifty years. The fact is, working for this right provided an opportunity (looking at it from the white point of view because that's what you're asking me about) for young whites in universities to work *with* blacks not *for* blacks—no patronizing proxy—in a productive and progressive way, that didn't require blowing up somebody or hurting anybody. These young whites began to work with blacks in trade unionism. Blacks have, perforce, had no experience of union organization. Trade-union affairs, as we know, are very complex. So, it became necessary for young whites to move in among blacks, to offer their expertise so that blacks could establish union rights.

Well, this has been done at great risk; ultimately, one white even lost his life. Neil Aggett was a young doctor who decided that he could do more for blacks if he worked as a trade-union organizer. He moved into this work and did it extremely well, stepping out of leadership as soon as people could take over themselves. Of course, to organize people in South Africa, to provide a rallying point, means that people do get a political training from the experience, as well. And when there's some trouble, when there are strikes, the usual thing that occurs is that the government looks around for "agitators." They don't believe that people are simply trying to assert their rights. So then, the police look for those who seem to know the most and who have the access to help from outside. So they round up these young whites. Many of them spent months and months in preventive detention last year, where all sorts of terrible things happened to them. Indeed, Neil Aggett was found hanged in his cell. That, of course, is tragic, as well as inspiring, depending on which way you look at it.

I'm quoting this to show you that there are some whites who, one way or another, are looking for ways to prepare themselves, to live differently under a black majority government in a non-racial state. They believe in a non-racial state and they think that the way toward it is through black liberation. I'm one of them.

R.B.: Are there external political models available to those who wish to create a revolution in South Africa? Would you yourself think of the revolutions that have been consolidated in other countries, in Latin America, in Africa, in Asia and so on, as appropriate models, or is the South African situation so very different that no external model will do?

N.G.: Well it gives me a little shudder when you speak of models for a revolution, perhaps because one's unlikely ever to hear of ideal revolutions in one's lifetime. These other models are pretty bloody and terrible, aren't they?

R.B.: Yes, they are. But do you hope to achieve the drastic changes which need to be achieved in South Africa without a revolution? And if a revolution is to come, wouldn't one want to consult at least some of the available models, however one regarded them?

N.G.: It seems to me that there are plenty of models, but they are not necessarily the models that one wants to follow. I have the obstinate utopian notion—and I'm not alone in this—that we must try to achieve this revolution without the terrible bloodshed that has happened in other places. But, whether one can do that or not, I don't know. I think the accompanying thought is that no two situations are the same. History *more or less* repeats itself, but never in quite the same way, though there are lessons to be learned from social upheaval elsewhere: things to be avoided, things to try to attain. However, South Africa musn't be confused with other countries in Africa. It's different because it is by far and away the most industrialized, the most advanced, and the most developed of any country in Africa.

R.B.: Of course, studying your portraits of Marxist revolutionaries, one has a sense that they are utterly different from the figures one reads about in novels by French and Soviet writers; as incomparable as the Rhodesian communists depicted in Doris Lessing's earlier writings seem to be. But let me shift direction a bit and ask what do you make of the idea, which is quite popular in some circles, that the most interesting writing, including your own, is almost inevitably produced under repressive circumstances? Of course, one can think of all sorts of exceptions here, but is there something about repressive circumstances that makes the writings of Solzhenitsyn, Kundera, and Gordimer, seem much more compelling than others? Is it only that they seem much more compelling to people who live in much more comfortable circumstances?

N.G.: I really don't think so. I almost interrupted you and said, "Of course we must remember Proust in his cork-lined room." I don't think that one should look to repression as something that nurtures talent or ability. But, in order to come up with a definitive answer, one would have to bring up a lot of names and conduct a sort of comparative study. In general, I think that this is an illusionary idea that we have; that a society under pressure produces better writers. Of course, you talked about the Soviet Union and the Soviet satellites. We know so few of the Russian writers, though we have reason to believe that the ones we know are the outstanding ones, and the people who are living inside under that repression produce a lot of mediocre work.

So what lesson are we to draw from that example? In South Africa and in Latin America, societies where there is repression and stimulation through the tremendous contradictions in society, an awful lot of indifferent and downright bad work is produced. Very often a writer writes pretty indifferently even though his heart is, so to speak, on the right side, particularly if he wants to ride the band wagon. Given the book of such an author to review, you and I would feel very bad about panning it because the sentiments are right. So, there comes this awful question of the morality of art and the morality of life, and it's very difficult for critics to find their way through this dilemma. I see it in French literary journals. It's amazing to see the kind of writers in France who are highly praised, beside the one or two writers, to my mind, of real genius. Consequently, a Michel Tournier novel will be reviewed on the same level as some third-rate novel that deals with what the French did in Indo-China, simply because the latter writer's sentiments are appealing.

C.B.: Among your many stories and among your many novels, what are your personal favorites and why should they be that?

N.G.: My choice has little to do with "merit," so you may agree or not. In other words, the book in which you've achieved most, often

might not be your favorite book because it might be connected with a
period in your life and private events in your life which were painful.
Whereas, you may have a very tender feeling for another book that is
connected with a pleasant time in your life.

But, if I tried, at least, to be objective I think that I would sit back
and say, "you did well with *The Conservationist.*" In that book, I
decided to ignore whether I was going to be understood or not, and I
decided to trust the reader, and to trust myself. By not bothering
about whether the transitions could be followed I was able to write
the most lyrical of my writings. I trusted to my own ability to carry the
reader across, and I seem to have managed, by and large, to do it,
though I've discovered that some people misunderstand the ending
of that book and think that the main character Mehring is dead. But
then they didn't read very carefully because a few days after the
incident where they think he died, the people on the farm telephone
him at his office to ask for money to buy wood to make that coffin. I
went over that book on a kind of tight rope; teetered now and then,
but didn't fall and that has given me a special feeling for it.

I had a different sort of feeling for *A Guest of Honour* because it is
not about South Africa. It's what I call a "post-South African" novel.
A Guest of Honour has little to do with "black and white," but rather
something different. In order to write that book, with all its political
and human complications connected around trade unionism, I had to
do research which I thought I was ill-equipped to do. Usually, I'm lazy
about research, but there I proved that I too can go to libraries if I'm
sufficiently motivated. I like *Burger's Daughter* for another reason
entirely. I had wanted *somebody* to write a novel of that nature for
years, someone directly from the center of that milieu. However
when the right people did write, they wrote non-fiction books and
never attempted novels. I had always felt that it would be presumptuous for me to do so. But, in the end, I decided to be presumptuous
and go ahead and do it . . . For me it's the only novel of mine that
has a purpose outside simply writing it. It is for me a kind of homage
to that group of early communists.

C.B.: Of all your novels, *Burger's Daughter* is the book that's
touched me the most. It seems to me to be a book that grows out of
The Late Bourgeois World. This seems apparent because of the
particular rhetorical style of that book. There's an obvious hunger, I

think, to convince and to persuade. There's an implied audience, a population, in fact, that is listening to Rosa's narration, to her appeals, which begin as a direct address to Conrad, her feckless young lover, who has no real political convictions, and who thinks of himself as an entirely free man. Rosa tries to tell him what is earnest and real in her life. Next she addresses her thoughts to Baasie: then—at the end— she addresses her father, Lionel. There are rhetorical flashes in this book that are pure dry narration; there are other almost surreal flashes that are hallucinated and are the expression of the extraordi- nary amount of personal passion she brings to bear. I'm aware as I read that book, as I am not so entirely in your other books, of the conviction that history, society and politics are as valid a point of departure for character, as psychology or personal experience. You have wedded psychology and history, as Faulkner did in *Absalom, Absalom!* You've achieved a kind of personalizing of history and politics, in a sense much broader than Faulkner knew.

How do you do this? Is it a reflection of that surplus of commitment and that habit of advocacy that is part of your experience in South Africa? Does it require the amount of disillusionment, the amount of suffering and tragedy that the South African experience entails, or is it art? In other words, is it an artful decision or is it your attempt to render the vastness of the experience?

N.G.: It's an artful decision because the vastness of the experience is Rosa Burger's, not mine. I have always been fascinated, astonished, and, in the end, awed, mystified by the incredible overriding passion and commitment in certain people. One hears talk about being a "new man" or a "new woman." These people anticipated that; they are already new men and new women who rose above so many of the personal conflicts that distract the rest of us in our own lives.

I'm interested in what you said earlier, that the point of departure is history rather than psychology. Indeed, you are right, but I would say that this was the psychology of history.

T.D.: I wonder if I could follow up on that with another question about *Burger's Daughter.* This concerns your description of the passionate engagement of the group of people that you're dealing with, in the context of Rosa's life and what happens to her eventually. The problem you explore with Rosa is that she doesn't have that kind of involvement, that kind of engagement throughout much of the

novel. To what extent does her problem arise from the fact that she is
Burger's daughter rather than Burger's son? Does it make a
difference that she is a female rather than a male protagonist?

N.G.: I don't think so because I've seen the same thing happen to
males, as well. Perhaps with a male, there is more likely to be a conflict between father and son. Had Rosa been her father's *son,* she
might have rebelled earlier, but otherwise, I don't believe her gender
was that important, no.

T.D.: I'd like to broaden that question, then, and apply it to your
work in general. Critics have remarked on your ability to speak
through both male and female characters. How do you decide which
to use in planning your work? Do you simply imagine the character
and find yourself speaking through that character, or is there
something that helps you to decide whether the protagonist is going
to be male or female, whether the voice is going to be male or female
in the book?

N.G.: The choice would depend on the type of experience. In *The
Conservationist,* for example, it simply wouldn't be possible to have a
woman portray the kind of businessman that Mehring is. So the story
occurs to me as the story of a man. There is no ambivalence in my
attitude, no moment of indecision at all whether this is a story about
a man or a woman. The story occurs to me simply in the way that it
has to be. It's similar to deciding whether you're going to tell a story
in the past tense, in the present tense, or in the first person. I don't
think any writer can explain this, and I think if the writer arrives at
this decision through trial and error, then there's something very
wrong with that story. You've got to hear it in the right voice.

T.D.: Since we've brought up the topic of sex difference, let me
ask you a social rather than a literary question. I think from an
American perspective we have a view of South Africa as a land which
is divided into an infinite number of categories. You have the Indians,
the blacks, and at least two separate groups of whites. Can such
divisiveness also be seen at the level of male/female relationships?

N.G.: No, it's all based on color, you see. I'm often asked this kind
of question by feminists and I have to reply—somewhat in the way I
replied to an earlier question about black and white writers—that the
white man and the white woman have much more in common than
the white woman and the black woman, despite their difference in

sex. Similarly, the black man and the black woman have much more in common than the black man and the white man. Their attitude towards life is much more similar. The basis of color cuts right through the sisterhood or brotherhood of sex. It boils down to the old issue of prejudice and the suppression of blacks of both sexes, to the way that they are forced to live.

The black woman doesn't carry a pass, but her movements are virtually just as restricted as a black man's are. If you're black, you suffer this restriction from the time that you are a little child. Indeed, black parents have to teach their children this, or they'll get hurt inside, damaged psychologically. They are taught that there are certain things they're not to do and there are certain ways that they must learn to address white people. Thus, the loyalty to your sex is secondary to the loyalty to your race. That's why Women's Liberation is, I think, a farce in South Africa. It's a bit ridiculous when you see white girls at the University campaigning for Women's Liberation because they're kicked out of some fraternity-type club or because they can't get into bars the way men do. Who cares? A black woman has got things to worry about much more serious than these piffling issues. White women have the vote; *no* black, male or female, has. White women have many more rights than black women. Black women are concerned with such basic things as being entitled to own a house or continuing to live in their house in a black ghetto when their husbands divorce them or die. Until just last year, a black woman had no right to have a house in her name, so if her man walked out on her she had to quickly marry somebody else in order to stay in her home.

Part II

J.E.: You have suggested that the goals of the feminist movement are trivial compared to those of blacks fighting apartheid. And yet you seem to look forward to a day when black women will have the luxury of becoming feminists as well. When you say that they will become militant and fight, do you mean that they will fight against black men?

N.G.: Against their own men, yes, because many are very much exploited by them. But at present they see it in the broader light: a

consequence of the exploitation by whites. A common position in
South Africa is one where a man living in one of the homelands—the
so-called national states, where only 13% of South Africa is available
to 80% of the South African people—will be recruited here for the
mines or by a large construction company, to come and work for a
year on a project. When that project is over, perhaps he'll get another
job in the same industry, and he'll be granted permission to continue
living in the town; he's wanted as a unit of labor. He will *not* get
permission to bring his wife and family. So the woman remains stuck
away in the country. As time goes by he will find another woman and
will probably have children by her. And then he'll have this conflict of
loyalty: to whom shall he send the money he earns? Will he send it
home or contribute it to the household of the woman he's shacked
up with? That woman in the country is being exploited by the male
because she's literally left carrying the baby; she's left to work the bit
of land, bring up the children, alone. Often the man disappears
altogether. Now, where does the blame lie?

J.E.: This was July's predicament in *July's People*.

N.G.: It was, and is a very mundane and terrible one.

J.E.: The West Indian novelist, V.S. Naipaul, talks somewhere
about "the dignity of the woman of Africa." Assuming he is implying
black women, as a white woman how do you feel you share that
dignity?

N.G.: There is no particular dignity attached to being a white
woman in South Africa! Far from it. However, it does hinge on what
kind of woman you are and how you live. There are some white
women with immense dignity attached to them. Helen Joseph[1] is
one of them. She has spent virtually her entire life fluctuating in and
out of house arrest. She is closely identified with the black cause and
with the left among whites. Most people can suffer house arrest for a
few years—Europeans I'm talking about—and then they leave South
Africa. It is not much of a way to live. If you are under house arrest

[1]Joseph emigrated from England and became a South African national in the 1930s.
Castigated by whites as *kaffirboetie* (a "nigger lover"), she was serving the last day of a five-
year detention sentence in 1967, when the government quietly informed her that the original
sentence, filed under the "Sabotage Act" of 1962, which charged that her activities furthered
the aims of Communism, had been extended for another five years. When government officials
indicated to Joseph she could escape her internal exile on a one-way exit permit out of South
Africa, she said: "This is what the government would like me to do. And that's why I won't go.
My home is here, not overseas."

your ability to act, to further the cause of liberation, is so obviously constricted that you become tremendously frustrated. You feel it's better to leave because you may be able to accomplish more on the outside. But of course there is a certain dignity about being immovable, about just sitting there, *if you can take it.* Helen Joseph is now in her mid-70s. She is very remarkable indeed, and people literally go on pilgrimages to see her, blacks and whites from Europe and within South Africa. Joseph is allowed to go out and work, but she has to be home by six o'clock every day. From six to six, all night in fact, and from Friday until Monday morning at six o'clock. She is not permitted to receive visitors at home. It's possible to go and see her at her place of work and to have lunch with her in a public place. But a banned person, such as she, is not allowed to go to any assembly (an assembly being three people or more). It is very hard to live like this for many years.

J.E.: Does she have the use of a telephone?

N.G.: She has a telephone; tapped, you know.

J.E.: Which must bar her the freedom of saying what she wants.

N.G.: Oh, she does say what she wants in any case. People like that are not afraid to speak out.

J.E.: I find many parallels in your personal life and your work. Your home, for instance, is open to everyone, as was Lionel Burger's in *Burger's Daughter.* A great number of whites and blacks involved culturally and politically in the anti-apartheid movement come to you free and unhindered. Why haven't you ever been under house arrest, or banned?

N.G.: First of all, I would say I'm not brave enough. I have never taken any direct political action. Someone like myself takes calculated risks. And everybody has his or her own particular ceiling of risk. Alas, for the majority of whites that ceiling is so low that they don't take any risks at all. And of course by being afraid to do anything they *help* a repressive regime. This is, I find, the worst kind of intimidation and loss of self-respect, for people of any race.

J.E.: Are your friends followed and suspected by the police?

N.G.: Yes, lots of my friends are in bad straits. But it is a point of honor for banned people to defy these political taboos. They are not supposed to meet other banned people but they often take the risk. If a banned person breaks the ban, then he or she may go to prison, and often does. Most of them are extremely brave people who would not otherwise be banned. They are not watching carefully to see that they don't break the ban—they are *trying* to break it.

J.E.: Baiting the authorities?

N.G.: Exactly. They turn tables. So, my view is that if they're prepared to take the risk, that's fine with me, and I am prepared to take the lesser risk my friendship involves.

J.E.: You are often questioned about your reaction to the banning of your books and once replied, "I've been protected all my life and still am." What did you mean by that?

N.G.: Well, I don't know the context. I haven't been protected. By whom? All their lives whites share a certain protection—not protection, privilege is the word: whether you like it or not, you are privileged. You don't carry a pass in your pocket. You can move around South Africa absolutely freely. If I want to leave Johannesburg and go and live in Cape Town tomorrow, I haven't got to go to an office and apply for permission to do so. I can just pack my bags and get on a plane and go. But no black can do that. That is what I meant, that I have been privileged since I was born. When it comes to protection, that is something else. I must have meant that if you are fortunate enough to gain some kind of reputation in the outside world, you are much closer to comparative freedom. If I do things the South African government doesn't like—and I'm always doing things they dislike—they will hesitate before taking away my passport, or doing anything of that nature with me. I have to make the calculation. Because the outside world will say, the writer Nadine Gordimer, et cetera.

J.E.: Raise hell.

N.G.: In the case of *Burger's Daughter* that occurred. You've got Heinrich Böll, Nobel Prize winner, writing from Germany, you've got John Fowles from England, you've got various well-known writers in America, all signing a protest against the banning of my book, or writing articles of outrage here and there. The government does not like that because they feel that so-called "bad press" does their image more harm than if they show "tolerance" and let a book like *Burger's Daughter*, which is a difficult book—you can hardly call it a rabble-rouser—be published.

J.E.: You're saying that not everyone is likely or able to read and discern the central conflicts in the novel?

N.G.: It is a calculation, yes. The book is unlikely to inflame the masses. So the government calculates that perhaps to let it go free in South Africa will inflict less damage for the government than if it were to remain banned and occasion a bad reaction in the outside world. Nevertheless, we still have censorship of books. There is still a list, each week, of books currently banned.

J.E.: Is this a public list?

N.G.: Well, it's published in something called the Government Gazette. The newspapers always pick up the list. Not only are books banned, but records, posters and even tee shirts, such as the one with the Black Power legend (a clenched fist, the logo of the African National Congress) across it. The ANC is a banned organization and so the tee shirt must be removed from the market. This Gazette comes out every week on Friday and one can see what is banned. There has been some relaxation when it comes to sexual explicitness in books. But then there are some surprising exceptions. They banned Updike's last Rabbit novel, *Rabbit is Rich*. The very same week that he got the Pulitzer Prize! But that ban was purely on grounds of sexual explicitness and has nothing to do with politics. Years ago they banned *Couples*.

J.E.: They also banned William Styron's *Sophie's Choice*.

N.G.: Released, finally. The censors are going through a strange period now. They've a great desire to show that they are worldly and enlightened. There is a new director of the Publications Control Board. And indeed, it's a crazy situation. The Director's committees, those that read the books and recommend a ban (whereby the book in question is Gazette-banned), are sometimes subject to an appeal by the Director himself: He appeals against his own committees' banning. The book will then be given fresh consideration by a commitee of so-called literary experts.

J.E.: Who are certainly not known publicly as anti-apartheid?

N.G.: No. There are some fringe figures who are not pro-apartheid, but who feel that if you can't beat them, join them. They offer their services to try to assure that books of literary merit are let through. A totally false position, in my opinion. I don't think anybody can tell you or me what we should or should not read. I don't care which professor he is or what knowledge of literature he may have. But there are people who think differently and who believe they are doing a service to serious literature by offering to serve on such an appeal board.

J.E.: Have they approached you to that effect?

N.G.: Oh no, they haven't asked me. That, of course, would be ridiculous. They do ask academics, some of whom are not government supporters, but who are still quite obviously conservative people.

J.E.: Why was the ban on your early novel, *A World of Strangers*, lifted after twelve years?

N.G.: Largely because it had become a period piece. A later book of mine was *The Late Bourgeois World*, published in the mid-sixties. By that time the sort of people you meet in *A World of Strangers* were disillusioned with passive resistance, with liberal non-violent action, and had started the Armed Resistance Movement. They were employing violence, so you see that by the time I wrote *The Late Bourgeois World*, which was banned immediately, these people were far more militant than those in *A World of Strangers*, which became an innocuous book by comparison.

J.E.: Mama Mkhonza, the wealthy black woman in *Burger's Daughter* who is a token example of black success in a white capitalist society: Is that character based on someone?

N.G.: There are many like her whom I've known. They are people caught within the power struggle. This kind of grey area is a very interesting one in South Africa. The South African government has to try to find friends among the blacks. From the outside it appears that they simply have the iron heel on them, but it is not as facile as it looks. No, they must try and win them over as well; the famous battle of the hearts and minds. A minister of defense told the South African government in no uncertain terms that the army has the sophisticated weapons and can hold the border (which is enormous and is totally surrounded by places where freedom fighters can set up camps and infiltrate), but that he cannot hold the internal situation. And that is where psychological warfare comes into play. The South African government is always looking for middle-of-the-road blacks. No good winning over a real Uncle Tom, because he'd be totally discredited by even the most moderate black opinion. There are these attempts to buy off, with a little bit of power, the blacks who falter between loyalties. Look at what we formerly called the "Bantustan" leaders, now known as the homeland leaders of these so-called national ethnic states which have been carved out of South Africa. There the government takes someone and begins by bestowing upon him the title of Tribal Authority. He receives a nice house and a big car and a monthly allowance. Stage by stage he brings his people to the day when they shall accept "independence." And on that day the new flag is run up. In the meantime a beautiful house of assembly will have been built with South African taxpayers' money. A border post is thrown up. And, finally, he is officially Prime Minister or President. There is an ostentatious handing-over ceremony. The puppet has been offered a certain measure of power and a lot of perks. When he travels—and this is something I can never get over!—when one of these chaps arrives in Cape Town, it's called a state visit! He is in his own country and he is moving only from one area to the next. But this is what the South African government has done. He arrives in Cape Town and he is honored with a 21-gun salute and members of the South African government run to the airport to meet him, bowing and scraping. A Balkan farce! But, as you can understand, there are always people who'll be tempted by this kind of pacification. There are others, certainly, who'll have nothing of it. The homeland leaders are despised among militant Africans.

J.E.: Are these chieftains-cum-prime ministers as unpopular in their own homeland?

N.G.: Their local situation is more complicated. All of a sudden people there are given the opportunity to acquire land, and as there is this tremendous land hunger, they nibble at the carrot, also acquiring all sorts of other little privileges. On the other hand, all suffer because they lose their South African citizenship. If they want to travel they never can because nowhere else in the world are the passports of these little puppet countries recognized. And thus, by the stroke of a pen, the entire population loses its citizenship and cannot get a South African passport. Eight million South Africans out of a total population of 26.5 million have been robbed in this way. All black.

J.E.: Are they not allowed to travel in South Africa proper?

N.G.: They may come to South Africa. But suppose somebody

from one of these "statelets" goes to school or university in South
Africa (there being little opportunity for higher education where they
live) and then turns out to be rather clever. He or she is offered a
scholarship to go to the United States, England or somewhere in
Europe. What's he to do? He can't get a South African passport and
Bophuthatswana or Transkei or Venda, whichever of these little
places he belongs to, can only issue him a passport which is invalid
everywhere in the world. So he cannot go.

J.E.: It's an awful hoax.

N.G.: It's a terrible hoax. Recently, while I was in Israel, I inquired
about a very prominent, brilliant and important black woman who'd
been invited to Israel. She'd accepted to go but when she applied for
a passport she was told that she is, by her tribal origin and by her
native tongue, a Tswana, and that she may not have a South African
passport. They say she is a citizen of Bophuthatswana, where in fact
she was *not* born and where she has never lived. She must apply
there for a passport. But the supposition is ludicrous, for you can't go
to Israel or anywhere else on a Bophuthatswana passport.

J.E.: As you're speaking of travel, I was wondering how you've
been able to combine the wife/mother role with all the traveling that
you do?

N.G.: My children are grown up now, so the mother role is much
more relaxed. When they were younger I didn't travel quite so much.
Indeed, I didn't leave South Africa until I was 30 years old, which
now seems incredible. I had neither the money nor the opportunity
to leave the country. I have been fortunate in that as I've published
more books and have more invitations and opportunities to travel,
this has coincided with a greater freedom in my private life. Insofar as
my marriage is concerned, it's the kind of marriage where I've been
absolutely free to do what I like and go where I please, on my own.

J.E.: Engagé writing: do you feel it is more paramount than vis-
ceral, personal literature? If, for instance, you did not write about
apartheid . . .

N.G.: I don't write about apartheid. I write about people who
happen to live under that system. I'm not a propagandist, I'm not a
reporter. I am a natural writer. By that I mean that I began writing as
a child, when I didn't know what apartheid was. Not only didn't I
know what it was but apartheid was not officially formulated yet. I

was obviously living in a society of intense racial prejudice, but I did not know. I simply accepted that that was the way of the world. I am not, you see, a writer who has been made by my situation. There are some writers who became writers because they became so indignant and were stirred to creativity. I began writing out of a sense of wonder about life, a sense of its mystery, and also out of a sense of its chaos. To me, all art is an attempt to make a private order out of the chaos in life, whether you're a painter or a musician or a writer. So that is how I started, and then the other thing came in implicitly. I was writing for a long time before I stood outside and could analyze what I was doing in terms of politics.

J.E.: André Brink said something I wonder whether you would take issue with. He believes that whether you are writing in Afrikaans or English in South Africa, if you're white you cannot write convincingly of the black situation, and vice versa.

N.G.: I disagree. I think that is too broad a statement. I have said, and I stand by it, that there are certain areas of life, on both sides, which each side cannot write about in terms of the other. There are areas of white life, a kind of ivory tower white life, that are so remote from black experience that I doubt if any black writer could write very convincingly of them. I have had several black characters in my novels and occasionally in a short story and have dared to do it from a black point of view. This has always been within my orbit of experience, my close experience of blacks. But there are some areas where I know I wouldn't succeed. Take the Soweto Riots of 1976, the uprising of young blacks. If I were to sit down tomorrow and write a novel from the point of view of a 15- or 16-year-old boy or girl who lived through that experience, it would be false. It is not a matter of generation gap or age difference; I've been a child myself and I've had children of my own. And writers have very strange powers of identifying themselves with other people and lives different from their own. I think they are strangely androgynous beings as well. But I know I couldn't write about those particular children because they experienced the kind of childhood and adolescence I haven't experienced myself nor really been close enough to anyone who has, to know. I'd never attempt such omniscience.

J.E.: Brink referred to the fact that white and black childhoods are too dissimilar.

N.G.: Yet to say we *cannot* write about each other . . . This is very much concurrent with the black-consciousness view. I am not afraid to contest it as untrue. For over 350 years we have been kept apart in some ways, but locked together in many others. After the working day is over, blacks stream to their ghettoes, whites to the suburbs. And yet for years, for generations, because South Africa is a highly industrialized country and blacks have gone through this industrial revolution, whites and blacks have worked alongside one another. Observing each other, absorbing each other's "vibes." We know a great deal that is never spoken and this is a whole area rich in material for any novelist.

J.E.: Could you speak about the "white-consciousness movement" which purportedly is turning away from European culture and trying to establish roots within Africa?

N.G.: Yes, I am for the white-consciousness movement and in my own way I belong to it. It was actually initiated by young whites, university students who, becoming adults in the seventies, inherited a situation where those movements of the left to which they would have naturally belonged were all banned. Blacks were near the beginning of the present period of disaffection with white liberal organizations. They no longer wanted to sit on committees talking about change with white liberals and they even withdrew from student movements. All through my childhood and adolescence the fight among students, primarily in the National Union of South African Students, was to prod the government to allow blacks to belong to that movement. Blacks were with us on that issue, then. By the time my children's generation came along, black students were saying, we don't want to belong to your union. You stem from the ruling class: you must in some way harbor self-interest. You cannot look upon questions of repression from the same point of view. Thank you very much, but don't bother to campaign to let us into your NUSAS because we do not want to join. And we're starting our own student organizations. Which they did. And they have worked out their own black-consciousness philosophy. They had their publications, alas, all banned now. Steve Biko was eminent among them. There was an extremely interesting publication called *Black Review,* published twice a year, where they went into every aspect of intellectual life, conceptualizing what their lives were in a completely new way, divorced from the preconceptions put upon them by their association with whites. It was a period of great self-doubt and soul-searching as well as assertion, and I think it has been imperative for blacks. They were influenced by people like Frantz Fanon, and Fanon watered-down by Americans like Eldridge Cleaver and the Soledad Brothers. Fanon's books were bibles for them. Their ideas were also imbued with Negritude, from West Africa, the teachings of Gandhi (important in the old passive-resistance movement), Marxism, Maoism, you name it, though their fracture with whites mainly came about through the separation of the black-consciousness movement in America.

J.E.: The fact that blacks split themselves off from white liberals encouraged whites to form their own consciousness movement?

N.G.: Well, these young whites were in a vacuum. What were the choices open to them? They might either join the thinking of the laager,[2] with its white separatism and the perpetuation of white supremacy, or the laager of liberalism, which favored change only insofar as allowing blacks into the existing capitalist system of South Africa. They had come to the conclusion that capitalism and racism in South Africa are totally integrated and entwined, and tried to find a way to convince blacks that, although white, they could opt out of class and race privilege.

J.E.: They were accepting the fact that the rise of "democracy" has always run parallel with the rise of slavery?

N.G.: There was certainly this feeling that you cannot solve the problems by letting blacks into the system. You've got to change it because the country's economy is based on it. Here you've got these younger whites who could not give any allegiance to the white setup, whether conservative or "liberal," and who sought a third way for themselves, and who went to the blacks and said, we believe in what you believe in. We know that we shall only be liberated when blacks liberate themselves; whites shall implicitly be liberated from racism. But what can we do? We can't just sit here, living under privilege, which we can't help. Can't we work with you? And the blacks said NO.

J.E.: Is it over?

[2]Now a figurative term, a laager was the Afrikaaner encampment of pioneer wagons Boers formed to protect themselves from marauding black tribes.

N.G.: Over. But what you *can* do is work among your own people to change them, because if white people are to survive in the true sense, which doesn't merely mean saving their necks, it means learning to live in a new way, then they must rethink all their values. It is on this rethinking of values that white-consciousness is founded.

J.E.: And are they repudiating European culture?

N.G.: No. You can't repudiate European culture because some of the very concepts even blacks themselves are using come from Europe. In literature, for example, you cannot say "we are going to throw off European influence." Blacks in South Africa are writing mainly in English: what forms are they using? They are writing plays, short stories, novels and poems. These forms come from Europe. Blacks have a rich oral tradition but they did not have a written literature. It came with conquest . . . Each country and nationality has borrowed from another. There is a commonwealth of literature and it belongs to all of us. A Shakespeare sonnet belongs as much to a black man writing poetry as it does to you or me. This is all ours, the entire world of literature is ours to use as we please. There is no question of negating that, though there are other values. A simple example: When I was a little girl growing up in a mining town, I would go on Tuesdays and Thursdays to learn to play the piano and to dancing class. On Sunday mornings when I woke up, I would hear the drumming and singing drifting over from the black compound, the barracks where the mine workers lived. This was regarded by my parents and by the people around me as noise blacks were making. Nobody ever told me it was music. The drumming was marvelous.

J.E.: When did you grow to appreciate it?

N.G.: Oh, years afterward. I came to it, like my understanding of apartheid, from the outside. This is the kind of thing we must recognize, that there is a black cultural heritage which we, as whites, have been deprived of. We were never told that this wonderful drumming was part of being born in Africa. I had a right to regard this as my musical heritage, but it was never given me. Whites are beginning to think this way now. There are many who want to strike down roots into a new culture, a third culture. Whether that'll come off, whether politics will sabotage it or not . . .

The Clash

Diana Cooper-Clark/1983

From *London Magazine*, 22.11 (February 1983), 45–49. Reprinted by permission of *London Magazine*.

Although Nadine Gordimer had never left Africa until she was thirty, she had preconceived the world outside through reading. When she stood in London for the first time, it was familiar because she had seen it through Virginia Woolf's eyes. But the landscape of Africa is ever-present in her writing, lived and remembered with what she calls her "purely subconscious recall."

She has been through many changes as a white woman in South Africa, from apologizing that she is white to an honest response towards blacks that accepts the limitations of what she can *know* as a white woman in a rigidly structured society. Her stories and particularly her novel *July's People* illuminate her belief that the vigour, the "virility" in her country resides in the clash between white and black cultures. Unfortunately, she lives in a country where the white culture superimposed foreign literary forms upon the rich oral tradition of the blacks, without any attempt to incorporate those forms. This has been the white people's loss. Africans, white or black, are connected by a basic cultural link and the land itself—the quality of light, the kind of mud people play with, and the kind of trees they climb. In 1972, she said that "it's the superstructures that are different, but the underpinnings, the earth is the same."

Her writing has moved from the nineteenth-century form of *A Guest of Honour* to the more open-ended structure of *The Conservationist* for which she received the Booker Prize. She has said that in South Africa, "society *is* the political situation." However, instead of giving the reader political nostrums, she creates a fictional world that is powerful in its personal and public conflict, a world full of compassion for the ineptitudes and vicissitudes of human beings. She writes not with the didacticism of Solzhenitsyn, but with the acute insight of Proust. Nadine Gordimer says that he changed her view of the world; a film was peeled off her eyes. Her stories create a picture of what the literary critic, Leslie Fiedler, has called "the relationship between the truth of art, the truth of conscience, and the truth of facts."

This interview took place in Toronto where Nadine Gordimer, along with such writers as Josef Brodsky, William Styron, Wole Soyinka, Yehuda Amichai and Edwardo Galeano, was attending a conference on "The Writer and Human Rights."

D.C.C.: You have stayed in South Africa when other writers have left because, as you have said, "the roots of other countries, however desirable, were not possible for a plant conditioned by the flimsy dust that lies along the Witwatersrand." You have also talked about the way white culture superimposed foreign literary forms upon the rich oral tradition of the blacks, without any attempt to incorporate those forms. Blacks suffered the suppression of black culture; whites, in turn, now suffer the deprivation of never having had the good sense to appropriate anything from those traditions. Have you ever benefited from the tradition in your writing?

N.G.: Not in the style because you must remember that there was no written literature in South Africa . . .

D.C.C.: I thought in hearing . . .

N.G.: Yes, of course, I benefited enormously from the human contact, from coming in contact with different attitudes to life which arise out of the African tradition. I do believe that we are all basically exactly the same in our *needs*. But these needs have been formulated and dealt with differently by different societies and it is always extremely enriching to make this contact. This is the charm, for instance, of being in an Italian village, of seeing how people deal with their children, of the way young people behave when they are in love, the different patterns of life. All express the same thing and all, when it comes to art, seek to explain the inexplicable in life, seek to find a form that transcends the business of being born, living through life, procreating, dying.

D.C.C.: The political nature of your work is often stressed. Yet, in 1965, you said that: "I am not a politically-minded person by nature. I don't suppose, if I had lived elsewhere, my writing would have reflected politics much. If at all." Do you still hold to that view now?

N.G.: Yes, I wonder! I think I would cross out the final phrase, "if at all." Obviously if I had lived elsewhere, even in apparently happy countries, like Sweden and Canada, shall we say, there are always particular trends in society, particular problems, that would again affect people's lives, that would have come into my work, so that there would have been perhaps directly or indirectly some kind of political concern. But I certainly think it would have impinged much less upon my imagination.

D.C.C.: Grigori Svirsky, the author of *Hostages: The Personal Testimony of a Soviet Jew,* said to me that unpolitical writers have been invented by American literary scholars. I got a feeling from you that you would agree with Svirsky that writers are political, if you live in the world, if you live in a certain historical context.

N.G.: Yes. Novelists and short-story writers provide implicitly a critique of their society. The proof of that is the importance given to Balzac's *Human Comedy* by critics in the Eastern European countries, critics who stem from the extreme left. Balzac himself was an extremely conservative person politically, very reactionary, but in his *Comédie Humaine* he gave such a truthful, marvellous picture of that very society of which he was a part, that in the eyes of the leftist critics, socialist critics, he gives an unbeatable picture of what was wrong with the bourgeoisie at that time, of the seeds of its own destruction that were within it. A good writer can't help revealing the truth that is in his society and by that token there is a political implication and he is politically committed.

D.C.C.: In your writing the life of the imagination is often a public creation. You have commented that: "in a certain sense a writer is 'selected' by his subject—his subject being the consciousness of his own era. How he deals with this is, to me, the fundament of commitment." How do you differ from writers whose subject is not their own era but rather themselves?

N.G.: It all depends upon the range of the writer. There are some people who may be wonderful writers but they are their own principal subject. There is a whole school of writing like that. Names immediately spring to mind, people like Céline and Genet. There are many writers like this. In a sense, one can say that such work is narrow, that the writers apparently cannot go beyond themselves, but on the other hand there is often so much *within them* that perhaps in the end to know one human being fully is enough, even yourself. . . .

Other writers with a different approach and a different kind of scope often choose to write about people very, very different from themselves and I have been that kind of writer. The main character in *The Conservationist* is somebody who is extremely unlike me and lives a life totally unlike the life that I live. There are other characters in my books who do live the kind of life that I live and would approximate somehow to my opinions and my convictions. I would dismiss any suggestion that my fiction is spun entirely out of my own life. That it is spun out of my own society is another matter. Goethe once said: "wherever you live, if you thrust your hand deep into the life around you, what you bring up will be something of the truth." I think the key phrase there is to stick your hand into the muck or into the rose petals or whatever there is *there*.

D.C.C.: Your work has evolved from a literary tradition that was South African to one that is defined as African or what you have called, an "African-centred consciousness." Your later novels, *The Conservationist, Burger's Daughter* and *July's People* reflect this change. Because there are so many different cultures on the continent of Africa, what are the links between such varied societies, over and above the experience of colonialism?

N.G.: Oh, I think there are very deep links and they are in the African peoples. There are strong threads that run from country to country that characterize African life. There is, as you know, a Tower of Babel of languages and there are many different religions and many different ideas in African societies but there is a greater similarity, a greater instinctive understanding between people of different countries within the African continent than between the people in African countries and the people of Europe or of North America or the Far East. There is some kind of basic cultural link. I distrust people—writers, too!—who lean upon a mysticism of the land and the earth but the fact is that there is something that comes through from the earth itself in each continent. And I think that even if you are white, if you were born in Africa and you have rejected both consciously and subconsciously the colonial consciousness, if you are not just floating on the surface of the society in which you live and ignoring its true entities which are the overwhelming presence of black people—if you don't ignore this then you too share in the real sense of Africa, the human sense of Africa and the physical sense of the land. It enters into your work through your perceptions. Where do writers get their earliest perceptions? They come from the quality of the light, the kind of mud you play with, the kind of trees you climb. Well, I am white, but those trees and that mud were Africa, so they are inside me and they come out, I suppose, in one's work.

D.C.C.: In most of your novels and some of your short stories, you seem to ask what kind of white commitment and participation are morally and realistically possible for white men and women during and after black revolutionary struggles. Elie Wiesel has written that "some words are deeds." In a novel: "In taking a single word by assault it is possible to discover the secret of creation, the centre where all threads come together." Do you think that the act of writing itself is a physical act in a political sense?

N.G.: It is. In a country like South Africa, as in Eastern European countries and the Soviet Union, writing is an act. It is an act in the way that a novel by Saul Bellow is *not* an act in America. It may be a revelation, but it is not an act. But the revelatory function of literature becomes an act in a country where much is suppressed or where much is called by the wrong name or much is concealed; where so much is double talk. However, I would still draw the distinction between that and the kind of other direct act that I was talking about, in a sense the nonverbal act, though it may also involve words— joining a political party, appearing on a platform, being active in an underground organization, even being a fellow traveller with an underground organization. In countries like Czechoslovakia, like South Africa, like Argentina, guilt by association is a fact and therefore the friendships you form can be a political act. This circumstance, way of life, is very complex. People think that a political act is signing a declaration or planting a bomb, but there are all kinds of political acts in countries where there is a great political struggle going on.

D.C.C.: In his Nobel prize address, Solzhenitsyn said: "It is within the power of world literature in these troubled times to help mankind truly to comprehend its own nature and to transfer concentrated experiences from some of its parts to others." In *July's People*, Maureen discovers that "no fiction could compete with what she was finding she did not know, could not have imagined or discovered through imagination." That character seems to be contradicting Solzhenitsyn.

N.G.: Yes, there is a contradiction there but that contradiction is indeed the very challenge of literature, the very challenge that your work gives you as a writer. It comes back to something you quoted from me before: to find the right form and the right words to contain what you discovered, what you *know*, what you are in the process of discovering. Now, Maureen tests a writer or writers and finds them wanting. Perhaps that is a message even to myself in that book because I am writing that book. I am writing her story. Have I written her story in a way that she would find meaningful, that would relate to the experience itself or would it fall far below it?

D.C.C.: The personal life of many of your characters is often drained by their political life, recently explored in *Burger's Daughter.* Is it inevitable that one obliterates the other or are they one and the same?

N.G.: I don't think it is inevitable but I think, from life-long observation and involvement with people affected by politics by one way or another in South Africa, that radical political involvement imposes an enormous strain on personal life. Let us take an extreme example. I know a couple who were both highly involved in politics, active in the most active sense of the word and the husband received a long sentence. This is a white man and he went into jail. It was apparently a good marriage, they were young, they had a small child, they were in love, they appeared to be happy. Naturally I am sure (here is a gap that the writer fills) that she must have assured him— "seven years—you know I will be here, it is all right, this is part of our life, of being politically active here." But the fact is that while the seven years were passing, she was young, she met somebody else and indeed she divorced that man while he was serving that long sentence. Now how are we to judge her, how do we know how he feels about it? He was shut up in prison, he couldn't fall in love with somebody else. She was outside, young, good looking, in exile, struggling to look after their child and still taking part in political action in exile, and she met somebody else and fell in love with him. Perhaps she lived with him and felt, "it will be an affair, and when my husband comes out it will end." Maybe the affair became stronger than the memory of the marriage and they married. Well indeed, there is a novel I am giving you there. But this shows you the kind of strain, the kind of complication that a dedication to politics (this is an extreme level) brings into people's lives. And then again there is the question of how different people deal with it. She divorced and married someone else; and when her husband came out, he had to start his personal life all over again. There was a political case a few years ago involving a black man and the man got twelve years. It isn't easy for people to go and see their relatives when they are in jail. And his wife, a simple woman, as we say, a country woman with a blanket around her, jumped up in court and shouted, "twelve years, my husband it's nothing." I still am moved when I think of it. It was such an extraordinary thing. Now I wonder what happened to her. Did she stick by that cry, "It's nothing!"? I don't know because I did not know them. These are some of the strains imposed by the political on the personal life. In *Burger's Daughter* I have looked into what happens to the children, what effect does the political faith and involvement of their parents have upon them.

D.C.C.: The children of radical parents sometimes do not want the legacy. They have a desire to distance themselves from the tradition of radical political commitment they are born to. Bobo in *The Late Bourgeois World* wishes his family were like other people— that they didn't care. Rosa Burger understands that "even animals have the instinct to turn away from suffering. The sense to run away." Is the legacy of radicalism sometimes as oppressive as the legacy of conservatism?

N.G.: I am proposing something there. I am asking, I'm not stating, whether or not they want the legacy. I am asking whether there isn't sometimes resentment at that legacy and whether there isn't a point where a young person wonders why this legacy should have been imposed, why other people can live more easily. That, of course, is the point for taking off with Rosa Burger in *Burger's Daughter.*

D.C.C.: That novel illustrates the way in which black activists have been ignored while white South-African activists attract world attention. Whites articulate black grievances—they become their voices. Lionel Burger is memorialized on television and in the papers, whereas no one seems to remember that Baasie's father, too, had died in prison for fighting apartheid. Is it changing now?

N.G.: Yes. Apart from the prominence of black political martyrs, such as the great Steve Biko, there is a whole new generation of black writers coming up to speak for blacks. I welcome this as absolutely right and necessary. But I think that if terrible things are happening in a country, let whoever has the talent and the know-ledge bear them forth. Black or white, painter, writer or musician. White and black live separated and there are areas of life lived by blacks that I don't think a white writer is qualified to write about. And the same applies to blacks writing about whites, though it's mostly academic because few blacks attempt to do this. Perhaps they feel they have enough subject matter among their own people. But, at the same time, for three hundred and fifty years and more, we have been not merely rubbing shoulders but truly in contact with one another, despite the laws, despite everything that has kept us apart; there is a whole area of life where we know each other. And I really say the word *know*. Yes, we know each other in ways that are not expressed. We know the different hypocrisies that come out of our actions and our speeches; indeed we know each other in the sense that we can read between the lines. Sometimes if I am with a black friend or an acquaintance, there are two sets of conversations going on. There is what is being said and what is unspoken. But each understands what the other has not said and this is truly *knowing*. Now there is so much of that *knowing* that it is a subject in itself. I talked recently to a young black playwright called Moise Maponye, and he was very bitter. He had got up at a writers' meeting. His remarks were directed against white writers generally. He said, "whites take our lives and make their books out of them, and these books are published and everybody reads them and nobody wants to publish my play." It was a typical statement born of confusion, literary and ideological standards and all sorts of strains and under-currents. So after this gathering I went up to him, because I know him well, and said, "Look, do you really think that you cannot write about somebody like me and other whites that you know? You have lived among us so long, we talk together, we have rows, and moments of empathy. . . . There are other areas in which, obviously, you have mixed with whites and there are other relationships in your life; you can't tell me that you are not fit to write about us. Of course you are."

D.C.C.: Toni Morrison has said that you write about black people in a way that few white writers have ever been able to write. It is not patronizing, not romanticizing, it is the way they should be written about.

N.G.: I would say the answer is that I don't romantize because I don't feel patronizing. The relationship that I have with blacks I am prepared to deal with honestly, and indeed I am having to question myself all the time because I have been brought up like every other white South African—I would say everybody else of my generation. I think of my children who have been brought up with a very different attitude toward people who may have a different colour. I feel I have gone through the whole bit, you know. I have gone through the bit of falling over backwards and apologizing because I am white. I have thought about it all, worked my way through it all, and achieved a position which as a human being is unsatisfactory, but at least I hope is honest. I feel inadequate as a human being in my situation as a white South African but as a writer I think I have arrived at a stage through my work where if I write about blacks or I create black characters, I feel I have the right to do so. I know enough to do so. I accept the limitations of what I know.

D.C.C.: You have written that "the human condition is understood dynamically, in an historical perspective"; that themes are statements or questions arising from the nature of the society in which the writer finds herself immersed and the kind and quality of the life around her. What are the aesthetic requirements of 'the novel as history'?

N.G.: I think the aesthetic requirements are the requirements of the novel *per se*. It is the attitude of the novel as history that sets the novel on a particular grid, so to speak, on a particular framework. Again this slippery element of the truth comes into it. We come back to Balzac. What he wrote was history, a remarkable social history of part of nineteenth-century France. The requirements there are not just truth to events, you could check the dates in any history, but an attempt to discover what people think and feel and most important, the most important requirement to my mind, would be to make a connection between their personal attitudes and actions and the pressures of the historical period that shapes such actions. So that if you are living during a time when one portion of the population is

extremely affluent and the other is very poor, the historical importance of that work of fiction would be in how it would show that that
extremely affluent group managed to justify their existence to
themselves, never mind the world, while round the corner they knew
there was a starving mob, in their houses they had the daughters of a
starving family scrubbing floors. I think that is where the novelist goes
much further than the historian. The historian can tell you the events
and can trace how the events came about through the power shifts in
the world. But the novelist is concerned with the power shifts within
the history of individuals who make up history.

D.C.C.: The details of life.

N.G.: Yes.

D.C.C.: Georg Lukács defined critical realism as a work in which
"everything is linked up with everything else. Each phenomenon
shows the polyphony of many components, the intertwinement of
the individual and social, of the physical and the psychical, of private
interest and public affairs." In *A Guest of Honour*, you quoted
Turgenev as a central motif to the novel: "an honourable man will
end by not knowing where to live." In *Occasion for Loving*, Jessie
turns to the novels of Joseph Conrad and Thomas Mann. One of the
epigraphs is a quote from Mann: "in our time the destiny of man
presents its meaning in political terms." Do you see your work in
relation to the European critical realists, particularly Balzac, Stendhal,
Conrad, Turgenev and Mann?

N.G.: Not really, not in relation to *the* critical realist, Balzac. As
time has gone by, certainly, I have sought more and more to find the
one form to fit each particular novel and it is always a different form,
so the nineteenth-century novel of Balzac can't contain what I want
to say. The last novel that I wrote in that way was *A Guest of Honour*
and even then it had elements obviously influenced by my great
mentor, Marcel Proust, and many others whose work I read when I
was young. But they go unacknowledged because, as someone said,
they taught you something and then you forget that they taught it to
you and you carry on from there. Indeed, people are rather amazed
when I say that I had and continue to have this feeling that I was
tremendously influenced, like so many writers, by Proust. My view of
the world was changed by him; a film was peeled off my eyes and I
understood my life and my own emotions in a way profoundly

influenced by him. People would think that the Proustian view of life, when one is looking at and living in a country like South Africa, would seem unsuitable. Proust does not deal with that kind of event, really, at all, except perhaps the Dreyfus case and that was drawing-room politics, wasn't it? But influences are part of the whole business of finding your own style as a writer. You experiment on the basis of all sorts of things you have learned, to find a way to express your particular vision. For me, style and content must be married completely or the approach to a piece of writing does not work. I couldn't write *The Conservationist* the way I wrote *A Guest of Honour.* The style for *The Conservationist* essentially had to express the kind of disruption, the disjointed consciousness of the central character. And there I had a big problem. I was writing about an unfamiliar country whose laws bring about certain morbid forms of behaviour. Can one leave out entirely an explanation of these laws? Well I did it; I decided that I must find some way of assuming the reader will make the jumps from the consciousness of one person to another to achieve understanding of the effects of the colour-bar laws if not the letter of the law itself. So indeed I used (if you want to look for models out of the past) a Proustian, Joycean, Woolfian approach and mode; one just can't say how one evolves these things but I hammered out what was to me the only voice in which to make this book find its particular tone and tell its stories. When I came to *Burger's Daughter*, once again I evolved something for myself. I have moved on stylistically in challenge to new themes that couldn't be expressed in the way the earlier books were. In *Burger's Daughter*, I could not ignore direct information, the way that I chose to do in *The Conservationist.* The theme *would not* allow it. Well, if you want to be very technical about it—and I didn't think about it in a very direct way at the time—it came to me as I was writing the book. The early life of Lionel Burger, his history—how would this reoccur naturally in Rosa's life when she is at that stage when she is concentrating on the past? And then it came to me, well, her father is dead, probably some people or several people are wanting to write about him and they will come to her for the hard facts. Here was a natural, inevitable way of imparting this information, and also of showing how inadequate bald information is. When the future biographer of her father comes to talk to her and he presents her with dates and factual

accounts of a political trial in which her father was one of the
accused, she relates this to the man she knew, to little incidents at
home and references that were inexplicable to her as a child; and
now they fit together. . . . The personal history and the documenta-
tion mesh. So these are the ways in which, for me, the form and
style of a book come about, through the demands of the content.

D.C.C.: Graham Greene has written that the revision of an
author's novel seems endless because "the author is trying in vain to
adapt the story to his changed personality—as though it were something he had begun in childhood and was finishing now in old age."
John Fowles rewrote *The Magus* and Toni Morrison said she would
love to go back and rewrite all of her novels.

N.G.: Something I don't understand!

D.C.C.: If you could go back to *A Guest of Honour*, it would have
to be written the way it was originally.

N.G.: Yes. There is an inevitability when I write the last word of
the story of a book. Unless there is an inevitability about the way it
has come out, then I have failed. I do believe that there is always only
one way to write a book. I can't understand people who re-write. If
there is something in a book that I fail to see in the theme at the time
that I wrote it, that is indeed part of the book.

D.C.C.: This is in part what you were saying about searching for a
new way of saying something—a search for a new vocabulary. In
July's People, the irrelevance and inadequacy of our present vocabulary is emphasized. Bam Smales uses formulas like "counter-
revolutionary pockets" and "rural backwardness" when confronted
with an old village chief who wants to help the white government kill
the revolutionary blacks. Words like this obscure rather than
illuminate. Does the use of symbolism, memory, fantasy and many
voices in *The Conservationist* partly eliminate this?

N.G.: Of course, *The Conservationist* is a book that people make
tremendous mistakes about. And I don't mind, really, because life is
open to countless interpretations. I like books to be open-ended so to
speak.

D.C.C.: Some critics have questioned your use of narrative point
of view in *The Late Bourgeois World*. I can't agree. Elizabeth's
limitation reflects precisely the problems of self and the society she
lives in. She doesn't have Max's courage to fail at trying to change

the world. She is inclined to play safe. The narrative viewpoint
reflects that search for the self, her pseudo-liberalism, her inconsis-
tency as a rebel. Do you feel that critics and scholars react best to
narrators who are coherent, rather than to those who are less well
defined voices. Voices that are searching, fumbling, failing, finding
and then losing again.

N.G.: I have never thought about it and of course you are using
the term "react to" pretty broadly. There is the real critic, somebody
who has spent his life reading and evaluating literature, and when he
looks at a piece of writing, he comes to it with a whole body of
literature with which to compare it and evaluate it. Oppose this
approach to that of some cub-reporter on the Hicksville *Enquirer*
who reads a book like a school-primer, an isolated taste without
reference to the purpose of literature, which is to make experience
transcendent. I know that there are some real critics indeed who do
welcome any writer's attempt to trap human consciousness in a new
way or to take from traditions and recombine them in a way that
perhaps somebody else hasn't done because somebody else doesn't
need to do it. Critics find different things in the same work and that is
satisfying too. For instance, Conor Cruise O'Brien reviewed *Burger's
Daughter* at length and he reviewed it as a profoundly religious book.
This aspect of the novel never occurred to me; I myself am an atheist.
But in a way I think that he is right, if we take the doctrine of suffering
and redemption which is explored in that book. In that sense an
unbeliever may write a profoundly religious book. Perhaps, indeed,
that was what Rosa was struggling against: a doctrine of suffering as a
revolutionary for the redemption of a classless freedom. The imposi-
tion of faith coming from a profoundly religious background since the
kind of Marxism that her parents accepted so uncritically was indeed
a religion; it was a demand for faith. So I don't think that one can say
that critics worthy of the name respond more to a simple straightfor-
ward narrative than to the other one.

D.C.C.: You have said that a writer should write as though she
were already dead. What do you mean?

N.G.: It is something I first said long ago and I keep repeating,
particularly for myself, because it becomes more and more true to me
as my life goes on and as things happen in the world to me and to
other writers. I really think that this is the one freedom that the writer

must hang on to desperately. Whether writers are in the Soviet Union, declared mad and put in asylums, whether they are in prisons, whether they are forced into exile, whether they are censored in countries like South Africa and the Latin American states, the writer must claim that freedom. The writer shouldn't be pressed into any kind of orthodoxy—a critic's orthodoxy, a political orthodoxy, a regime's orthodoxy, even the orthodoxy of friendship and loyalty imposed upon him/her by family and friends. The taking of this freedom is both the bravest and the monstrous side of what a writer is. You must give yourself the freedom to write as if you were dead. It is very difficult, and nobody can carry it out to the hundredth degree because you are still alive; you care about your relationships with other people and there are some insights you have but cannot use because you would hurt and destroy, and you would end up by being totally isolated as a human being. But given those extreme cases, I really think that you have in the end to ignore what people say about your writing. I do read reviews, though certainly not all of them. There are a few critics whose opinions I value, whose praise elates me and whose criticism, although it might hurt, although it might annoy me, helps me to stay self-critical. Learning to write comes from your own recognition of what is wrong in your own work. But I think you must claim freedom to do it; that is the way you discover for yourself. Graham Greene has put the claim best: "To a novelist his novel is the only reality and his only responsibility." Not everyone will understand that this reality is a transformation of the substance of reality into its essence, and the responsibility is nothing less than an attempt to take on the truth. Kafka said of writing that "the more independent it becomes, the more incalculable, the more joyful, the more ascendant its course."

Nadine Gordimer: An Interview

Marilyn Powell/1984

From *Canadian Forum*, 63 (February 1984), 17–21. Reprinted by permission of Marilyn Powell of CBC. Originally produced for the Canadian Broadcasting Corporation.

Nadine Gordimer has become, at least for the English-speaking world, the preeminent South African writer. André Brink, Wessel Ebersohn, Elsa Joubert and J.M. Coetzee, who won the English Booker Prize for 1983, have also captured international attention, but it is Gordimer who, after Alan Paton, has taken most of us inside that complex world of the white South African who is in Gordimer's words "a non-European whose society nevertheless refused to acknowledge and take root with an indigenous culture. He is also the non-black, whom blacks see as set apart from indigenous culture." Nadine Gordimer has been writing since 1953. Her most recent novels are *Burger's Daughter* and *July's People* (both published by Penguin). When she was in Toronto to take part in an Amnesty International Conference, she was interviewed by Marilyn Powell.

Marilyn Powell: *Recently you said of yourself "I've passed the stage of worrying." Can you explain what you meant?*
Nadine Gordimer: It is very difficult to explain for people who don't live in South Africa. First of all, I don't give any message. I'm not a propagandist, not a politician; I'm an imaginative writer, but I take my material from the society around me, from the world I know around me, and it is an intensely political world and I don't close my eyes to anything that I see there. So if there is a message it comes out of the content. It is not a message dictated by me. It is a message carried in the lives of people there and the way they are lived, in their actions—it's implicit, in other words.

A lot of South African writers, we are told, do disguise their

*messages, by using images or allegories. But you don't do that; you
say you write very directly what you see and what you feel.*

Yes. There has been a move lately among some South African
writers to use allegory, but there's another question that comes up
here. I think when you use allegory, it can be extremely effective—
you've only got to think of Camus' *The Plague* and many others. I
think there are some forms of writing where allegory is particularly
effective and pointed and carries punch, for instance, satire. An
allegorical satire is often far more impressive than a direct one, but I
think that to lean too heavily on allegory can remove your work and
what it has to say, what it is expressing about the society you live in—
it can remove it from the understanding of quite a large section of
people. I think that allegory implies a certain sophistication in approaching literature. It is a very literary device, this kind of indirection,
and it also sometimes gives the reader an opportunity not to apply
the book to himself, not to identify with the book because the book is
set in an imaginary country or is set in the past or a distant future.
And this allows the reader within that society, reading a critique of the
society of which he is really part, to distance himself—whereas if
imaginative writing can do anything at all in bringing about certain
changes, it achieves this by confronting the reader with himself or
herself.

May I ask you then, am I right in thinking that, in your novel,
Burger's Daughter—*Burger was a real man?*

No, you are wrong. People always play this game of—

Guessing who it is?

Yes. And of course in every society this is confined to perhaps 100
people who know the writer, and the writer's acquaintances. The
game is certainly being played with *Burger's Daughter* because the
circle of the extreme left in South Africa was a small circle, *is* a small
circle, what is left of it, and obviously people are eager to say this is
so and so or that is so and so, and of course people seem to think
that Lionel Burger is Bram Fischer. I knew Bram Fischer; I admired
him tremendously and in a way this book is an act of homage to
people like Bram Fischer. But heaven knows I didn't know Bram
Fischer inside himself. I didn't know him intimately. My answer to the
guessing game is to say to people, "Well, if all one has to do to

produce a work of imagination is simply to take a living being and flesh out the facts of that person's life, then why didn't you do it yourself?"

It's not going to surprise you that a lot of people on this side of the world will not know who Bram Fischer is. That prompts me to ask about Lionel Burger in your novel as well.

Yes. First of all, Bram Fischer, Abraham Fischer, was an Afrikaner from a very prominent, very distinguished Afrikaner family. He was a highly intelligent young man; as a child, he was extremely sensitive to what was going on around him and had a searching and curious mind. He became a lawyer and was interested in politics, and clearly had he joined the Afrikaner establishment, had he joined the National Party and followed the apartheid line, he probably could have one day been Prime Minister. But as a young man he became tremendously troubled by what he saw around him, by the inequalities in life in South Africa, became very troubled about the position of blacks and the way he saw South African history evolving, repressing them more and more, became very interested in his reading in leftist ideas and eventually joined the Communist Party. Why did he? Perhaps he would have joined the Communist Party in any country. But there is a big question mark over that. At that time, there was indeed no political party he could have joined which did not have a racial bias and that was the only one that was open to mixed membership.

Bram Fischer became a very prominent lawyer indeed, and he continued to work in the Communist Party as long as it remained a legal party. It was outlawed in 1950 and it dissolved; a small section of the party went underground, not literally—they didn't disappear, but they continued their activities underground, and he was one of them. He did this so successfully that he continued to defend people in political trials, and very prominent political trials. Nobody knew that he was indeed a sort of mastermind behind some of the campaigns that these people were engaged in. Eventually he himself was discovered, shall we say, and put on trial, and he disappeared during that trial and he lived truly underground for, I think, about nine months in disguise; then he was betrayed and brought into court again and received a life sentence. Before he received the sentence, he made an extremely moving speech about his reasons for having got to the extreme stage for a lawyer, someone who had great respect for the rule of law—what evil there was in a society that had brought him to the extreme measure of actually skipping bail and, before that, of going underground. So, as you can see, there are similarities between my character and the life of this actual personage who died later, not in prison; indeed when the South African authorities were satisfied that Bram Fischer really was dying (he was dying of cancer), they let him come out to spend his last days at the home of a relative. He was one of a small group of people who lived lives on that level of sacrifice, and one could say that any novel that deals with lives like that of course brings in the elements. It's a sort of composite picture of how such people, their children, their wives, their families and their friends live.

In your novel, Lionel Burger is a doctor who puts himself on the line as well, in involving himself in the cause of racial justice.

Lionel Burger is a man like Abraham Fischer, with a similar sort of background. I don't know much about Bram Fischer's family background, about his parents; I don't know whether he lived on a farm or where he lived as a boy, but it would be very likely for my fictitious character, Lionel Burger, to have that kind of background— many Afrikaners do, and so I gave it to him.

What is fascinating to me is that you begin by saying that you're not a political writer, you are a creative writer. But I was thinking as you were talking that Burger's Daughter *was banned in South Africa; and it was returned to its home in published form because of outside pressure—international pressure.*

Yes, that's true. *Burger's Daughter* is of course an intensely political novel and a very contentious one, and not only in South Africa. I found when it was published in America and I was there at the time of publication and I was being interviewed, there was a kind of cover-up move on the part of people who were interviewing me, the media. They kept referring to Lionel Burger and to Rosa Burger, his daughter, as liberals. Then I would interrupt and say, "No, no this is a misapprehension that you are under or that your readers or listeners or viewers are going to be under. The point is that he is not a liberal. He was that uncomfortable thing a white communist, and if you

accept that he was a sympathetic character, that he was indeed
heroic, that he was concerned with suffering, in ways to ameliorate
suffering—you have to accept that in some countries, in some
situations, at some times, communists, in whose name terrible things
have been done (as bad as have been done by fascists elsewhere;
communists have done terrible things)—there have been intensely
heroic people who were deeply committed communists. Lionel
Burger represents exactly that kind of man and this mantle of heroism
doesn't fit the liberals.

*It is extraordinary—you were flushing out repression in another
society.*
Yes. The Americans found him an appealing character, admired
him, and could not bear to think that they were admiring somebody
who had been a card-carrying communist.

*Let's go back to this basic issue of a fiction and the power that it
carries—what danger would the South African government see in*
Burger's Daughter?
Oh, because it shows this group of white communists as intensely
self-sacrificing, as good people not dreadful monsters because that's
the official picture—dreadful monsters who want to take over the
whole country, who would persecute the blacks. And *Burger's
Daughter* of course gave another picture.

*So government doesn't make the distinction between fiction and
facts that you make.*
Oh no, they clearly enough admitted this was something that had
happened in South Africa. Indeed that the early small communist
party had a tremendous influence on the whole spectrum of liberal
thought. And even in a strange way now some of the mild reforms
which don't mean very much, but they nevertheless are reforms—
are being brought in by the present South African government, and
they were the kind of changes that were being demanded by the
radicals in what one might call their more moderate days.

*You know what is confusing is a society that will ban a novel—(we
are familiar with that in the Soviet Union or in many other countries
where fiction is banned) but then will allow it back in. It's a mixed
repression, if that phrase is meaningful.*

Well, you see, there are several issues that come up with a novel like that when it is banned. First of all, there is the assumption that if you choose the subject and present the people in it, objectively, insofar as you are able to, that means that you are a protagonist for their ideologies and their views. So if I wrote a book which doesn't represent white communists, black communists, as monsters, then that shows that I must be a card-carrying communist (which I am not and which I have never been). So there is that danger in it. But then, of course, *Burger's Daughter* was regarded as an inciting book—a book that's likely to incite people to some kind of revolutionary action. It ends up at a very difficult moment in South Africa's very recent history and that is the Soweto riots of '76. In the book there is almost a facsimile reproduction of an actual document—a little pamphlet put out by the black students, South African students' organization. Why did I put it in? Did I put it in as a provocation because I knew that it was a banned document? There are two kinds of banning of literature and documents in South Africa, and one is to ban a document or a book for distribution—which means you cannot sell it. If you bought the book last week in the bookshop and it is banned the following week, you don't have to burn the book. You can keep it, but you must not lend it to anybody, and the bookshop mustn't sell it. Then there is a stricter kind of banning, which is banning for possession, which means that when you read that the book is banned, you should destroy it. Otherwise if the police happen to raid your house for one reason or another and they find that book, you've committed a criminal offence. Now this little document I reproduced in this book was indeed banned for both distribution and possession, so it was an offence to own it—which I obviously did or had had it at some time—and it was also certainly an offence to publish it. So I was offending on two counts.

Well, I say, why did I put it in? I put it in after quite a bit of thought because I knew the book was pretty sure to be banned anyway, but, if I put it in, it had to be banned. But I decided in the end that it was absolutely necessary to put that document in because no description of a document of that kind, no made-up fiction of a similar document I could have thought of, could have had quite the force of that simple misspelled, ill-written, semi-literate, little pamphlet. Because that document itself, written by young people between the age of about

16 and 20, who were rebelling about the second-rate education they were getting, that document said more than 20 pages of description. Because people who are 16 and 20 years old and are just about finishing school, are so poorly educated that this is how they express themselves. So it was a very forceful document; it made a statement in itself, and I decided that I was not going to sacrifice the impact that that document would make and I put it in.

You put it in knowing the book would be banned in South Africa. Did you project what its future might be?

Well, I did think about it of course, and about strategy because I wanted it to be read. I spoke to my publishers in London, and, well, they knew the position in South Africa. They knew what kind of book it was. They had read the manuscript. And we did manage a little strategy that worked. The books that are brought in from abroad usually—if a book is by somebody who has already had a couple of books banned, the very sight of the author's name is sufficient for the book to be what is called embargoed—which means that it can't be sold until the censors have read it and decided whether it should be banned or not. So through a small deception, shall we say, the parcels of the book came in, several thousand copies of the book came in, without the appropriate document or letters. Perhaps there was the name of some other book on the document. And it worked, and so the book came in and orders were filled and a couple of thousand copies got around before the censors got wise to it and plonked an embargo on the bookshops who had slipped them onto their shelves and boldly into the window. They had to withdraw them. The censors took five weeks, and then they banned it. They banned it on all five counts that can offend. It was calculated to be harmful to race relations. It was obscene—I still don't quite know where it was obscene. It was blasphemous. What was the one other count? The fifth I've forgotten, but in any case it was damned five times.

Is this according to the act that was passed in 1974?

Well, the first act was passed in the early sixties, and then there was a new act in 1974.

By this time—this novel—you are an established writer. What would have happened had it been your first novel?

Well, precisely, this is really the most important question. First of all, it was a novel published well on in my writing life. I was established. I have a readership abroad, so even though it is very sad not to be read at home, it still means you are being read, and one day the book will be coming back into the country. But if you are a new writer—if it had happened with my first book—this can either set a young writer back many years or can indeed even crush that writer.

It is very discouraging. Probably you've only had one book published, and the publisher has lost money on it. And every other publisher knows that; they are very reluctant then to take on another one. And probably an overseas publisher has never heard of you. And perhaps your first book isn't terribly good. You're going to improve and your work is going to get better, but there are a lot of counts against you.

You are not Afrikaner, and I wonder if you feel isolated vis-à-vis the Afrikaner government and Afrikaner society.

Well, you belong to a minority group, consisting of all sorts of people: Afrikaners, English-speaking people, blacks, whites, who are opposed to the policies of our government. And, you know, there is a solidarity within that opposition; so you don't feel alone. Except that of course there are people who are under ban. Sometimes you have friends—indeed I have friends—who are banned which means you can see them, but under difficulty. If you have a party—you want to celebrate something—those friends cannot come, because they cannot attend the gathering.

There are several kinds of ban, but the most common one works like this: suppose you're a teacher or a journalist or a publisher. The most serious part of your ban will usually be that you cannot enter any teaching establishment, so that's the end of your career teaching in a university or school. If you are a publisher, you cannot enter any premises where any work is prepared for publication. You cannot function as an editor. If you are a lawyer, you cannot practice law. So very often people who are under ban have to do something quite other. Indeed I think there are a few people in *Burger's Daughter*— there is a woman who is working as a dental nurse because she isn't allowed to teach, if I remember rightly, or because she is not allowed to work in a publishing firm. And this is what does happen to people.

But for all these people, under provisions of the ban specific to their profession, there is always an overall provision, and that is: you are not allowed to write or publish anything, and you are not allowed to be quoted; you cannot give a newspaper interview; you cannot get up in a public meeting and speak.

You don't exist.
No. You don't exist. And of course your passport is always withdrawn. Some people have a geographical ban as well; you have to stay within the magisterial district of, say, Cape Town or Johannesburg or wherever you happen to live.

Obviously, you are not under ban; you have your passport. Is it prestige that allows you to come abroad and speak as candidly as you do and write as candidly as you do?
I hope so.

Can you go further with that? What do you mean?
Well, I mean that one never knows. Writing is one thing. Speaking on public platforms abroad, especially on public platforms such as the one here, under this sort of auspices, is not a very healthy thing for a South African.

But you'll go on doing it as long as you are able?
Yes, and I think that as long as those of us in South Africa who are articulate—are asked to go abroad, and we know we are going to be interviewed, we cannot refuse. There are so many people in South Africa, within the country, who are muzzled. And there are others who may not be muzzled within South Africa but whose passports are withdrawn, people like Bishop Desmond Tutu—a very important voice; you know, a writer is nothing compared with him. He is a big figure, a real leader, and he can't go abroad and speak. So I think that those of us who can, as long as we can, we have to use the opportunity.

May I ask you about your novel, July's People? *Because what we've been talking about now are acts of faith and optimism that things can change. The thing that strikes me about* July's People *is that you present a very different vision there; it's almost prophetic; that is, if things don't change, what would happen if black Africans in*

South Africa take over; what would happen to the whites? And I suppose that says—what would happen to people like yourself?

It is impossible to say, but let's look at the nearest comparison which would be Zimbabwe where there has been no animosity towards whites. The government is trying very hard against all sorts of odds to conciliate those whites who have stayed with the black population after the terrible rift—greater even than the years of racialism that went before, the great rift of 11 years of terrible war.

You know it's a sort of Pascalian wager. I think that if you stay in South Africa and look at the future, you have to accept that wager, that the society under a black majority will be a real democracy for everybody.

Talking to Writers: Nadine Gordimer

Hermione Lee/1986

This is a transcript of an interview broadcast on 15 October 1986 by London Weekend Television in the "Talking to Writers" series. Printed by permission of London Weekend Television.

HL: Hello. This week on "Talking to Writers" my conversation is with Nadine Gordimer, one of South Africa's leading writers of fiction. Nadine Gordimer is a white South African from a Jewish family who's lived all her life in or near Johannesburg, although she has also travelled widely. She published her first story in 1939. Her most recent collection, *Something Out There,* came out in 1984. In the 45 years between, she has published not only a large number of marvellous short stories but also eight novels, most notably *The Conservationist,* a brilliantly subtle study of the white need for power, and *Burger's Daughter,* which powerfully examines the legacy of the Communist martyr. One of her critics has said that Gordimer has never let up on herself ideologically. In her life she is one of the minority that opposes apartheid within the white minority, and in her writing, from her investigations of liberal guilt in her early novels, like *Occasion for Loving,* down to her apocalyptic vision of the future for South African whites in her last novel *July's People,* her fiction has risen to the demands of history. These demands partly require a moral commitment. "If you write honestly about life in South Africa," she said in 1977, "apartheid damns itself." But the writer also has to make a total onslaught on life as it is in South Africa. As she puts it, you have to stick your hand into the muck.

Nadine Gordimer, South Africa seems now to be at a crisis point. What is it like to be living there now for you?

NG: Well, for a white South African things have changed very much. I'm not only talking for myself, I'm talking generally. Indeed I would almost except myself because I've been aware for a long time of a great sense of uneasiness there. But I've never felt that I found it difficult to work for instance. People have said, how can you work in that country, even as a privileged white? But we writers are very selfish beings in any case. We sit down and pull out the telephone, close the door, and work. But now I do feel there are so many tragic things going on, just not sporadically as they did before, but all the time. And if you're white, it's happening very near you but not to you. But I think you have to be of a particularly obtuse kind of temperament and have a very thick skin, very thick white skin to ignore it. When you think that something like 1,800 people have been detained since the 12th of June, life is not at all normal there for anybody, even for privileged white people.

HL: Is it possible for privileged white people at all to go on thinking that nothing is happening, that they are living their lives as they did before?

NG: Yes, it's still possible . . . but the crisis is reaching them, through fear, because now we have had what was surely inevitable. So much violence has been done to blacks; now there is counter-violence mostly directed against other blacks but also spilling over into white areas. So there have been incidents in supermarkets. At Christmas-time last year a bomb went off in a supermarket; a white child was killed and someone else was killed. There was a tremendous sense of shock over the death of one white child. The death of a child is tragic and terrible and should never happen. But the fact is, the death of that one white child shocked the white population more than the death of thousands of black children; apparently one white life is worth more than a hundred or two of blacks.

HL: It's a situation that obviously creates martyrs and heroes. In your novel *Burger's Daughter* you say it's strange to live in a country where there are still heroes. What kinds of demands does that fact make of fiction?

NG: Well, it doesn't make any particular demands beyond the usual demands on a writer to understand what makes a person what he/she is. And, of course, since heroes are not too common in the world, there is, I suppose, some kind of a challenge there. And I think that for fiction writers, one has to go beyond the public profile. The public profile shows the great courage, the bravery of the person who has gone to prison, who has perhaps spent half a life in prison. But for the fiction writer, there is the whole dimension of that person overcoming ordinary human weaknesses, a desire to live like everybody else. This is the interesting part for the fiction writer and this is the kind of miracle. This, in the end, is the core of the heroism.

HL: Do you think it would be true to say that many of your novels have the characters work towards a point where they either have to rise to the demands of history or fail those demands? I mean, I notice very often at the ends of the novels there is a point of choice. There is a point of imminent political decision where the characters are going to get involved or not, or make a commitment. Is that right? Is that a right description?

NG: I think so, and I think it simply rises out of the circumstances of the lives of these people which is the life that I live myself, that I see lived all around me. I am not saying I am a heroine, of course not, but I am talking about the texture of a life. One is constantly faced with decisions. When I come to Europe or I am in America, I am amazed to see that we forget how peaceful and how subjective life can be, the choices in life. Whereas for us, these choices are always invaded by social and political events that can't be put aside, that simply have to be faced, and choices have to be made about them.

HL: One of the things that you have to do as a writer of fiction is to penetrate inside the minds and the attitudes of characters who are completely alien to you, completely remote from you. Is that right? Is that something that you find yourself doing?

NG: Yes, I suppose it's true. Except that the thought crosses my mind, is any one of them alien? Isn't there a bit of a murderer, isn't there a bit of a prostitute, isn't there a bit of a thief, in all of us? So maybe writers create characters unlike themselves out of suppressed instincts of these kinds. Partly I think; this is partly the explanation.

HL: So if you are writing, as in a recent story "Something Out There," about a white police interrogator, does that in a sense express something that is buried in your real life?

NG: Well, perhaps it's something by the grace of good fortune didn't happen to me. I might have been born that little boy. Probably he was born in the same town that I was, and through different circumstances and different instincts, I turned to the local library and read a lot and became a writer. But he probably left school at 14 or 15 and went into the police force and was brought up thinking that white was might and right. So I could have been that boy, and perhaps that helps me to create him—unpleasant, obtuse, thick-headed bully that he is!

HL: But the very fact of doing that, of penetrating an alternative life or of trying to find out what it would be like to be someone quite other, is in itself presumably a resistance to apartheid.

NG: Probably, but I think it would be a little precious to claim that as a resistance to apartheid. I think that it's things that one does outside the function as a writer, speaking for myself anyway. I just see my life divided in this way. I'm a writer and I'm a natural writer. I've been writing since I was nine or ten years old. I simply fell into it, the way people who've got a voice sing. It was the only thing that I could do, and so I do it. But the other thing has demanded a conscious choice, and that is to take up some sort of responsibility for being born a white South African, in that country, in my country to which I'm devoted and committed. But you can't just say I'm devoted, committed, and leave it at that in a country that is in the state that South Africa's in.

HL: But you're suggesting by saying that, that the act of writing is not necessarily a political act—

NG: No, I think that it's become implicitly political. Because if you try to tell the truth about your society and that society is in political turmoil, and it's a racist society, what is going to come out of that will definitely be in some ways a political novel or a political story.

HL: Could there be a pro-apartheid fiction that was any good, do you think?

NG: It's such an interesting question, because despite the fact that the majority of the white population (the only people who have the vote) have put this government and previous governments in power—that out of this mass of people who are for apartheid in one form or another—there is not a writer who is an apologist for this, no writer of any consequence, not even a writer in the Afrikaans language. I always feel heartened by this; I think it says something about the truth that lies at the heart of all art, that it's difficult in the end to lie.

HL: Do you think that you've moved in the writing of your novels from a kind of writing which is more perhaps didactic or explanatory? For instance, in the early novel *The Lying Days* you describe a lot of what it felt like to be under the first nationalist government in the late '40s and early '50s. Do you think that your novels have become less explanatory and more ambiguous?

NG: Oh much more, because I was very young when I wrote that novel. I'd hardly lived, and most writers at that stage, you know, have the great idea that every little thought they've thought is the most original thing in the world and has to be written down. But as you get older and you write more, so you're much more selective and find you're always trying to find a different approach to "net" reality. People talk about style; to me there's no such thing as a style for a writer. Each book requires a different approach, and the style is dictated by the theme.

HL: Are you read very differently here and in America than you are in South Africa, do you think?

NG: I think so. I don't think I can ever get an idea of how I'm read in South Africa because there is really no body of criticism within the country that you can judge by—professional criticism. Among the people I know—nobody ever tells you the truth, do they, about what you write? You know, you feel they are either praising you because they're a friend or for some reason; there's something wrong there. So I really can't judge. I can judge much more clearly in America and in England or wherever than I can at home.

HL: But do you not get letters at home?

NG: I very rarely get letters at home; I get many letters from abroad but not from home.

HL: So you don't know if you have a black readership for instance?

NG: Well, . . . it's not in the tradition for people to write to a writer much in South Africa, whether black or white. I do get quite a lot of comment and talk in person from black readers.

HL: Do you ever get fed up with being, as it were, venerated in America and England as the good white writer? I mean as the person who is on the side of the angels. Is it ever a liability to be a writer who, you know, your western audience is going to assume is on the right side, if you see what I mean?

NG: Well, it's a liability; something else is a liability and that is to be the subject of a moral rather than a literary judgment.

HL: Quite.

NG: Being an opponent of apartheid or of racism doesn't make you a good writer; alas, there are some terrible writers who are very good opponents of apartheid. So I think that there's a confusion there that I sometimes resent. But as time has gone by, I don't really worry any more, because I see as part of my role as a South African, to be glad of any interest in fighting apartheid in my country. And so whether I am welcomed for my political views and stance, at the expense of concentration on my books, I feel it doesn't matter; if I'm interviewed and only talk about South African politics and I can then get in a strong statement against apartheid, at least I've done something for the political opposition, for the black liberation to which I adhere. And so the books should speak for themselves.

HL: Sure, but I wondered if there was a kind of, not exactly self-consciousness, but a sense of responsibility or a sense of duty, whichever comes over you, as you start to write another novel or another story, if that doesn't strike you.

NG: Never, never. That falls away. I write just what I like, and I never think will it further the cause, will my own—the people on whose side I am—approve of it or not. I think that as soon as you start worrying about whether it's going to be on the side of the angels or not, you lose your freedom as a writer. And if you lose your freedom as a writer, you betray whatever little talent you have, and you're useless.

HL: Your newest book which is about to be published is called *Lifetimes: Under Apartheid.* It's a collection of photographs by David Goldblatt interspersed with text from your work—right across the range of your work—and it's got some extremely striking and impressive images of South African faces and places and people. Do you think, in a way, that to evoke those places is perhaps the strongest way to get at the truth of South Africa?

NG: Well, I always think that people are very closely related to their places, that indeed they remake the natural landscape according to things that are deep inside themselves. So I don't think that I could separate them from their landscape. I've always had a very strong feeling for the landscape; I was born in what is probably the only ugly part of South Africa—right in the middle of the mine dumps on the bare, high veld. But the sense of it, and the sense of it being something that formed my sensibility and my way of seeing landscape, I think has been useful to me.

HL: Something that comes through very powerfully in the book and in the novels and stories is the extraordinary contrast between the environment of the white people and the environment of the blacks.

NG: Yes, you see, what I've come to realise eventually is that I have lived along with all other white South Africans in a kind of country club—these wonderful beaches which were never crowded—the parks I was taken to as a child which were absolutely manicured. Such a small percentage of the population was using these facilities compared to the great mass of people who should have been using them and who should have been throwing around their ice cream cups and filling up the beaches we were enjoying exclusively. But they were not there, and so what seemed to be one of the beauties of South Africa [became] one of the most ugly things about it. That's another reflection on the landscape.

HL: Is it a problem that now and increasingly perhaps, there are going to be black readers, black writers, who are going to be saying to you, "Let us get on with it"? Is there going to be an increasing divide between what black writers feel ought to be said about South Africa and your own works as a white, radical writer?

NG: No, because the black writers are writing what they know, and I'm writing what I know. In many instances the stream meets; sometimes it doesn't. There are areas of life I don't know sufficiently well to write about. But I have lived there all my life, and I've always mixed with blacks, and they've mixed with me. They know things about me as a writer that I don't know, that are revealed subconsciously. So I see no reason why black writers shouldn't have created white characters. They should have no inhibitions about it; it's in the nature of writers, just as we are androgynous I think. So there *are* other barriers we can cross to a large extent. Of course, there is the barrier of the totally different circumstances of life. And that really is something that black writers have to be responsible for telling the world about.

HL: At the beginning of *July's People*, your last novel, there's a quotation from Gramsci, the Italian philosopher, who says that when the old is dying and the new is not yet born, what you have is morbid symptoms. It's as though now, what you are describing at this latest point of South African history are these morbid symptoms. I wonder what you think is going to come next, and what you think you'll next be writing about?

NG: Well, I just hope it's not going to be some dull kind of social realism, but I don't think so. It's interesting that in the 70s when there was a black separatist movement very strong in South Africa, there was no *official* set of rules by which black writers had to write. Yet there was an implicit orthodoxy about choice of subject matter and treatment: treatment had to be heroic; characters always had to be shown in this heroic light. Every mother was Mother Africa; every man was a hero. Well, it's very limiting for writers, who really are writers and who know that indeed this is not the way revolutions are made and this is not the way people are. So the best of them, again, were never happy under it, and indeed didn't really follow this. Now fortunately it has fallen away again, and recently there have been—I can think of two good books of short stories by black writers who've broken away from this completely, who show the whole man, the whole woman.

HL: You once said that you must give yourself the freedom to write as if you were dead.

NG: I still believe that.

HL: What do you mean by that?

NG: Well, partly what I said before, that because you're on the side of the angels, you mustn't fear to show that they're not all so angelic. That's why in *Burger's Daughter* Burger himself in his domestic life is shown to exploit his daughter for the cause and so on. And I think that this moves right into the heart of your personal life. You can't consider whether you're going to annoy this one or that one or whether they are going to identify. Sometimes it's a very difficult choice and, of course, to wait for everybody to be dead so that they cannot identify, you may be dead first. So I think you have to indeed write as if you were dead.

HL: So what you're saying is that really, although the circumstances in which you are writing are always present and are always in a sense pressing upon you, you have, in a way, to go outside them when you write.

NG: You have to go outside them.

Nadine Gordimer
Junction Avenue Theatre Company/1986

From *Sophiatown Speaks,* Ed. Pippa Stein and Ruth Jacobson (Johannesburg, South Africa: Junction Avenue Press, 1986), 25–30. Reprinted by permission of Nadine Gordimer and the editors of *Sophiatown Speaks.*

As you know, we are making a play about a Jewish girl who goes to live in Sophiatown in the fifties. Could you talk about what it was like to be a young Jewish girl in the fifties?

Well, I'm not such a good person to talk to about that, because I never had much sense of identity with the Jewish community. As you know, I was born and brought up in Springs. I find my mother a very interesting character. She was the dominant member of the household and a sincere do-gooder. She was one of those people who started a crèche in the black township near us. We led a very free kind of life in the community, and it was through my mother that the amateur dramatic society I was in arranged to go to a hall in a black township. A "great adventure": a performance of—guess what—*The Importance of Being Earnest!*

My mother was born in England and educated in South Africa. My maternal grandmother had an extraordinary background for a woman born in the late 19th century. She worked for the court wardrobe—and what did she do? She was a feather comber! You had to curl and clean feathers and keep them groomed because, of course, the court wore so many feathers. She and her sister did this, going off to Buckingham Palace every day. They were quite independent for middle-class female Londoners.

My father came out to South Africa alone, as a boy of thirteen, from Lithuania, having had only three or four years of education. He was running away from Tsarist oppression; you were not allowed to go to high school if you were Jewish. So when you had finished your primary schooling, you had to learn watchmaking or tailoring. He learnt watchmaking and came to South Africa. He had a great sense of inferiority in relation to my mother because, first of all, she was

247

able to speak English as a mother tongue; she had had a good
education in Johannesburg. To understand his feeling of inferiority,
we must remember that he was an immigrant boy coming from some
tiny village in Russia and, in a way, making it here—wearing a suit
and having a bathroom. He had been brought up in exactly the way
the majority of Africans are brought up here. His mother was a
dressmaker and his father was a shipping clerk; both parents worked
in the city of Riga and the old granny in the village brought up all the
children. I'm only one generation away from that. I think my father
felt very inferior culturally. Although he had a normal Jewish village
religious upbringing, my mother more or less forced him to abandon
all that. We kept only the Day of Atonement: he had a new suit about
every two years and off he would go to fast—and my sister and I
would be sitting in our shorts in the car, waiting for him, looking at
these people coming out of the synagogue!

My mother's attitude towards black people was maternalistic, but
there was always an uneasiness there. She saw the need to collect old
clothes and so on. Whereas my father I'm sorry to say—and this
again has something to do with class and his culture shock, of coming
into a new country at thirteen and not knowing anyone, it must have
been really awful—I remember his attitude towards blacks was that
they were beyond the human pale, an extraordinary attitude for
someone who had fled from Tsarist oppression.

Yet it was the Jewish Socialists and the British Labour Party who
started the Communist Party in South Africa in 1921. Some people's
struggles in life produce a strong political awareness; in others
struggle produces merely a desire to get what you can and just hang
onto a cosy life.

*How did you come to a growing awareness of what was happening
in this country?*
Well, in the convent where I went to school, there were no blacks.
But we lived about 300 yards across the veld from a gold mine, and
between the mine and the suburb where we lived there were
concession stores. On the corner of the stores there was a little cafe
and we white kids used to wander up there to buy sweets and
chewing gum. That's perhaps my earliest awareness of black people.
Of course we had a black woman working for us in the house; she

wasn't really a nanny but she looked after our family for about forty years.

I used to go up to the stores, and then the mine workers would come down from the compound. Now in those days, they still wore tribal dress. They came from all over the place, Northern Rhodesia, Tanganyika, Mozambique; and they would come in their blankets. I remember the Shangaans with their clay-braided hair. There were all sorts of things about them which were so exotic to me.

And of couse we white children were always told, "Don't hang around there. Little girls mustn't hang around there," and I grew up with the feeling—nobody explained really why—that because you were a girl and you were white, every black man was in some way a threat to you.

So how did you come to meet black people eventually?

Well, when I came to Johannesburg in 1949, it was a kind of revelation to me when I actually got to know journalists and musicians through friends, many of whom came from Sophiatown. Zeke Mphahlele was my first black friend. We got to know each other when we were both quite young and it was an extraordinary thing for me to meet a black person who was not a servant or a delivery man, but someone who was struggling with the same problems of being a young writer. This is such a bond, yet it simply did not exist across the colour bar for most people.

When Anthony Sampson took over DRUM, he had, from the beginning, an extraordinary ease which a middle-class white like myself certainly didn't have. Through him, I got to know the whole group of DRUM personalities, starting with the famous Henry Nxumalo, Bloke Modisane, Lewis Nkosi and Todd Matshikiza. They were absolutely extraordinary people.

I remember going to parties with Anthony. I had never been in a black township in my life except when I was in amateur dramatics. Anthony really put us all to shame because here was this young man from Oxford rushing around on his motorbike as if the differences of colour and taboo didn't count at all. I think he influenced a lot of white journalists and people in the arts, making us realise that you could live in another way.

I got to know Can Themba—who didn't?—and one day he turned

up at my house and had with him a rather snooty-looking young man, Lewis Nkosi, who had come up from Durban and was going to do some work on DRUM. Lewis sat around looking very bored and finally said to me, "Any music in this place?" "Yes," I said, "There are the records." "This is not music," he said. "It's all classical!"

He was quite exceptional among the DRUM group because after living about three months in Sophiatown in Can Themba's famous "House of Truth," he got very friendly with a white girl and went to live in a white suburb, Parkview! He didn't care a damn and would simply come out of that house in the morning always looking extremely well-dressed. And nothing happened to him. He had a way of staring at people . . . if whites started any nonsense, it just fell away.

It was a time of tremendous, memorable parties I'll never forget for the rest of my life. We women were all extremely dressed-up with high heels, make-up, real party-going clothes! Nobody ever went home; people were not in any condition to go home! We danced kwela solidly. There was a great crowd of musicians and that's how I met Todd Matshikiza. If there was a piano, Todd would play like a dervish all night. Kieppie Moeketsi played until he fell over. Todd was the first black man I ever danced with. He had the distinction of being even smaller than I am! We were quite a midget couple.

We would visit shebeens in Sophiatown. They were shabby, friendly places—just rooms where people gathered and drank. Sometimes we went on pub crawls in Doornfontein with Jim Bailey. The shebeens there were really rather dreary because they had bourgeois pretensions. I remember one with a cut-velvet covered sofa with a hole in the arm and an ashtray and little doilies here and there. I must say I found them very dull. They were so stiff; everyone sat around in a little room and it was such solid drinking I didn't find it enjoyable. I much preferred the parties. Of course, there were a lot of voyeurs at the time. It was the great experience for people from Europe to come to South Africa and to be taken by people who had black friends, to shebeens. I think this still goes on.

One of the things Sophiatown is remembered for is its intellectual and cultural life . . . .

And yet when you look back at it, what was happening in the theatre? Today there are hundreds of plays by blacks and whites. There were little groups active in the black townships at the time, but they never came to town. Whites never saw these shows.

I don't think there were any theatre workshops, then, although there were music workshops. In the fifties black musicians were leading the cultural drive. People like Kieppie Moeketsi belonged to two worlds, the world of musicians and the world of gatherings where class and colour didn't seem to count. Whenever anything went on, there was somebody there playing. It's interesting how the music spread because the mixing spread.

There was Kurt Jobst, a jeweller, who wasn't a Jew or a leftist but had quit Austria because of the Nazis. He hadn't ever had any black friends. He was a middle-aged man and let part of his house to an English friend of ours called Robert Loder. Loder became active in the African Music and Drama Association. And he loved the old farmhouse where Jobst lived. Jobst had a stormy love life: he was divorced and he was there alone. Loder went in and out of Sophiatown and other townships. So in Johannesburg we were quite a mixed group of people. Then Nat Nakasa and I became good friends. He and others started the *Classic* magazine and we worked on it together.

The DRUM school of writing, as it's now known, had a certain style—an ironic, witty way of attacking apartheid. As a style, it would be frowned upon today among many black writers. In my own experience most black writers today regard that work as too much influenced by whites in the sense that it wasn't overtly, sufficiently committed. But I think that kind of ironic approach to attacking apartheid has now been taken over by the theatre. You see it in *Bopha, Woza Albert,* in the things you people have done, and it's interesting that it has passed from the journalists and fiction writers to the theatre.

Can Themba, for example, was a great reader. He knew his Shakespeare well and his Dostoevsky. I find that young black people who write today don't read much and if they do, it's mostly black writers. Literature began about 20 years ago for them. But the Fifties intellectuals and artists read anything and everything. They were city people, educated before Bantu Education, and their English was wonderfully, tremendously lively. Illiteracy didn't pass as innovation then!

Why do you think so many of the writers and journalists from that period went into exile?

It all began really with the Defiance Campaign. People were arrested and the whole political scene got tougher. There were two things that happened: I think there were some, like Lewis Nkosi, who were not really politically involved, who went into exile. Some of them became more politically involved when they were out of the country and were drawn into the ANC or PAC. But there were people who left out of sheer frustration, for example, teachers. When Bantu Education came in, it was a point of no return for them. Look what happened to the cast of the black musical of the Fifties, *King Kong.* They went off, had a moderate success—less than we thought they would have overseas—and then the bubble burst. Some of them, like Miriam Makeba, made it. Others disappeared from view; others drifted back. But it wasn't as it is, as it has been now for more than 20 years, that people went into exile because they faced imprisonment or internal exile if they stay. In those days, people left South Africa out of intense frustration rather than danger.

A Voice from a Troubled Land:
A Conversation with Nadine Gordimer

Peter Marchant, Judith Kitchen, and Stan Sanvel Rubin/1986

From *Ontario Review,* 26 (Spring-Summer 1987), 5–14. Edited
by Earl Ingersoll and Stan Sanvel Rubin from a transcription of a
videotape produced by the Educational Communications Center on January 24, 1986 and sponsored by the Brockport Writers
Forum, Department of English, SUNY College at Brockport,
New York. Copyrighted © 1986 by SUNY. All rights reserved by
the State University of New York. Not to be reprinted without
permission. Reprinted by permission.

The following conversation is a transcription of a video-
taped interview which took place January 24, 1986, during Miss Gordimer's visit to the State University of New
York, College at Brockport, where she received the
Brockport Writers Forum International Award. Speaking
with Miss Gordimer were novelist Peter Marchant, poet
and fiction writer Judith Kitchen, and poet Stan Sanvel
Rubin, who is the current director of the Brockport Writers
Forum.

Marchant: I know that you are a very busy woman. There are
tremendous demands on your time and energy—political involvement, teaching, and speaking. How are you able to be so prolific as a
writer?

Gordimer: I don't think that I'm prolific. I regard myself rather as
a slow writer, but I suppose if you count my books against my age, I
do seem to have written quite a lot. But I never really have a program
in mind; a book must take as long as it needs to get itself written. The
other things are merely political obligations: a writer has a voice, a
writer is known, and you can't live in a country like mine and not
speak out.

Marchant: But do you keep your mornings for writing? Do you
have a routine in which you write something every morning?

Gordimer: Yes, I always do my own writing in the morning, but living where I do I have an increasing burden of correspondence, so many letters to write that simply cannot be dealt with by anyone else but me. Writers have very personal letters to write. You have young writers writing to you with problems. You cannot just ignore these things. You have people who want to put together anthologies and if they want to bring in writers from South Africa, whom are they going to ask for addresses? They're going to ask me. All of this takes time.

Marchant: You began writing at the age of nine? How did that happen?

Gordimer: As I remember, we had a choice at school, to write an essay or a poem, and I don't know why but I decided to write a little poem. I think it was a very bad poem, and I've never written a very good one. That's the first thing I remember writing. Then I used to compose entire newspapers, I suppose modeled on our weekly paper—the "rag," as we called it—in the small town where I grew up. I would invent weddings, engagements, openings of municipal buildings, and things like that, and actually draw the columns and photographs. That's how I really started, but I didn't really turn into a journalist after all.

Marchant: You have a wonderful eye for detail and obviously a great relish for what people wear and how they live and the rooms they live in and the foods they eat and their mannerisms. Did you always have that?

Gordimer: Always. As a child, one of the things I enjoyed doing and was encouraged by adults to do for their amusement was to mimic people, and I was really rather good at it. I had a parrot-like ability to mimic an accent or way of speaking, so sometimes when my mother's friends were there, I was mimicking other friends. I now think it was rather an unpleasant thing, but I enjoyed the limelight. Fortunately, these instincts to show off—I was also a dancer and did some amateur acting—all fell away, and whatever this projection of the imagination was and this ability to observe people closely that all writers must have became concentrated on writing quite early on.

Rubin: Your fiction reveals a spareness, an efficiency in getting at the essential. How did that develop in your writing?

Gordimer: That strictness comes from the discipline of the short story. When I was teaching myself to write, it was the short story I was working on, and I think my first two novels lacked narrative power because I knew how to condense but not how to make the links properly, so that the first novel fell into segments that didn't quite knit. But the getting to the essence of things and the looking for the significant detail come from the discipline of the short story.

Marchant: You said that you read Upton Sinclair's *The Jungle* when you were fourteen. Did it have an effect upon your writing?

Gordimer: It certainly had an effect upon me as a human being. It was the first thing that I read that made me think about where I was living and the way *we* were living in this small town. I lived in this gold-mining town, and there were very big mines all around us. About a mile from our house was an enormous "compound," as we called it, or barracks, where the black mineworkers who came from all over southern Africa lived. They had no wives or children with them. Nothing much has changed: they were migratory workers, as they are today; this iniquitous system was already in place. I began to think of them not just as "mine boys," who had been brought there to do their labor and spoke incomprehensible languages, but as workers, as people who were living in a really inhuman way. I think this came from reading about the conditions in the stockyards; I began to understand how people can be used as units of labor.

Marchant: Did you start to ask awkward questions of your family or at school?

Gordimer: Certainly not at school. I went to a convent school, and I can't remember any questions of this nature coming up. There were no black children there, and nobody ever dreamt of asking why there weren't. It's very difficult for children brought up in that atmosphere, because your parents are your models—we know that from our own children; it's a tremendous responsibility, both touching and frightening—and one thought that life was as presented to one by one's parents. There were these divisions. I went to an all-white school, and the library that meant so much to me as a small child was segregated—no black could enter that library. The cinema, a great treat—I saved my pocket money and went every Saturday afternoon—allowed no blacks. I simply thought, "This is how it is! just the way the sun rises in the morning and sinks at night."

Marchant: Was there a moment of sudden consciousness?

Gordimer: I don't think so. One might invent that afterwards, but I don't think it really happens that way. My mother felt guilty about the way blacks lived and her way of dealing with this was quite often to say, when she saw them maltreated or deprived, which one really saw all the time, "Well, you know, they are human beings, after all." So she was beginning to think of black people not as ciphers, and she herself did some good things—she was one of a small group of women who started a crèche and clinic in the black ghetto near our town—but she didn't take it a step further; she didn't realize that it was the social order that was responsible for the condition of the people whom she pitied.

Kitchen: In last week's *New York Times,* you are quoted as saying about a party you overheard people discussing: "Maybe when I was twenty-five, I wouldn't have made all these judgments; I would have gone home and written a short story about the party." Do you feel that time is running out—that the ways of art are long and that your country and you can't wait any longer?

Gordimer: No, I think I was speaking rather regretfully then. As I have grown older, so much has happened around me and, of course, has changed my consciousness. I hate using these psychologically and politically loaded words, but I can't think of any others.

I'll give you an example. When I was about eighteen years old, I wrote a story called "The Kindest Thing to Do," about a child who finds a pigeon that's obviously been shot by some kid with a catapult. It's injured, and it's suffering badly. You can't put it in a cage and feed it, as children will do, and nurse it back to life. The child is faced with the choice of watching it suffer or killing it. The child takes off her shoe and bangs it on the head. When I looked at that story for some particular reason a little while ago, I realized that what I was doing there was thinking about the responsibility we have for life and death, that we can actually kill somebody, that we can take life away. I think that was my first confrontation with this moral problem, but I had no idea I was doing anything as high-falutin' as that. But I think I was; I was dealing with life and death.

Marchant: You said you taught yourself to write short stories. Who were your teachers? Did you go back to the English nineteenth century?

Gordimer: I read truly omnivorously. I can remember distinctly winning an essay prize, a book token with which I bought *Gone With* *the Wind* and Pepys's *Diary.* It didn't seem to me an odd combination at all.

I read Chekhov, de Maupassant, Eudora Welty, and, I might add with some hesitation, Hemingway. Without them, and many others, I could not have found my way to my own voice.

Kitchen: Could we look a little more closely at your last two collections of short stories? These stories seem to have some new, underlying themes. One is betrayal—not only the betrayal of blacks by whites but also whites' betrayal of whites and even blacks betraying blacks.

Gordimer: When I was reading the proofs of *Something Out There,* the latest collection, I was absolutely stunned by this sense of betrayal. I realized that there is an obsession with betrayal in the stories. Even the one about the couple in Europe, "Sins of the Third Age," is all about different forms of betrayal—political, sexual, every form. I seem to have been obsessed by this, and I asked myself, "Why?"

In the last few years, it's been so much in the air at home; you just never know, really, to whom you're talking. You're among friends, and then you may discover later that there was somebody there who was indeed *not* a friend. The most extraordinary things have happened. I have two young friends; he and she are lawyers. They are people who work terribly hard in the liberation movement. The young man who was so close to them that he was best man at their wedding turned out to be a master spy. He's been a principal State witness in a number of very important treason cases. They had no idea. He had their total confidence.

Kitchen: So the "something out there" is really something *in* there.

Gordimer: Yes.

Marchant: I'm astonished that you didn't see that theme of betrayal until you got the galleys.

Gordimer: When I publish a collection of stories, they've usually been written over a period of years—often as many as five years— and I haven't read them all together. When I look at them together, I may see, as in this case, that I've been obsessed by a particular theme, exploring it from different viewpoints, as it affects different people. In a society like ours, one thing that happens to me and to the subjects of my stories is a distortion of sensibilities. Just as a baby's head is finally formed in the birth canal, so by living in South Africa, your personality, your perceptions, are constantly under these pressures that shape you.

Rubin: You write both novels and short stories. What are your varying commitments to those two forms? What are the kinds of truth that each can get at?

Gordimer: I don't think there are different kinds of truth that each can get at. But now I tend to write fewer stories. I recognize with some sadness that I have been neglecting the short story. The themes that interest me are becoming more and more complex, perhaps because life is becoming more and more complex—the life around me from which I draw my sustenance and my subject matter.

Rubin: So you can't deal with terribly complex themes in the short story because of its limited development and the number of characters you can handle?

Gordimer: No, no, it's a matter of thematic layers. Even in my stories, I'm not satisfied with one layer. It's really like peeling an onion: once you begin to invent an alternative life for others, once you begin to find out why they are as they are, you just go deeper and deeper and deeper, and sometimes it seems the story doesn't give enough space to do that.

Rubin: You are, particularly in your more recent work, an absolute master of what isn't said. How conscious is this sort of reticence or control, this avoidance of the explicit?

Gordimer: That's just the way I write; it's not a matter of something I cut out afterwards. Indeed, sometimes I have to go back and think, "Now you've held back so much there, you've given so much breathing space. Will the reader really make that jump?" particularly in a novel of mine, *The Conservationist,* where I decided, "To hell with it, I'm not explaining anything! If it's full of unfamiliar terms and unfamiliar situations, I'm not going to put in any kind of authorial direction. It must carry itself, or not."

Kitchen: Your recent novel *July's People* is a visionary novel. Does it reflect what you actually think will happen, or are you just playing with the future?

Gordimer: I was playing with the present, looking at what we were doing in South Africa that could very well bring about that kind of consequence. In the few years since it was written, of course, many of the things which seemed like science fiction *then,* have begun to happen, and it's not because I'm a seer or prophet, but because it was there. We'd been doing things that would bring this about.

Marchant: I find a theme—the condemnation of detachment—running throughout your work. You point out the wishy-washy liberal, whom I feel myself to be much of the time, not wanting to make life unpleasant. It seems a self-condemnation too, as though you're spurring yourself to be involved. Am I right?

Gordimer: Well, you're right that it is a self-condemnation. I'm often indeed criticized for this "cold eye" that I cast particularly upon white South Africans, but I'm also saying, "I'm one of you. If I'm castigating anybody, I'm castigating myself." Not from the point of view of self-improvement. I don't write to improve my morality. It's part of the *knowing* process, of getting to know why we are as we are, what our behavior really means, in all sorts of situations. Not only political ones. In my story "Siblings," you have a cousin in the family who is a dropout, a drug addict, and the various attitudes of the family to this child. I often deal in my stories with the relationships between children and their parents. That brings us to what I think is one of my central themes—power, the way human beings use power in their relationships.

Marchant: You do something that I find extraordinary: you manage to avoid being shrill or overtly didactic, and it seems to me because you're writing about people as people who happen to be in particular circumstances. I find such a wide range of characters, and some part of you loves them all.

Gordimer: Yes, I think that's true—even of the character in my novel *The Conservationist,* who is just exactly the kind of man I hate in South Africa. But, once I began to write about him and got under his skin, I began to understand him better. I don't believe that to understand all is to forgive all. Certainly in a country with conflict like my own, that's a very dangerous attitude. But for a writer, it's absolutely essential to understand all, and once you do, you cannot be entirely unsympathetic. Unless you're a propagandist and you want to draw cardboard figures.

Marchant: Because the monster is not another person, absolutely divorced from oneself, but it's oneself in those circumstances, if one doesn't watch out.

Gordimer: Absolutely. I agree. The monster is always there, inside, in all of us.

Rubin: To follow through on this point, you have written and said numerous times that you are not a propagandist, and don't want to be; you're not a reporter, and don't wish to be. You said that you are a "natural" writer. Is the language of politics truly distinct from the language of art?

Gordimer: Oh, I think so, and one has to watch out for these words and phrases coming in. One has to cleanse poetry and fiction of them. They're like old pieces of soap: they're worn right down; there's really nothing there any more. I prefaced an essay that I wrote by saying, "Nothing I write here in this essay will be as true as my fiction," and I believe that with all my heart and mind. I write non-fiction only for political reasons, because I believe there's perhaps something I have a little wrinkle on that you don't get in the newspaper; but I always feel that the writing is self-conscious, somehow tailored by some other force in me. I'm never happy with it, and I really mean that it is never as true as what I imagine.

Rubin: Just this year you've had a number of essays appear in this country—in *The New York Times* and *The New York Review of Books*. Does the necessity to be moved to this kind of writing detract from the time and effort that you could give to your imaginative writing?

Gordimer: I do as little as possible. But as a white South African writer, when my country is in crisis and I know that more immediate attention can be drawn to this by one piece in something like *The New York Times Magazine* than by any fiction, then I feel that I cannot refuse. Who am I to say, "No, no, I'm writing my novel and I can't do it"? In certain special cases, it's the one thing I *can* do. It's better for me to write something than to sit on some committee— although I have also done that.

Kitchen: Do you see yourself as a female writer or as a writer who happens to be female?

Gordimer: I have to be honest. I'm not at all conscious of being a female writer. There is a special kind of *male* writing, and there's a special kind of *female* writing, and then there's another kind which allows the writer to be what the writer really is—this strange creature who can get into the skin of all sexes, all ages. I think that's something a writer really has to give himself or herself the freedom of.

Marchant: You have a very strong sense of nature, as though you were someone with bare feet in the soil. Have you always had that?

Gordimer: Yes, and I don't know why. South Africa is a very beautiful country, but I happened to grow up in one of the few ugly parts of it—this ugly little mining town, very flat, above the tree belt. In fact, it was a little town that had been thrown together because the mines came up. But I always had this strong feeling, first of all for minute things in nature—worms and bugs and the petals of flowers. Then, when I grew up and was free to move around my country, it opened up tremendously my sensuous response to nature. In my early stories, it's indeed the motivation for writing. Unfortunately, as you get older, that goes, because you don't see that flower or drop of dew for the first time. Once you've seen it umpteen times, it doesn't have the same impact.

Rubin: How has your sense of your audience changed over the years that you've been writing?

Gordimer: Not at all. I never think about it, truly.

Rubin: Do you do a lot of revising?

Gordimer: Not much. If I'm writing a long novel, I will usually go straight through, and although I may go back a chapter, I don't keep going back to the beginning. When I finish, then there will be the grand task of going right through it.

Rubin: Do you read your work aloud at any point in the composition process?

Gordimer: Not usually. And I never show it to anybody. I've got a feeling that it will all disappear if I show it to somebody.

Marchant: Not to anybody? You don't read it to your family?

Gordimer: No, never. I'm always amazed to read in the correspondence of nineteenth-century writers, such as Flaubert and Turgenev, how they trapped their families and friends and made them listen for hours. Of course, they really had something to read to the family.

Marchant: Do you listen to criticism? Family, friends, the critics?

Gordimer: My family is very blunt, and I can get the truth from them, especially from my two children, who are grown-up, of course, and from my husband. Friends, I think, never tell you the truth, because if they love you, they do not want to tell you that they don't like this latest book as much as the one before. So really I think they smile and kiss you on both cheeks, and doubtless I do the same thing. Critics? There might be one or two in the world that I know of who, if they wrote a critique of a book of mine, I might be interested in reading it. It would mean something to me, and I should be wounded if they had very strong criticisms of it, because I would feel they knew what I was trying to do and I had failed to do it. In the general run of reviews, very often you get praise for the wrong things, because somebody has failed to see what you were doing.

Marchant: What happens if your blunt husband and children don't like something?

Gordimer: It's too bad, because the book's published by then. They hadn't seen it before.

During the time when I was writing *A Guest of Honour,* there was one person with whom I discussed the book while it was being written and whose opinion of how it was going was important to me and who is somewhere in the shaping of the book psychologically, but that was the single exception.

Rubin: You have also of late adapted your stories for television in the USA and Europe. Is this rather like essay writing, a necessity for you?

Gordimer: Not at all. I'm very interested in film, and every now and then, somebody comes along who wants to make a film of one of my stories. But what happens then is that they want to bring in a Hollywood writer who wants literally to have "lions on the freeway"—indeed, running around the streets of Johannesburg. It's never got beyond the first stage of negotiation, because I couldn't agree to just give my work over to anybody.

The seven television films that you're speaking about—from seven of my stories—were the idea of somebody who loved the stories, had no money, but managed to raise a little through German television and Channel 4 in England. In return for my giving the rights to my stories—really, for a tiny token—I had wonderful control: I chose the directors and wrote four of the scripts. I enjoyed doing that, and I think I learned something.

Rubin: Although you're frequently described, very positively, as being in the mainstream of English fiction, I noticed an expansion of stream-of-consciousness technique, or interior monologue, in your more recent work. Where do you see yourself in twentieth-century fiction?

Gordimer: I think that all of us who write today were very much influenced by Joyce, and by Proust. Without Proust, Joyce, and Thomas Mann, where would we be?

Marchant: What do you find to be significant about writing in terms of social change? Obviously your strength lies in writing fiction and not in journalism or in making political speeches. Do you have any faith that your fiction makes change?

Gordimer: I don't think that fiction can *make* change. I don't think that writers are taken that seriously; I know they're not in my own country. Black writers are regarded as enemies, and most white writers as well, because we all oppose the state. You won't find *one* writer who will covertly or overtly defend apartheid.

Books make South Africans, black and white, see themselves, as they cannot from inside themselves. They get a kind of mirror image with which to compare their own feelings and motives. I think fiction raises their consciousness in this way. In the case of blacks, it has raised people's self-respect and pride in bad times.

Long before and in between the times when South Africa is headline news, fiction writers have given a sense of the daily life and in that way influenced the outside world's awareness of what is happening in South Africa.

On Writing and the Liberation of My Country:
A Morning with Nadine Gordimer

Jan Askelund/1987

From *Vinduet* [Oslo, Norway], 41.4 (1987), 2–7. Norwegian title:
Om Alle Tings Samanheng Og Frigjeringa Av Mitt Land: Ein
Formiddag Med Nadine Gordimer. Reprinted in a revised form
by permission of *Vinduet* and Jan Askelund. Translated by
Thomas F. Van Laan.

Nadine Gordimer is a tiny, sprightly woman. A book in her hand, she
walks toward me in a flower-filled garden in Ndola, the capital of
Copperbelt Province in Zambia. Her name is known the world over.
She has been for many years among the leading candidates for the
Nobel Prize for Literature. It is stated and accepted that her novels
and volumes of short stories are strongly political. It they are no
longer banned in her native country the instant they come out, it is
no doubt because the rest of the world has its eyes on her.

As it says about Nadine Gordimer in the *The Oxford Companion
to English Literature:* Most of the work of this South African writer "is
concerned with the political situation in her native land; her protests
against apartheid and censorship have been outspoken." And that is
true enough. But that statement indicates nothing about the quality of
her short stories and novels, about why or how they are written. One
Saturday morning in August, Gordimer shared her thoughts with me
about her own writing and, in particular, about her latest novel, about
her support for black African writers, and about translations.

Nadine Gordimer was born in 1923 in South Africa, the daughter
of a Lithuanian Jew who came to that country when he was thirteen.
Gordimer is glad she has been able to remain in South Africa. South
Africans, black and white, who live in political exile, are cut off from
their roots. To have to experience that, she regards as a nightmare.
She lives in Johannesburg with her husband Reinhold Cassirer, who
is an art dealer. He is originally from Heidelberg, Germany and has
been in Africa for fifty years. So one can figure out when and why
he went there.

By the way, the book she was carrying that morning was *The Valley of the Elephants* by Norman Carr, an old-hand, big-game hunter who now organizes hikes and other tourist activities in Central Africa. Nadine Gordimer and her husband had just been on a week-long safari in Luangwa Valley, the valley of the elephants. She and her husband were enthusiastic about their trip. In many ways it had been a marvellous experience, but it had also been upsetting. The hippopotamuses there had become victims of a disease that no one had been able to diagnose. "We saw at least ten dead hippopotamuses, on land and floating in the river," Reinhold Cassirer recounted. "All the other animals were lively and in fine form, elephants, zebras, rhinoceroses, antelopes, lions. . . ." "Not the lions," Nadine Gordimer commented. "I don't think we saw any lions on the whole trip."

Gordimer's speech and her observations are in keeping with what one might come to expect from reading her works. She speaks her mind directly and candidly; yet everything she says seems carefully shaped, with no loose ends.

It took her three and a half years to write *A Sport of Nature*, the novel that came out this Easter. It consists of 396 big pages. Now she needs time to replenish, perhaps a vacation. She and her husband have been in the bush and visiting good friends in Zambia. That which in its origin has been intended as recreation can easily be remodeled as artistic material for novels and short stories by an author who has greater social and geographical points of contact and insights than most people who write. *A Sport of Nature* concerns the Republic of South Africa (RSA) and the history of black Africa through more than a quarter of a century. The protagonist and title character is the white South African Hillela, born in 1944. The novel deals with Hillela's life story from her birth through some years further on than 1987; yet, Hillela's history is the history of our era: how it has been; how it could be; how people have to accommodate themselves to the way things turn out.

Hillela is a stubborn rebel. She rebels through her sexual nature. From her youth on, she is a passionate person. She is driven by her natural impulses rather than her intellect. She is flexible, indeed chameleon-like, adjusting readily in her relationships with a series of men to a variety of lifestyles. She is open, honest, affectionate, and erotic.

If Hillela's sexual revolt does not shock us cold Norwegians in the same way it would South African fundamentalists, we nonetheless probably confront with some wonder a novel that fits into a tradition that most of us have forgotten—that of Kjartan Flogstad. *A Sport of Nature* is a picaresque novel—i.e., a type of novel that represents the life of the protagonist through a series of loosely-connected episodes. While she, through multifarious adventures, gains insight into multifarious circumstances, the story acquires the stamp of a realistic depiction of society which invites satiric commentary. In keeping with the genre, the protagonist less often distinguishes herself through her virtues than through what the average citizen might call the opposite; in that sense, the novel might be labelled "anti-heroic."

Not that Hillela is immoral. She is amoral, with a never failing nose for what is right for the whole society but what at the same time most satisfies herself. Hillela is unconventional. She makes up her mind to ignore all the restrictions being white would normally impose on her in South Africa. She indulges her emotions, instincts, and fantasies. Men are her specialty. She marries two of them. The first is a black ANC politician who is murdered in their apartment in Lusaka. The other is a black general who becomes chief of state (and Hillela first lady) in an unnamed African country.

Before Hillela rises to the status of a first lady, we go through a long and intricate story. What is shocking for Hillela's society is not merely that she marries blacks and thus breaks a taboo—for that could be interpreted as expiation or subjugation or a quest for identity; rather the most important thing in Hillela's marrying a black and desiring "a rainbow of children" is that she rips away all the mystique about race and blood. She repeals apartheid in the private sphere. With her persistent happiness, she proves that what she does is right. Furthermore, she proves the rightness of her instincts through her daughter—a picture-perfect, internationally celebrated model. Politically she proves the "rightness" of her behavior through becoming the influential wife of a president. She is in truth the sport of nature that the title refers to—a mutation, an aberration.

Hillela travels and works in Rhodesia/Zimbabwe and Mozambique, the Republic of South Africa and Swaziland, Tanzania and Great

Britain, the United States and West Africa, Zambia and Eastern
Europe. While readers of A Sport of Nature follow Hillela about the
world as well as into her intimate moments with a black spouse, they
begin to realize that Hillela herself intuits how what she discovers and
experiences elsewhere is interrelated with the situation in her native
land. Still, even though Hillela's brain appears to absorb without
difficulty everything she encounters on three continents, it is
unsettling to find a novelist as cerebral and disciplined as Nadine
Gordimer portraying a character who lives by instinct and sexual
impulse to the degree that Hillela does. Through this amazing
protagonist, Gordimer takes us along to South African independence
in a very near future. She takes us into the dream. She moves us
along from questions about justice to questions about power.

Gordimer utilizes fantasy but she also uses historical facts. A Sport
of Nature is, to some extent, a documentary novel. Through the close
to four hundred pages wander Oliver Tambo and Nelson Mandela,
Nkrumah, Sadat, and many, many more.

*How imaginary is your writing, how autobiographical are your
books?*

Most first novels are strongly autobiographical, I should think. [She
notes that as the author of a first novel published in 1987, I am
blushing.] But now that I'm an experienced writer, it won't do to have
my characters recognized on the streets of Johannesburg, Dar es
Salaam, or Lusaka.

A friend of mine who has read A Sport of Nature *maintains that
you could not have written about Hillela as you do without having
had a black lover yourself. Is she mistaken in that?*

My lovers are my private business. But the emotion must be
firsthand.

*Your novel includes such real people as Oliver Tambo and Nelson
Mandela. The female protagonist, Hillela, eventually marries a man
who becomes the president of a West African state. What country is
it?*

Your guess is as good as mine. You can yourself decide what
country suits best and put the name on the map.

May I assume that Hillela is a purely fictional figure created without a living model? Is it really possible to take one's character out of thin air?

They all come from oneself. I have learned much from observing my own children. I have been a child; I am a mother. I can see myself through my own children just as I have in retrospect come to know my own mother.

Nadine Gordimer has two children, a daughter and a son, one each from two marriages. She collaborated with her son on the filming of seven of her short stories, which were shown on Norwegian television three years ago. She wrote four of the scripts for the films herself: "It is very instructive. No matter what or how I wrote in the script, the whole thing was made in the cutting room."

She is fascinated with how one can take material from all kinds of sources, particularly when one isn't seeking it: "I had considered a different title for my last novel. I had thought about giving the book Hillela's name with only the one additional phrase, 'a sport' (an ambiguous word for a person who responds to adversity with joy and cheerfulness, especially a good loser; but which can also as easily mean a 'gambler'; but which can just as easily mean someone who follows the rules and never cheats). Then I happened to read a dictionary definition for 'a sport of nature' (a mutation, an aberration from nature). I saw that I had written a case history, and the title was given."

When you refer to places and historical personages and events, do you reimagine them so they fit into your own story?

No. Since my short stories and novels are also concerned with larger experiences than those I invent, with human life in a factual external reality, such things have to be correct in the least detail. An example: Hillela in *A Sport of Nature* was born during the last world war. She rejects the white culture and goes to bed with several Africans, black Africans. So it is important to be careful about what words one uses. "Native" won't do. Nowadays Negroes want to be called "blacks," but "Africans" used to be the term in favor. I have to remember to use the appropriate word for the time and not, for example, to make the change in usage before it actually occurred.

*You are historically and factually correct in your novels' treatment
of the reality we all have in common. You perhaps don't like the
concept "intellectual writer," but you seem extremely conscious of
everything you put on paper. A device you use often is allusion. In
spite of the large printings of your books in several parts of the world,
are you perhaps dependent on having qualified readers?*

Qualified readers? Yes. Did you notice, by the way, how I put Rosa
from *Burger's Daughter* into *A Sport of Nature*? I can't remember
that I've seen the critics remark on that.

Did you use irony in your depiction of Hillela?

It is ironic how Hillela, the mutation or aberration, succeeds and
achieves self-fulfillment.

If, like Hillela, you were growing up in South Africa right after the
war, you were educated and brought up to not appreciate African
things, African history, Africa itself. Europe was the great thing, the
splendid thing.

In the context of this residual, colonial attitude—idealizing Europe
and denigrating what was African—Gordimer went on to discuss
choices made by Hillela's mother. She had run away from home with
a lover when Hillela was about two years old. She had gone to live in
the capital city, Lourenço Marques, in the Portuguese colony
Mozambique, which was the most European-like city she could
reach. Gordimer explained:

"Later she drifts away from the sweet life in Lourenço Marques on
the East Coast only to end up managing a rundown hotel in a West
Coast city. Her life goes downhill just as abruptly as Hillela's goes up.
When they finally meet in a coastal city in the west, Hillela has
nothing to say to her. She has long since finished with her."

*Hillela reflects her times; and there can be no doubt about your
discussing real problems. Do you perhaps have a political message
that you use your characters to get across? Do you write about
politics under the guise of fiction?*

No. My books are not political pamphlets. It is not my intention to
prove but to show. Writing fiction is an attempt to organize life, to put
it in a meaningful context, isn't it? I want to tell a story, and hopefully

it will be an experience for the reader to see how that story comes together, how lives turn out and blend together into a work of art. It is important to show the connections between human lives—how things, people, and events interrelate.

That Nadine Gordimer does. And when she shows the interrelatedness of all things, she also shows the social, economic, and political connections. She does not do so in the form of slogans, true enough; yet long chunks of *A Sport of Nature* are authorial commentary. However, her novel is not politics camouflaged as fiction but rather fiction that must also be read as politics. Gordimer does not merely narrate in well-crafted works of art; still, the stories are her contribution to what she calls "the liberation of my country."

All the same, Gordimer is perhaps more political outside of her books than in them, for instance, when she uses so much time and energy to support other writers and when she speaks enthusiastically about friends and acquaintances who do the same thing in South Africa. Recently, she helped create a new progressive association of authors. As she said: "In that way I am involved with working for the liberation of my country."

She has no illusions about what she can accomplish. She does not at all expect thanks and praise. She is aware of the liberal dilemma. Her novel *The Late Bourgeois World* deals with that. The Norwegian edition came out in 1975; but the original is from 1966. It can be worth recalling that it appeared prior to 1968 and is therefore not an unoriginal presentation of later ideas, of the revolt of '68 and those who participated in it. In a fictional framework of a single day Nadine Gordimer reveals her concerns. Neither the author nor the white characters in the novel can escape being aware that they live in a mad society which necessarily creates pangs of conscience. Gordimer says that she has been at times wrong, at times cowardly. When she was young, she believed that socializing with blacks and other so-called nonwhites was a contribution to the battle. That liberal perspective was an inadequate and at times hurtful response to the situation that existed. Nor can there be rewards for "nice" whites in South Africa. As she said elsewhere, we must accept that we cannot live respectably in a rotten society.

The dilemma in *The Late Bourgeois World* becomes the dilemma of the whole white population of the Republic of South Africa. Whites live in an irresolvable conflict. Thus, the political life of the protagonist Max becomes the story of a defeat in the face of forces that he cannot control. He proves to be unable to withstand pressure and torture by the authorities. The blacks and "coloureds" cannot rely on him. Nonetheless, he does the right thing by fighting against the system, by working for a revolution. The fact that Max is a bad revolutionary does not invalidate the idea that revolution is right and necessary. Good causes can have bad advocates. But no matter how much one looks for hope, this is a deeply pessimistic novel.

Gordimer's critical book, *The Black Interpreters,* is indicative of the work she does to support other authors and their causes. As a writer, she herself works in a systematic and disciplined way: "When I'm writing a book I work on it four hours during the morning. [I know from others that she broke her morning writing routine for the first time after the shock of the Sharpeville massacre, which deeply moved her personally.] In the afternoon I write letters and so forth. [She has no secretary or other assistance for her writing but does have servants to take care of the housework.] Before I go to bed, I look over what I have written in the morning. I make few changes. I have pretty clear in my mind what I will write before it gets as far as being set down on paper. For *A Sport of Nature* (396 pages), I had perhaps ten pages of notes. But I am absolute about the demand that whatever stays must be right in terms of the external reality, history, and topography."

She often finds it difficult, however, to persuade talented black authors to adopt a disciplined work routine and an exactness that can be beneficial to them. Gordimer not only helps others in finding publishers and getting published, but she also helps them with the writing process. Down to the last detail, she insists on craftsmanship. However, her emphasis on discipline is not always fruitful. She laments that black Africans are often one-book authors:

"When an author gets out a novel that also comes out through a European publisher and the author is being read, he is usually invited to Europe. He is celebrated, and he gets more money in royalties than he is accustomed to handling. That's often the end of the writing as far as he's concerned. There's just one book."

Gordimer keeps up with writers such as those she discusses in *The*

Black Interpreters. I had tried to track down a South African author
whose first novel was published in several European countries,
including Norway. At his place of work they did not know where he
was: "We haven't seen him for six months. He'll pop up somewhere.
I believe he's in England—or the United States." But Nadine
Gordimer knows where he is. She knows what country, and she
knows what his personal reasons were for going there. How it is
going with his writing, she does not know. Nor is she offended that
this man, as I understand from others, can be difficult and rather
ungenerous. She takes into account that colleagues are people with
their faults and idiosyncracies. She accepts this and remains fond of
them.

"And while we are talking about writers, do you know my good
friend Sara Lidman?" Then she talks about the Swede Sara Lidman,
an author who urges her readers to feel responsibility for their fellow
human beings, who is very much concerned with human existence
and human problems, whether they exist in northern Sweden,
Africa, or Vietnam. Gordimer tells about the two times she visited
Lidman in Sweden. "A series of Sara Lidman's novels have come out
in Norwegian, always to critical acclaim, usually in several editions. I
recall her documentary work *Gruva* [*The Mine*] from 1968."

"Unfortunately, I've never gotten to read *Gruva*. There isn't any
English edition, is there? It seems to be different with translations in
your country; Scandinavians read a great deal in English, don't
they?"

I express agreement but only up to a point. While Nadine
Gordimer herself has many readers in Norway, most of them wait to
read her when the Norwegian editions come out.

*Even closely-related languages like Norwegian, Danish, and
Swedish must be mutually translated before people will read the
literature of their neighboring countries. At the same time, your last
novel was construed as news by my own newspaper, Stavanger
Aftenblad. We requested a couple of copies from London and
managed to review the book only a few days after it came out in
Great Britain. Other Norwegian newspapers have also written about
A Sport of Nature (which came out in a Norwegian edition from*

Gyldendal in the first half of 1988, under the title Et villskudd,
translated by Johan Hambro).

I don't know whether that's a very good idea, Gordimer observes.
It's fine as far as my getting readers, but that way don't most of them
make the effort to get a copy of the original in English to the
disadvantage of the translated edition? Wouldn't it perhaps be better
if the newspapers waited to write about the Norwegian edition when
it comes out?

I reassure her that the first edition is presented as the new, great event
that it is, but that this does not happen to the neglect of newspaper
space when the Norwegian edition appears. The Norwegian version
will be reviewed then, not least in order to evaluate the quality of the
translation. Gordimer is concerned about translations: "I can myself
verify only the French translations properly. There has been, I'm
sorry to say, a lot of awful stuff produced by the translations into
French. My husband checks up on the German editions. But it is
difficult, if not impossible, to keep in touch while the work is actually
being translated. Unfortunately, I have neither the time nor the
opportunity to do like Günter Grass, who keeps in direct communication with his translators and gets the publishers in the foreign
countries to arrange seminars for the translators to meet the author."

I would like to reassure her that her Norwegian editions are fine
but, in my opinion, they are not all equally good. It is striking that the
six novels and the big collection of short stories in Norwegian have
seven different translators.

Poetry is the only genre that Nadine Gordimer says she has not
written in. But, as is evident in her book *The Black Interpreters,* she is
nonetheless genuinely interested in the work done by writers who are
poets. Moreover, she is full of praise for people who use their time to
cultivate work by budding authors in South Africa with everything
from research to typing; and she mentions them by name.

An author must, as Gordimer says, find her material within herself.
Writing and authorship are a matter of personality. With Nadine
Gordimer it is so cerebral—yet so full of feeling. Her spoken words
come without hesitation, precise and forthright. She does not ramble

on. If there are digressions in the conversation, she leads herself back
to the main topic, which is writing and writers and the liberation of
her native land: "As I was saying before I was so rudely interrupted
by myself: it's in the theater that it's happening in South Africa. You
must come and see."

Nadine Gordimer: Choosing to Be a White African

Carol Sternhell/1987

From *Ms.*, September 1987, 28, 30, 32. Reprinted by permission of Carol Sternhell.

Lying beside him, looking at pale hands, thighs, belly: seeing herself as unfinished, left off, somewhere. She examines his body minutely and without shame, and he wakes to see her at it, and smiles without telling her why: she is the first not to pretend the different colors and textures of their being is not an awesome fascination. How can it be otherwise? The laws that have determined the course of life for them are made of skin and hair . . . . It has mattered more than anything else in the world.

—from Nadine Gordimer's
"A Sport of Nature"

A woman and a man of different races lie in bed after making love and think about skin and hair. "Sex and politics," says Nadine Gordimer, who created the man and the woman and the bed in her latest novel, *A Sport of Nature* (Knopf). "Politics and sex—I don't know which comes first—have been *the* greatest influences on people's lives." In South Africa, of course, where Gordimer lives and writes, "politics" means, quite simply, skin and hair.

"I think when you're born white in South Africa, you're peeling like an onion," commented the 63-year-old novelist in a recent interview in New York. "You're sloughing off all the conditioning that you've had since you were a child."

Her own childhood in Springs, a small gold-mining town about 30 miles from Johannesburg, was solitary, lonely, apolitical, bounded by books. Gordimer frequently describes herself as "a natural writer." By "natural," she has explained, "I mean I began writing as a child, when I didn't know what apartheid was . . . . There are some writers who became writers because they became so indignant and were

275

stirred to creativity. I began writing out of a sense of wonder about life, a sense of its mystery, and also out of a sense of its chaos." She first wanted to be a dancer, Gordimer recalls now, then began performing original dramas with her friends, "so when I began to write, nobody took any notice and I think that was a good thing. It was just Nadine scribbling away the way she had danced or put on a play."

Gordimer's immigrant Jewish father, who escaped Lithuanian pogroms to become a South African watchmaker, was concerned only with the small jewelry shop he owned, Gordimer says. Her mother—also Jewish, but born in England—had a social conscience but not a political consciousness. "She didn't connect her feelings that something was wrong with politics. She made me conscious I was privileged, but the fact that one might have to live *differently* because of that, that one might have to think differently, all that came to me from reading."

Now, however, Gordimer—the internationally acclaimed author of nine novels and eight collections of short stories—believes even a "natural writer" (particularly one whose canvas is South Africa) must do more than write, however finely crafted or passionate her words.

"I resisted it for years," she explains, "but in the last ten years or so, I've realized that you can't just say, 'Well, I'm a writer, you know, I'm too busy to sit on committees or go to meetings.' So I do that kind of thing now, because I feel I must. Because I live there and I'm white and I have a kind of inherited responsibility for what whites have done there.

"When I think back to my childhood in that little town," she adds, "would I ever even be a writer if I couldn't have gone and used the public library? But no black child could use that public library."

Nadine Gordimer, tiny and elegant in white shirt, slacks, neat grayish hair, shows up early for our scheduled interview, but that's just because she hopes to get it over with more quickly. In New York recently to talk about her ninth novel, *A Sport of Nature,* she would rather be somewhere else—preferably writing. She answers questions fully, precisely, courteously, rapidly, occasionally checking her watch. Probably because she dislikes the process so much, she is strikingly well prepared, unfailingly articulate.

"It really is very draining, you know," she says. The woman who once wrote that fiction should "spread an intensity on the page; burn a hole in it," talks with that same fierce concentration.

Gordimer is not a feminist.

The Women's Movement, she says, "doesn't seem irrelevant to me in other places in the world, but it does seem at the present time to be kind of a luxury in South Africa. Every black woman has more in common with a black man than she has with her white sisters. We may share the same convictions, but after we've finished talking about it in a sisterly fashion, I remain the privileged writer and she goes back home where her children are being attacked.

"Whenever something terrible happens to young people," she adds, "to children in South Africa, you get well-meaning white women saying, 'We are all mothers. This is something we have, no matter what color we are, that men cannot have because we bear our children.' But these organizations, which call themselves Women for Peace or whatever, they always break up because of what has happened to the black women's children. White women's children are going to school every day, working peacefully, and the black women's children are taking on the burden of political responsibility, boycotting school, having tear gas thrown into their classrooms. They are in the battlefields. So it *cannot* be the same thing."

A woman and a man lie in bed after making love: Hillela, the puzzling, disturbing heroine of *A Sport of Nature,* lies in many beds with many men. A sport, or spontaneous mutation, she thrives wherever she washes up. She adopts the manners, customs, ideas, *life,* of whatever man she happens to be with. A middle-class white Jewish South African woman with no particular political or intellectual commitments of her own, Hillela becomes a legendary figure in the revolution that destroys apartheid. The young girl expelled from boarding school for inadvertently socializing with a "colored" boy is transformed into the regal wife of the new African state's black president. But she'd been so many women to so many men. What if she'd simply married someone else?

Hillela's passionately political Aunt Pauline (who nevertheless throws her niece out of the house when she catches the girl in bed with her cousin Sasha) remarks, "Hillela's field was, surely, men."

And Sasha tells Pauline: "Don't you see? It's all got to come down, mother. . . . It will take another kind of person to stay on here. A new white person. Not us. The chance is a wild chance—like falling in love." A wild chance, a sport, a spontaneous mutation.

"I'm fascinated by people like Hillela," comments Gordimer. "There are people who live instinctively, who act first and think afterward. And they are great survivors. And I think that cerebral people like myself have often been inclined to look down on them. And then you find that really you've been quite wrong."

I wonder if Hillela ever becomes a genuine political activist. "I don't know, because I ask myself, 'What is a genuine revolutionary?'" comments Gordimer. "Revolution is people who bring about change—some people do it in one way, some people do it in another. I see a relationship between Hillela and the true courtesan. They were always politically powerful; and their field was always men.

"So many people," Gordimer adds, "who have never known real political activists, imagine them as either monklike or nunlike. And I know that they're not like that at all. Having the revolutionary temperament, the daring, usually goes along with very sexually attractive personalities, strong sexuality in both men and women."

I wonder in what sense Hillela is a "sport," isn't normal. "Well, I think she's a critique of what we at home regard as normal, you see," responds the novelist. "Think of the choices she was given. She was given all the quote advantages unquote. But they weren't normal. South Africa isn't normal."

Gordimer isn't a "woman writer." She has said more than once that "all writers are androgynous beings." A woman writer, she explains now, "is somebody who is setting out to make a point about being a woman. But to me, the real thing that makes a writer a writer is the ability to intuit other people's states of mind—to get inside the skin of a child, to imagine what it is like to be old. Writers do this all the time. I think there is a special quality a writer has that is not defined by sex."

In the same way, a writer's art is not defined by race. "Probably," she says, "it would be easier for me quite subconsciously to slip into writing from the point of view of a white man whose general range of living experience I was familiar with, than it would be for me to project into a similar black person who lived perhaps in an area of life that was truly out of my range of possibility. But to decide simply on grounds of black and white, again, I find incomprehensible."

Except for the mysterious changeling Hillela, none of the white characters in *A Sport of Nature,* not even the radicals, find a place in the new black African state. In *July's People,* published in 1981, a similar revolution forces liberal, arrogant Maureen Smales, her husband, and children to seek refuge with their black servant July in his native village. In the novel's last scene Maureen is running, running, running, away from the future, for her life. But Gordimer, who believes black rule in South Africa is inevitable, does not feel whites must run, hearts pounding, like Maureen.

"Some, I suppose, will leave," she says. "But you know we're an old, sick population. So there is no question, I think, of the entire white population leaving, but it may go. The great mistake so many of them are making is not to prepare themselves for the future and not to join with blacks in some way in the struggle to bring that future about instead of hanging on to this dead, old, bad, cruel system.

"The African National Congress," she adds, "has reiterated again and again that whites are white Africans there if they wish to be. But you've got to do something to prove that you really want to opt out of your class and color and throw in your lot with the future."

Gordimer's own children—her daughter Oriane, from a brief first marriage, and Hugo, her son with her husband of 33 years, Reinhold Cassirer—do not live in South Africa. Neither is politically active.

"My daughter married a Frenchman and lives in France," says Gordimer. "I think if she'd stayed at home she would have been involved because she's very much a person involved with people. She has a great love of children—she's a teacher. And my son, I think it's not yet decided in his personality because he has had, like my daughter, a feeling of 'well, I don't live there anymore, so I want to cut it out of my life.' But I can see that he's really torn. And of course, being a filmmaker, there is also the feeling that you'd like to put into film some of the things you know. So I don't know about him."

Motherhood, Gordimer says, has been astonishing. "Women, of course, have been oppressed, but in the end I think that women have got the edge over men because of the fact that we can bear children and it's an absolutely extraordinary experience that I wouldn't have forgone for anything." On the other hand, she missed a good deal of her children's childhoods.

"Writers are ruthless people," she admits a bit sadly. "I sent my children to boarding school. Now I think, 'Oh, my God, it all happened so quickly.' They seemed to be such a nuisance—and then they were grown up and gone."

Thinking about skin and hair: living in South Africa, says Gordimer, is "a manic/depressive sort of life." Because there are heroes, and as Rosa says in *Burger's Daughter,* "It's strange to live in a country where there are still heroes." And because there is destruction. "Such terrible things happen," says Gordimer. "People who have nothing to do with your liberation movement always seem to get killed at the same time. And then you think, good God, how can one be part of this?"

Nadine Gordimer, fragile and powerful, looks at her watch. Her smile is gracious. Her intense concentration smolders, and seems to burn a hole through my notebook.

"It really is very draining, you know," she says.

Arts and Africa: An Interview with Nadine Gordimer

Alex Tetteh-Lartey/1987

Transcription of "Arts and Africa" program # 694G printed by permission of Alex Tetteh-Lartey and BBC's African Service.

AT-L: Nadine Gordimer was born in South Africa a little over sixty years ago. She's white. She's written many novels and short stories and won many literary prizes. And now her ninth novel has just been published. Nadine Gordimer, welcome to "Arts and Africa." Your new novel, *A Sport of Nature,* roams around the African continent, following in the footsteps of the young white girl, Hillela. Are you now wanting to feature more of the continent or is it a new way of focussing on the South African situation?

NG: Well I think it depends upon the character. What happened to her and what was going to happen to her demanded that she should move around in Africa, as well as have experiences in her own country where she was born. But perhaps it also symbolises, in a way, my feeling that more and more South Africa must become conscious of being part of Africa.

AT-L: How much travelling have you actually done outside South Africa?

NG: Well, I've been really very lucky because being a writer means one has friends who are also writers. My political stand is well known, not just through my writings but through my actions at home, so it's known that I am a strong opponent of apartheid, with the result that I have been lucky enough to travel in other parts of Africa. I've been to Ghana; I've been to the Ivory Coast; I've been to Tanzania; I've been to Zambia, Zimbabwe, and Angola. I've travelled widely in Africa. It's really only in extreme North Africa and Arab Africa I haven't had the opportunity to go.

AT-L: And have your views been formed by the travelling you've done, or did you have your ideas right from the beginning?

NG: Well, your ideas as a writer—writers being mostly great readers—your ideas of the countries you have visited come from the literature. And I've always been very interested and read everything I could that came out of other parts of the continent.

AT-L: Do you consider yourself an African writer?

NG: Yes, I do. I'm an African writer in the English language and therefore I'm also part of English literature. I consider every black writer writing in English part of English literature as well.

AT-L: What is most important to you as a novelist? Is it the telling of the story or is it bringing to the fore historical truths and facts?

NG: The story comes first. For me the characters come first, because I believe that the story comes out of the characters. But since I've lived my whole life in a country in which personal life is so imbued with political meaning, of course the political side comes into it very strongly—political ideas come in. But I think a novelist is not a propagandist; a novelist is not a journalist. You begin with human beings and you begin with the mystery of life. Where I live, the mystery of life is very political.

AT-L: And do you think the novel is influential enough to change people's ways?

NG: It's a very difficult question. I think in some countries novelists count and have been influential. I think that the influence of novelists within South Africa is not very strong, whether they are black or white. But I think when their books are read outside, they have helped to show the world what really happens to human beings under apartheid and under all the new names that apartheid now has and its so-called reforms. They show this to people in depth through human beings the way that newspaper and television reports never can. I think that's all a novelist can do.

AT-L: What lesson would you say there is in *A Sport of Nature*, which is the book we're now talking about specifically?

NG: Well, to try and sum up a rather long and complicated book is difficult, but I will try to look at my book from the outside. The title, *A Sport of Nature,* comes from genetics, the science of genetics or heredity. Nature sometimes plays a trick, is "sporting," and produces an off-spring that is completely unlike the parent type. I am suggesting that my character in this book, Hillela, doesn't run true to type—as determined by her family background and as a white in South Africa. And she instinctively rejects the various solutions that her white background offers her, the kind of solutions that, it is

suggested, will serve when there's black majority rule. She has a kind
of healthy instinct about that, and she solves this problem in her own
way. She succeeds in becoming identified with South Africa as
indeed a white African, but in a rather original and unusual way that
would not be approved of by many whites who see only certain ways
of reaching an accommodation with black power.

AT-L: And when you place her in these different countries in
Africa, is it so that you can spotlight certain facts about these
countries, or is it just part of the general drifting process?

NG: Well, for instance, when she's moving among refugees from
South Africa, it is a way of examining what has happened at home
and also what happens to people in exile. I've become very
interested in what exile does to people, how some survive, some
grow; and particularly among writers there have been some
tragedies, in that we've lost some wonderful black writers who simply
haven't been able to survive the pressures of exile. Others have
continued to grow and to write.

AT-L: Would I be right to say that you have admiration for Hillela?

NG: She fascinates me because she's so unlike me.

AT-L: I was wondering if she reflected some of your own nature or
some of your aspirations or dreams.

NG: Maybe I would like to have been like her.

AT-L: You seem to be very sympathetic towards the liberation
movement in South Africa.

NG: I'm not only sympathetic, I identify completely with the
liberation movement in South Africa.

AT-L: You're not actually a member though of these movements.

NG: Well, as you know, you cannot be a member of the ANC in
South Africa; it's a banned organisation. I'm close to the United
Democratic Front, which at present is still not a banned movement
but which adheres to the Freedom Charter.

AT-L: Nadine, there's this President Nomo in the book who has
become the chairman of the OAU and to whom Hillela is married.
You say of him that "he was a man of high intelligence whose style
makes him popular in Africa and the Eastern Block and whose
humour and sophistication do the same for him with the West." Now
is this the sort of man who you hope or expect, when liberation
comes about for the blacks in South Africa, will govern South Africa?

NG: No, I hadn't thought of it, but this is not a bad set of

characteristics for a President, and indeed it's the kind of characteristics I've observed in black leaders when I've travelled about.

AT-L: Well, Nadine Gordimer, I would like to thank you very much
indeed for this most interesting conversation. I've really enjoyed it.

NG: Thank you.

Writers in Conversation: Nadine Gordimer

Margaret Walters/1987

Transcription made and printed with permission of Margaret Walters and the Institute of Contemporary Arts. This ICA Video (Writers Talk #62) is available from The Roland Collection, 3120 Pawtucket Road, Northbrook, IL 60062.

MW: Nadine Gordimer, I'd really like to welcome you very much to the ICA. I'm not going to say much in introduction because I'm sure everybody here knows your work very well. It's certainly been an important part of my life for about twenty-five years now. I knew nothing about Nadine Gordimer when I first picked up *The Lying Days.* It turned out it was her first novel. Being young at the time, I took it as a novel about simply adolescence, about a girl growing up; and I still think it's one of the best I've ever read of that kind. When I went back to her short stories and then read *A World of Strangers* and *Occasion for Loving,* of course I realized that she was intensely and distinctively a South African writer. I think my next favorite one was *The Late Bourgeois World* in 1966, about which I'm going to ask later; it did seem to me to be possibly a turning point in Nadine Gordimer's work. It's the first one, it seems to me, in which one of the central characters, a woman living on her own, was actually drawn into politics, half reluctantly. Since then, of course, Nadine Gordimer has become very, very widely known in England and in the States. *The Conservationist* won the Booker Prize in 1974. Since then there's been, in 1979, one of my favorites *Burger's Daughter,* and then *July's People.* Nadine Gordimer lives in Johannesburg as she's always done; and, I think, in recent years she has been increasingly speaking out about the political situation in South Africa. She's just published a new novel *A Sport of Nature,* which we'll talk about a little bit later. But, I wanted to go back to how you began writing. You wrote short stories for quite a long time, I think.

NG: Yes, I started writing short stories when I was a child. I published my first story, adult story, when I was fifteen in a small journal in South Africa.

MW: Did you find, as I think other African writers have said, that in a sense you had to invent a language to get the physical feeling of Africa. You'd been brought up, presumably, on European literature.

NG: Yes I had. I didn't feel that it was necessary to invent a special language; it's just the small problems of certain names that meant something to us in South Africa but wouldn't be known to people outside—words like donga for ditch and the names of plants and birds and so on. But I myself was used to reading; for instance, I liked very much some of the writers from the Deep South in America, but I didn't know what a Judas tree was, I didn't know what a chinaberry tree was, and I'd never heard anybody speak like people in the South. But I always feel that it's up to the writer to make it intelligible so that the reader makes that leap in his mind. A novelist can't have little asterisks and explain things all the time, so I didn't feel that was necessary. What I did feel, when I was very young, was I suppose the experience of any white person in a colonial situation beginning to write, that literature was somewhere else. After all, as a child, when I was reading children's books—these were, of course, the children's books that all of you in England read—and there were stories about what happened, pancake-tossing, Ash Wednesday, Christmas with snow, our lives were physically different from that. So there was just that to overcome when one began; there was a different physical atmosphere in which one lived. As a child, I was unconscious of the *really* important thing, which wasn't whether Christmas had snow or sunshine, but the social situation in which I was living in that little mining town. When I really began, very young, to write, I wasn't aware of that yet; it was the physical world that concerned me.

MW: I've always thought there is a very intense feeling for place, for the land, in your work. Ironically, you gave that sense of the land to one of the least sympathetic of your characters, the man in *The Conservationist.*

NG: True, horrible man, but I had to grant him that, that he did have that feeling. But I think as time went by, I found how it's such a paradox really because we're all for conservation; we all have this concern about the natural environment in which we live. But in the South African context, it often becomes something very unpleasant and almost evil, as it did in *The Conservationist,* because there's the question of whose land? Can you own the land with a piece of paper, a deed of sale? So the concern for the birds and the beasts and the lack of concern for the human beings become another issue.

MW: You've talked about a short story that you wrote when you were about eighteen called "Ah, Woe Is Me," which is about a white woman and her relationship to a former black servant. You said that that was one of the first short stories that ever showed some sense of the political situation you were living in.

NG: Yes, I think it was; I was moving in a very unconscious kind of way to the real issues in my country, and obviously I could only approach them from my very limited experiences of that time. And since I was a child brought up in a household where there was a black woman servant, when I began to think or to question relations between black and white, it would naturally be on that level. I went to a convent school for white children only; the cinema that we went to once a week with our sixpence in hand was for whites only; and most importantly, the library, the municipal library, was for white people only. And I often think now, if I had been a black child, would I ever have become a writer? Because I wouldn't have had access to that library; my parents were not rich; we didn't have a library in our house. I would ask for a book as a birthday present or as a Christmas present and look forward to those two books the whole year. I would save up pocket money and buy a book. But the library was really my training ground as a writer; if I'd been black, I would have been cut off from it. And I've only realized that late in my life.

MW: You were nearly thirty, I think, when your first novel *The Lying Days* was published; what provoked you to turn from short fiction to a novel? I assume in some ways it was an autobiographical novel.

NG: *The Lying Days* is my only autobiographical book, and it did have a strongly autobiographical basis. But I had wanted to write a novel and had made a few attempts in my late teens and beginning of my twenties, but somehow I didn't like what I wrote. Of course, the reason was clear to me later on: I hadn't lived enough. Perhaps that's a limitation of my own experience; but I felt my life was really too narrow, and emotionally it was too constricted for me to be able to write a novel. Whereas there were small striking incidents, things that could be contained, you know, like an egg. A short story's like an egg; it's all there. Whereas a novel, when I write a novel, it's an unknown territory that is staked out, and it can take time to move from one part of the territory to another. I began to write short stories and always wanted, really, in the back of my mind to write a novel and began to write that novel when I was about twenty-five.

MW: I don't think I was wrong in taking it as primarily a novel about emotional growth, but what I didn't realize then was that the 1949 Nationalist government was a very important factor in Helen's growing up. She does, in fact, talk about its importance but also about the slowness with which the real importance of that filtered through to whites and their more intimate lives. I think she says that it takes a long time before that kind of change permeates through to actually affect most intimate relations.

NG: Yes. I don't think that novel really reflects adequately what that election meant. I think that my preoccupations were still very personal, emotional, very adolescent, as so often happens in first novels.

MW: Yes, all I was saying was that she was registering that it had happened, but she was still much more preoccupied with her personal life.

NG: Yes.

MW: That was one of the points. I think that at the end she goes abroad, but knows she'll come back too. That's the other decision that she's made.

NG: Yes.

MW: Did that follow any pattern in your life? When did you go abroad?

NG: Not in my life, no, no. But perhaps it was a kind of wish fulfillment, something I wanted to experience; I wanted to see Europe and didn't have the opportunity to do so. And so many of my contemporaries were doing this! It was a time when you still felt that literature, culture, art, it couldn't possibly be where you were. You had to go to London or Paris or somewhere. You had the same phenomenon among Americans of Hemingway's generation and earlier generations, that you couldn't possibly be a painter or a writer right where you were in Ohio, or Wilmington, Delaware, or Springs, Transvaal. Of course, we were quite wrong, and now there isn't really that view at all. And people feel quite the contrary, that it's a terrible deprivation when people have to go into exile for political reasons.

MW: It has been very important, obviously, for you that you have stayed there.

NG: Yes. I think I would have been a writer anywhere because I've been writing all my life. But I probably would have been, perhaps, a different kind of writer.

MW: Do you think there are advantages for writers being in exile? In *The Lying Days* there is a novelist called Isa who is going to go off to England and write.

NG: No, I can't see any advantage. I think that some, greatly talented, have continued to develop in exile but obviously do not write the books they would have written if they had stayed at home. I'm not saying that exile is a disaster that kills talent; if the talent is there, very often it continues to develop. You've got Doris Lessing; you've got Dennis Brutus; you've got a number of other people. But I know of so many others who have left at a point where somehow exile became stultifying; because of a certain fragility in themselves, in their personality, they have not developed at all. Their lives have been tragedies, and they have come to unhappy ends.

MW: You said a moment ago that your first novel was still looking at life from a fairly adolescent and rather private point of view. But the next two novels, leaving aside the short stories for a moment, do seem to be more and more about the way politics are affecting personal life. *Occasion For Loving* is about a love affair between a black man and a white woman. And one of the characters talks about how in South Africa the personal is always driven back to the social, and the private has to become political. Were you conscious of that?

NG: Oh, very much so. By the time I wrote that book, I was living then in Johannesburg, and I was mixing in a completely different milieu from the one that I was brought up in in that mining town. By that time, I had black friends as well as white ones; you must remember it was a time of great political turmoil on a mass basis. In the fifties, you had the great Defiance Campaign; I myself was not taking part. I'd been a very slow developer politically, I think, very. But I was tremendously aware of this ferment around me, and so many of the people I knew, whose lives affected mine, were involved.

MW: I believe the first character of yours who is really political is in *The Late Bourgeois World*, which I've always liked very much. It's a very short novel about a divorced woman. She doesn't do very much politically. I think she just makes available an aunt's bank account.

NG: Oh my dear, to make available a bank account for a banned movement—[Gesture of cutting her throat]

MW: What I was going to say was, that felt like the beginning of something for her rather than the end of the story.

NG: Yes, oh it was. It was indeed a beginning. We don't know what happened to her, but she made a very big and dangerous decision there.

MW: Did that mark a turning point in your work? It did seem to be the first time you were writing very directly about—

NG: As for all writers who don't seek exotic locations, so to speak, who work from within their own society, whatever is changing in that society is going to come into my work—implicitly. So that kind of thing was happening, that kind of agonizing decision was coming to people and was absorbed by me, I suppose, and went into the work. So that what happened to the young girl, the preoccupations of Helen in *The Lying Days,* were then bypassed. They belonged to the past, to another era. I think that the historical connections between fiction and fact are always stronger than we think. It may not be conscious in the writer's mind, but it is there.

MW: I think it's very marked in your work, isn't it, because you said you were slow developing politically, but in fact the novels have become more and more political and more directly—

NG: Well, I think they probably went ahead of me as an individual.

MW: In a sense, if you take *Occasion For Loving* and go from that to *The Late Bourgeois World, Burger's Daughter* is the one that really tackles head on the problems of whites working politically and working with blacks in South Africa, doesn't it? Was that again in response to what was happening in the seventies?

NG: *Burger's Daughter? Burger's Daughter* was in response to—I don't want to sound pretentious—it was really the only book I've written that had any motive other than the desire simply to write what I knew. It was an act of homage to people like Rosa Burger's family. By that time I had become so fascinated, amazed, admiring; I had become, well, fascinated is the word, with people of that kind. I was always waiting for someone who was right within that milieu to write about them, but it happened mainly in nonfiction, in personal accounts, and I've always believed that there are so many inhibitions even in the most honest autobiographical works. People fear—even if they will reveal themselves, they cannot reveal others or hurt them too much. So there are tremendous inhibitions in fact. But you are free in fiction, and I took, then, the freedom of fiction to put what I knew of fact in a fictional form, in a form of imaginary characters.

MW: It is a very painful story because Rosa spends a lot of time almost trying to escape that political heritage in South Africa, doesn't she? She's been brought up in such an intensely political family; it becomes a problem of whether she's—

NG: Yes. I was also by that time fascinated, having teenage children of my own. You see your children get to the stage when they break away, and they *must* break away because you've gone through that stage yourself. Sometimes it's done easily, depends a lot on the parents as well as the children, and sometimes it's a very painful and difficult process on both sides. But I had noticed, and I still see something amazing about families who are totally politically dedicated: that it simply goes on, seems to go on from generation to generation. It's like a very strong genetic strain. Very often, one can't generalize entirely, the children and grandchildren of such people take up the torch so to speak.

MW: Yes, I know. I've heard communist families in America and Australia say about that book, "I mean, that's exactly it!" I know it's also very much about South Africa, but I think you did get a certain kind of, as you say, political heritage, quite remarkably. It's also though, isn't it, about the problems of whites working with blacks; that becomes increasingly an issue in the course of that book.

NG: Well, in the '70s it was becoming an issue because you have the growth of the Black Consciousness movement, and the feeling of—First of all, the black liberation movements were banned and working with great difficulty underground. It was a dormant time, an unhappily dormant time, until the Black Consciousness movement in the '70s began to build up a black sense of identity, began to inspire black people with a sense of being themselves. And following the Black Consciousness movement, *everywhere* this meant drawing away from working with whites. There was also the feeling that there had been a failure of liberal motivation to change in South Africa. To put it crudely, many blacks felt that liberals had sold them down the river. If you don't succeed, it doesn't matter how much you've done.

If you don't succeed, then you don't count anymore. It does seem indeed that liberalism did not achieve. We *know* that it didn't achieve the end of apartheid in South Africa; indeed, things just simply got worse during the '60s and '70s. It didn't meet the historical demands of the time. So part of that comes into that book, whereas Rosa's parents, who were not liberals of course but radicals, had worked so closely with blacks. She grew up in a time when the separation was coming.

MW: In fact, one of the crucial things is when she meets the black child she had grown up with and he rejects her, which, in a sense, turns her back to South Africa and politics.

NG: Yes.

MW: Your latest book, *A Sport of Nature,* again covers a very long period. Like *Burger's Daughter,* it seems to be looking at South African history over 20-odd years, isn't it, or longer.

NG: It's more. She's a couple of years younger than Rosa.

MW: Actually, Rosa appears briefly.

NG: Yes, Rosa pops up. She pops in for a cup of tea or something.

MW: Hillela is an extraordinarily different kind of heroine from Rosa—Rosa with this serious family background who thinks every-thing out with a conscience. And Hillela is, well you called her a sport of nature, she does act instinctively, sexually. Why were you interested in that kind of heroine in what is a very political book?

NG: Well, because I think that we make, especially those of us who consider ourselves "serious-minded people," we decide who is effective and who is not. Perhaps there are more ways of being effective than we would allow. Over the years, in what's now a fairly long life, I've observed this sometimes. Someone about whom I've thought, "Well, really, you know, that person is really a lightweight," has turned out to be quite different. And then, so many people, heavyweights, in the serious sense of the word, in the political sense of the word, or the spiritual sense of the word, have been such disappointments to themselves and to others, and have taken the wrong decisions or had bad luck or landed up not achieving their goals at all. And the most unexpected people, who you would have never thought could have done anything, have done this, have become effective in unconventional ways. I've also been fascinated all my life with women who have been the power behind the throne so to speak, the Madame de Pompadours and the Maintenons, all sorts of figures in history who seemed to have had a strong political influence. But because they were women, they are just remembered as so-and-so's mistress. We were discussing last night with some friends, every time a woman's name comes up in connection with a famous man, somebody says, "Oh well, she was so-and-so's mistress," and we were trying to think of somebody, of some famous woman, and one would say, "Oh, do you know so-and-so," mentioning a man, "he was so-and-so's lover." I popped up with Simone de Beauvoir and Jean-Paul Sartre, but it was not acceptable. They were too evenly balanced. So I had this fascination with a woman who I think will perhaps annoy some feminist circles very much, because she works like a courtesan, doesn't she? She climbs her way, at the beginning, from bed to bed. She really hasn't much choice. I wasn't trying to create a modern Moll Flanders; I wasn't trying to jump on any kind of bandwagon like that. What I hope comes out of the book, and if it doesn't, well then I have failed with that, is that she has seen so much emotional and moral prevarication. If you look at the people that she's lived among, she finds so little to trust that she comes really to the conclusion that the only thing that you can trust is your own body and your own feelings. The bed, at least, is honest. You feel pain; you feel sexual pleasure. At one stage in her life, after all, she's in a very, very precarious position, going off as a young girl with a man that she believes is a hero, a political refugee, and then he—first of all he's a spy! This is not an outlandish tale at all; we who live there know that it happens all the time. And then he abandons her. She has no money; she is not attached to any cause, so nobody is going to look after her, so she's suspect. All she has is her spirit, her good looks, and her nice little body. And a measure of intelligence. So she's a very physical person, and she is trusting indeed on these elemental aspects of herself. Of course she changes later on; she develops later on. But from that starting point, I really wanted her to be stripped, in a sense, and she is; she's stripped of all the middle-class, all the bourgeois trappings that Olga could have given her, and she is stripped of the support of decent, middle-of-the-road opinions that Pauline—progressive opinions that she could have got from Pauline.

MW: In fact, she is the one who makes most political contact with blacks. In a sense the book ends very optimistically. She becomes more effective politically than say somebody like Rosa who's working more—

NG: Well, she and Sasha. Sasha's the one who comes to grips in one way, and she in another.

MW: I was quite struck by this book, because it does seem more optimistic than your previous novels, say *The Conservationist,* which did seem to be about the end of white possibility in South Africa, and *July's People,* which is a vision of a terrifying future, a violent future. This is a vision of the future by the end, isn't it, and yet it does seem to be a much more peaceful and orderly possibility that you are envisioning.

NG: Well that's because she isn't there, but think of Sasha; he's there. So what has happened while she's been away can't be assumed to be peaceful.

MW: No, though it's not a violent vision like *July's People,* is it?

NG: Well, I don't know. *July's People* covers a different, a shorter span in a particular stage. People always say that *July's People* is about what happens after revolution in South Africa. But it isn't; then they've misread the book because it is *during.*

MW: Yes, you use a quote from Gramsci, don't you, that "the old is dying, and the new cannot be born; in this interregnum there arises a great diversity of morbid symptoms."

NG: Yes, and that's the period in which that book is set.

MW: And this is a morbid kind of—

NG: I think it's born of people's fears and, in some cases, a wish fulfillment to say, "You see, this is what South Africa is going to be like when the blacks take over!" That book is not about that; it's about a time of civil war.

MW: And in this book you're going further into the future.

NG: Yes, in this book she does go further into the future, the character.

MW: And with an optimistic ending.

NG: Yes.

MW: Would you like to read a passage from *A Sport of Nature?*

NG: All right, if you'd like me to.

Hillela, after a series of adventures, marries a black South African revolutionary in exile. This is a little internal soliloquy.

Reads from A Sport of Nature

[This interview was conducted on stage before an audience at the

Institute of Contemporary Arts. Those in the audience were at this point invited to present their questions.]

Audience: One of the books you didn't discuss, which fascinated me because of my background probably, was *A Guest of Honour.* I'm Greek born, and I've known civil wars that followed wars of independence. I would very much like to hear Ms. Gordimer say something. You must realize the similarity, to me at least, with Zimbabwe. Was it your understanding of the African movements of independence that made you write this book which was almost prophetic?

NG: Yes, I didn't have any particular country in mind; I used the physical characteristics of Zambia and Zimbabwe, and little bits of Botswana thrown in and little bits of Kenya. But the kind of conflict was one I had read about and studied in many countries in Africa. For instance, the trade union aspect, that was really much more important in countries in West Africa, but the novelist has the great freedom to bring in all these issues in an imaginary situation.

Audience: You said it took you a long time to become politically aware. Do you think that women writers who are serious must eventually enter politics in order to take their place, first of all among men who have been, quote, serious writers and been political writers. Or can one stay within the private and still be a serious author?

NG: I don't think there's any difference there between whether women writers should become more political or men, because they live as human beings in a society—unless you're talking of women in the sense of feminist politics. I really can't give you an adequate answer, because I'm not a feminist writer. And I don't see myself in that spectrum at all. I'm a woman, and obviously what I write is influenced by the fact that I'm a woman, but so far as politics is concerned, I am concerned with the liberation of the individual no matter what sex or color. For myself, I don't see a particular role as a woman writer.

Audience: I'm very interested in your use of scientific metaphor. Often you look at personal behavior as if seeing through a microscope, and I wondered whether this was a certain distancing to achieve perhaps a closer view and whether you do this consciously in your writing.

NG: No, I don't do it consciously, and I think it's an interesting idea to wonder where writers get their images and metaphors from, where they occur from. Sometimes you'll find in a book by a man, some image that you wouldn't really think would occur to a man, something that comes from cooking or sewing. And in the writing of a woman, you get some reference to something mechanical that you really wouldn't think is in the normal life of a woman. But writers are such strange creatures; they're like magnets attracting all sorts of particles of what would be useless knowledge, perhaps, to other people, and I think that's, perhaps, where these images come from.

Audience: In *July's People,* I have some doubt in my mind about the final chapter. Are we to believe that Maureen escapes, alone, and leaves her family?

NG: Yes, she does. I think she does. It is what I call an open-ended book. I happen to like open-ended books, other people's open-ended books. Because I think that is how life is; there's no conclusion until death, and indeed the consequences of your life go on after your death very often. So that there is no end really; the writer, it's an arbitrary thing, you pick up a life here and you put it down there.

Audience: I wondered if the formation of a political organization like the UDF [United Democratic Front] has had any influence, tangible influence, on your work as a novelist. Has it, for example, enabled you to move towards a more positive ending in this latest book?

NG: Well, that's an interesting idea. If so, it's subconscious, because in my own life, not as a writer but as a human being, the formation of the UDF has meant a great deal to me and has been something that has revived hopes for a different kind of resolution in South Africa, a different kind of interim resolution to a new South Africa. So maybe in some subconscious way it has made me more optimistic. But even before the UDF ever existed, I had never lost my belief in the eventual future of a good and decent society in South Africa—not a utopia, nothing like that, but certainly a more just society than we've ever had. We've never had a democracy; I think we've got a good chance of getting one now.

Audience: Ms. Gordimer, I've read and indeed reviewed some of your books, but I haven't read all of them, and I don't know whether I've missed any references to your Jewishness. I would be very glad if you'd give me some idea of what part it's played in your life and in your work.

NG: Well, oddly enough, Hillela is the first Jewish hero or heroine I've ever had in my nine novels. But her Jewishness doesn't really play much part in her life, and that's the only connection with my own. It's really played no part at all in my life. I didn't come from a family where I had been given Jewish religious upbringing or been taught anything about the history of Jewish people. I read it for myself when I grew up. I'm conscious of the fact that I am Jewish, but it hasn't had anything much to do with the formation of my attitude to life, with my philosophy, or with my moral attitudes. For me, the formative thing has been being a white African.

Audience: Has there been any political criticism of your work in South Africa?

NG: Do you mean just from people generally?

Audience: From the government or the ruling party.

NG: Well I'm afraid the ruling party hasn't done me the honor. But I have had several of my books banned for quite a length of time and then released. And of course political criticism, we all fight amongst ourselves all the time, you know, why are you this and not that. This is just natural, I think, in all countries. If you belong, as I do, to the Left, there are different factions in the Left. This one tells you that your views are inadequate, that one agrees with you; this is part of the democracy we don't have. We only have it on that private level.

Audience: I just wanted to rather challenge your statement that you're not, at least at all, a feminist writer. Because I find that *A Sport of Nature* is a novel about "heroine-ism." It is Hillela who is the effective one; I know Sasha is too, but she refuses to go anyone's way but hers, and there's that very interesting contrasting scene between the two wives in the village—the black wife who is married to the white man and the white woman who is married to the black man. I'd like you to say something about that, because I found that absolutely fascinating.

NG: Well, I suppose that any piece of writing that concerns a woman or women as central characters, one can interpret it from a feminist point of view because of the positions that women have had over the years. What I meant by a feminist novel was something conceived with the idea of proving something about women. I think, probably subconsciously, there are a lot of things about women and what has been done to women and what has formed women's characters that come out in Hillela. But it was not something planned and intentional.

Audience: When the revolution in Zimbabwe gained power, there was a great emigration of white people outside the country. The same happened after the Angola and Mozambique independence; and when you were asked about the ending of your last novel, you said that it was a promising future for the character that had left the country but not as promising a future for the one that remained in South Africa. So, would you think that right now, white South Africans are considering to a large extent the possibility of emigrating in case of greater turmoil in the country?

NG: White South Africans have been emigrating since Sharpeville, since the sixties, in waves when something has happened to frighten them. Many of them, especially those with professional qualifications which enable them to earn a living elsewhere have gone. This is quite distinct from people who had to leave under political pressure, who had been extremely brave and who were in great danger, and I see some of them here today, and that is quite a different thing. But you were talking about people who leave because they fear to stay. I'm always interested in this analogy now with Zimbabwe. What is terrible that has happened to white people in Zimbabwe? Nothing. And some of the people who came to South Africa from Zimbabwe, now that things are going unhappily, for them, in South Africa, have actually gone back. But you see, I've said somewhere else and perhaps it bears saying again, because I, too, have lived in that white country club: South Africa has been a kind of exclusive club for white people. The beaches, the parks—they all belonged only to whites, which meant that they were tremendously underused. So now people throw up their hands and say, can you imagine how crowded, how dirty everything is going to be, because the whole population will be using what was a private domain. Well, the country club is closing down, because the whole country is going to belong to the people.

MW: Can I just say, on behalf of everybody, thank you very, very much indeed for spending so much time with us, and it's been fascinating.

NG: Well, thank you for having me.

Off the Page: Nadine Gordimer

Jill Fullerton-Smith/1988

This is a transcript of an interview broadcast on 5 January 1988 by Thames Television PLC in the series "Off the Page." Printed by permission of Thames Television PLC.

NG: When I come to France it's not just a holiday, a kind of artificial interlude; it has deep emotional connections, because my daughter lives here and so I come to her.

I live in South Africa. I'm always very disturbed before I leave. I don't quite know why. Well, there's a feeling of leaving behind my responsibilities there. At home there are always so many people in trouble, so that at the back of your mind you're remembering that there's somebody you know in prison or there is somebody who is living underground, sleeping in a different place every night. It's very difficult to relax in South Africa. There's a war going on there. It's an undeclared war, but it's on and, indeed, it's been going on for a long time, in moral aspects and in many different ways.

In that war, I know which side I'm on. But from my point of view, I must take my freedom as a writer to show human beings as they are, warts and all. And if you don't, then you're becoming a propagandist. Propagandists are necessary, but I'm not one; and I think as a writer I am—how shall I put it—too selfish to put what talent I have to that extent to any cause. I just couldn't become a propagandist. So there will always be the element of self-criticism in my work, coming out through my characters.

Reads from The Late Bourgeois World

The political content should be part of the essential truth. If the incident, the story, the book is placed in a milieu and at a time where part of the essential truth of that situation is political, then the political element must be there. But you can't judge a work of art by its political content.

JF-S: It happens to you all the time. I think you remarked that you feel an affinity with Eastern European writers.

NG: I do feel an affinity with Eastern European writers, because I

299

know that they suffer from the same thing. But no matter how subtly they may write something, what will be drawn out of that book—mainly by the critics—will be its pertinence to the political situation out of which they write.

JF-S: Were you aware of South Africa and apartheid when you were a small child?

NG: No, I don't think so. I think for most children, certainly up to a certain age, probably up to early adolescence, your parents are your models. The life that they live seems to you the only possible life, and their values and their attitudes you take on automatically. You only begin to question them and rebel against them when you become a teenager. I accepted the fact that I went to the local convent school and everybody was white there and that the black woman who worked for us, Lettie, who worked for us all my childhood, all my life at home, that she—I don't even know whether she had a child somewhere—that she was just an appendage in our house. The black children that I would see round about in the town—they lived in the location and went to school there, and it didn't occur to me that it was strange that they couldn't come to my school or that I could go every Saturday afternoon to the matinee of the cinema and there were no black kids there. It was a kind of god-given rule; white people were here and black people were there, and that was it. It was only later on that I began to see it and question it.

Reads from The Lying Days

JF-S: Helen remarks in *The Lying Days:* "I never read a book in which I, myself, was recognisable." Was that your experience as a child growing up in South Africa?

NG: Yes. Obviously, emotionally there were books that had relevance to my life. D. H. Lawrence was a tremendous favourite of mine when I was about fifteen/sixteen. His wonderful feeling for nature, all the minute things—the face of a pansy, a little tortoise, all these things that he wrote about so marvellously—the sensuousness I could relate to, because African landscapes are very sensuous, and I responded to those very strongly. But everything else was totally different. The obvious thing is the difference in the seasons. When I was a small child, brought up on Dickens and Angela Brazil and so on, all the festivals were celebrated in the wrong seasons for me in England; snow and so on, and there we were always out picnicking at

Christmastime. But this, of course, is an experience that Australians and New Zealanders have. And when I began to read Katherine Mansfield, I realised, here was somebody who was writing about this other world whose seasons, at least, I shared and that it was possible to be a writer even if you didn't live in Europe.

JF-S: Did you come from a literary background then, were your family—

NG: Oh, not at all. No, not at all.

JF-S: What was your family like?

NG: My father was a shopkeeper with a small shop; he sold jewelry. He sold commemorative canteens of cutlery for retiring mine managers and engagement rings and wedding rings and watches. My mother didn't work; very few women in those days seemed to work in South Africa. She just did the usual charity things. My mother was a great reader at a popular level. Indeed, I think I have to thank my mother for the fact that I was able to become a writer, because she saw to it that she read to me and to my sister when we were small. When I was five years old, I was a subscriber to the local municipal library. I was like a pig in clover there; it meant a tremendous amount to me. I've often thought since, there was I growing up, there were not many books in the house, and there was not much money in the house to buy them. But there was the library, and nobody tried to direct what I was reading. I could just read whatever I liked. But had I been a black child, I couldn't have gone to that library. So something like that can be of tremendous significance in a country like South Africa.

I was at school, and then when I was about eleven I developed some very slight—I've discovered since—heart ailment. But my mother, being unhappily married, reacted in a way that many women like that do: she became someone who clung tremendously to her children. And as my sister was older and went away to become a teacher, went to university, I was left at home, four years younger. I think my mother seized upon this illness, you know, as a way to keep me near her.

Reads from "The Termitary"

My mother took me out of school from eleven to about thirteen/fourteen—that's a big slice in a child's life—and took me to some woman who taught me for a couple of hours a day. That I absolutely hated. There's nothing more lonely. When I think of Victorian children with tutors, I realise what it must have been. I was all alone with this woman. And I discovered later on that it was really all about nothing. I should never have been taken out of school. But she did this, so that meant I was at home a great deal; and I think it was then that I began to write.

So the relationship that I had with my mother was very loving at the beginning and much too dependent. This made me very careful not to allow my children to become too dependent upon me. I realise the best thing you can do for your children is to set them free. Of course, like everybody else, I haven't always succeeded. I've done my children damage in some ways, I know that, because one isn't perfect—very, very far from it. But I think that I succeeded when they were quite small in making them independent, not overprotecting them the way I was, because that is the cruellest thing you can do, make a child defenceless.

JF-S: I want just to ask you about what appear to be minor decisions in ordinary life, but in the context of South Africa they became major moral choices.

NG: Well, I think you can't judge in your life what is a minor or major decision. Often, when you can't make a decision at all, at some very important point in your life, you make it through some kind of divergence, through a minor decision. You also, I think, begin to understand crises in your life or things that you haven't been able to interpret, when something apparently minor happens. I used that in my novel *Burger's Daughter* where Rosa Burger is leaving a political gathering, a women's gathering, and she's driving back across the veld near Johannesburg, a place where there are all sorts of little roads which are not on the city map. That detail in itself is indicative of the position of the blacks living round about. Nobody's even bothered to put these little roads on the street map of Greater Johannesburg. And she more or less gets lost. She can't quite find how to get back to the main road and, in the course of this, she hears a donkey. She sees a donkey cart coming along to cross her path. She sees it against the sun; she sees the silhouette of a man savagely beating the poor donkey to get it to pull this cart. And on the back of the cart there's a black family sitting there under rags. She has immediately the usual white, well-brought-up person's reaction, which is one against cruelty to animals. She brakes automatically, and she's full of indignation and rage.

Reads from Burger's Daughter

It's a small incident which makes her realise where she stands in her life there. She can go so far as to stop the cruelty to the donkey, but what about all the rest? This is really what I would regard as my method, using small incidents like that.

JF-S: You use descriptions of people very sparingly in your writing.

NG: Yes, I do use descriptions sparingly, because I think it's very difficult to describe people's physical characteristics. I prefer to let the reader imagine them from the way the person speaks, moves, reacts and from a few little clues if they have some outstanding physical characteristic one way or another. I think this comes from having started as a short-story writer; indeed, I still am one from time to time. In a short story you've got to find significant detail. You're not going to describe a person from head to foot, so just maybe the way that they move a hand, the way that they stand or stoop, the way that they sit, some little tick that they have that is going to create a line from which the reader can build up the whole picture. And I don't think it should be done all at once as was done in a nineteenth-century novel where the author started off saying so and so was born and then described every hair, colour of the eyes, shape of the nose, everything. But I prefer to drop these little sketches or hints through the work as it goes along, so that readers can build up their own picture of what this person looks like.

Reads from The Conservationist

Well, there I describe the Boer farmer in quite a lot of detail because his physical presence is the important thing. It isn't so much what he says or what anybody else says. He is just in that room, dominating that room by his physical presence. So for me then, it justifies a long description of him—also because I found his dignity at the same time rather funny and his hold over the family. I think the idea came to me from having met a young—not such a young woman—a woman in her forties, who was afraid to smoke in front of her father. She would slip off into the loo to have a cigarette, terrified. She had grown-up children, but she wouldn't smoke in front of her father. Of course, that's become one of my preoccupations, the

question of power. It seems that so much of life consists of people
seeking for ways to gain power over others. It really is everywhere.
Between parents and children, too, that has interested me very
much. Of course, in South Africa it is inclined to be connected with
political power as well. But perhaps writers perceive life in different
terms. In mine (I've had rather a long life) it seems to me that the two
greatest drives in people's lives, the two most important things, are
sex and politics.

Reads from A Sport of Nature

I think there may be a particular connection between sexuality,
sensuality, and politics inside South Africa. Because, after all, what is
apartheid all about? It's about the body. It's about physical differences. It's about black skin, and it's about woolly hair instead of
straight, long blond hair, and black skin instead of white skin. The
whole legal structure is based on the physical, so that the body
becomes something supremely important. And I think maybe
subconsciously that comes into my work too.

It's difficult to say whether staying on in South Africa has
strengthened my writing or had any effect, because it seems to me so
natural to stay on. I'm very attached to my country. You have to earn
that attachment if you're white in South Africa. You have to show
that you support not only change, but in my case that you support a
complete revolution, if possible a peaceful one. I use revolution in a
very broad sense, in a sense of completely changing at grass roots,
the social organisation and political organisation in South Africa. And
I think it isn't enough for the whites to say: "All right, I will be
prepared to live under black majority rule" and then sit back and wait
for it to come. I think you also have to work positively in whatever
way you can, as a human being; I'm not talking about as a writer.
Indeed, so far as that is concerned, that kind of activity as a human
being—working towards progress in South Africa—takes up time
and brings about all sorts of distractions that make writing there more
difficult. There are, admittedly, wonderful subjects. There are
wonderful mutations in human nature to see taking place, because
people are under such pressure; and this is food for every writer.

The function of the writer is to make sense of life. It is such a
mystery. It changes all the time; it's like the light. You see incidents in
your life differently. You're weaving back and forth between the past

and the present. And you are trying to make something coherent out of it. Isn't all art doing that? When somebody paints, whether it's an abstract painter using just pure form, whether it's a figurative painter, you are assembling amorphous things and putting them into an order; and it's the same thing with writing.

Fresh Air: Nadine Gordimer

Terry Gross/1989

Transcribed from an interview on "Fresh Air with Terry Gross,"
produced at WHYY-FM Philadelphia, distributed by National
Public Radio. Originally broadcast on 24 May 1989. Printed by
permission of Terry Gross.

TG: Nadine Gordimer is one of South Africa's best known writers.
She's a long-time opponent of her country's racist policies and has
written about the agonies of apartheid in her novels and short stories.
In *July's People*, she imagined life during the civil war; in *A Sport of
Nature* she projected a vision of black majority rule. Gordimer is the
vice-president of PEN, the international writers' union. Her latest
book, *The Essential Gesture,* has just come out in paperback. It's a
collection of essays written between the early 1950s and 1985. Many
of these pieces are about what it means to be a writer in South Africa
and where she sees herself fitting into the fight against apartheid as a
white woman. A few weeks ago, the anti-apartheid activist David
Webster was assassinated in South Africa. Blacks and whites
disregarded the law to gather together at his funeral. Gordimer told
me that she saw this as a cause for optimism.

NG: When you see black and white people coming together, in
the mass, out of respect and love for a man like David Webster, you
feel optimism vis-à-vis the fear that people express to me here in
America and outside—that there'll be no place for whites in South
Africa when we have black majority rule. I don't believe this, and I
keep seeing evidence that it is not so. It depends upon whites; it
depends how they behave; it depends which side they show they're
on now: not just out of their mouths, but out of their actions as well.

TG: I'm curious about when you became aware of apartheid. You
grew up in South Africa. Your parents were émigrés, your mother
from London, your father, I think, from Lithuania. You grew up in a
mining town.

NG: Well, I think I was quite a late developer really, when I
consider the awareness, political awareness, of my own children a

306

generation later. But in that small town, you know how it is, particularly in a small town where you're not open to many other mind-blowing influences, you tend to adopt the attitudes and the mores of your parents and your teachers and so on. And I just took it as natural as a child that I went to a segregated school. I went to a convent school; all the kids were white; and the only people, the only blacks that I was in touch with were people doing the menial jobs: sweeping the streets, acting as servants, messengers, and so on. I mean, they were all around. And of course, as it was a mining town, there were thousands of black migratory miners who lived in their compounds (as we called them), barracks, quite near where we lived, but were completely separate from us, not only by language, but they just had no part in our lives. But when I was about—I was a great reader—and I really came to think about apartheid in terms of class injustice from reading people like Upton Sinclair when I was a teenager. And then I began to look around me. I began to write very young, by the time I was seventeen, and the first published story that I wrote was indeed about apartheid, not in a direct, not in a formula form, but as it affected the lives of the people that I knew. It was about a police raid on a house for illicit liquor-brewing by the black servant.

TG: Did opposing apartheid also mean that you had to oppose your parents? Did your parents support the system?

NG: Well, my father, I think, did. You must remember that when I was a child, the word apartheid hadn't even been coined. The apartheid government only came into power in 1948 when I was grown up; I'm talking about the '30s. At that time it was a sort of colonial racism, with quite a lot of paternalism mixed up in it. My mother had a social conscience; she did good works, and I don't say that sneeringly. She was one of the people who helped form a crèche and clinic for black children in the nearby black ghetto, which we called a township then. And she was always uneasy and angry if she saw black people being treated badly, but it was always as a form of charity. She didn't connect it with the law; she didn't connect it with the fact that they didn't have rights as white people had.

TG: Was writing, for you, a response to injustice; or do you think you would have become a writer one way or another?

NG: Writing was not a response to injustice; I wasn't even aware of injustice. I began to write out of a sense of wonder at life, and also out of the mystery of life, wanting to find out what it was all about; it was my way of exploring life. I think this is true of all artists; that's at the base of what we do. I don't think that any real artist begins from a political stimulation, or conscience.

TG: In the 1950s you became friends with many black writers. Were there many obstacles at that time to developing friendships between black and white writers?

NG: Yes, there were, but I think as everywhere in the world, probably in the United States as well, writers and artists, actors, journalists have tended to be people who don't really fit into a conventional pattern of life and have more in common with one another and with the things that interest and absorb them which cross color, race, language, everything. I think this was true in South Africa as well. I had so much more in common with some young black person who was beginning to write than I had with the people in that mining town; it was community of interest.

TG: Do the people in your mining town see you as a traitor?

NG: Well, I left there when I was quite young, and I don't know how they saw me. While I was there and was quietly writing, it was very much a sort of secret activity. Nobody was particularly interested in it, which I think was a good thing for me, left me to develop in my own way. I think they were a bit annoyed when my first book was published—my mother was still living there—because it was set in a town like that, and first books usually have quite a strong auto-biographical element. So I think there was a bit of name-spotting. You know, this is so and so, and that's based on whatnot and tut, tut, tut, how could she have been doing this?

TG: In 1959, in one of your essays reprinted in the collection *The Essential Gesture,* you ask the question: "Where do whites fit in in the new Africa?" Your answer was: "Nowhere, I'm inclined to say." What was the vision of the new Africa in the late 1950s?

NG: Well, it was exciting, and it was strange that down in the south there, in the big toe of the continent, it seemed hardly to affect us at all, and this is partly due to lack of communication. It's always been much easier, whites in South Africa have always been very Euro-centric, and indeed when I was a young girl and a beginning writer, it was a dream of everybody then to go to London or to go to Paris.

How could you possibly be a writer sitting in Johannesburg?
Fortunately, I didn't ever have the money to go. And I think it was
very fortunate because why become an expatriate for no reason, lose
your background and your home? I'm a bit worried about that essay,
because many people don't notice, as you did, that it was dated '59;
it's a very long time ago. I didn't alter any of my opinions and bring
them up-to-date in that book, because I thought a personal book like
this shows the development of one's opinions and responses to one's
time in society. But, I obviously, in 1959, doubted whether there
would be a place for whites to continue to live in Africa. But, so far
as South Africa's concerned, I certainly don't believe that now, and I
haven't believed it for many years. I'm quite sure that there is a place
for whites. The African National Congress, the premier liberation
movement, has always been nonracial, still is. And it's simply a
matter—it's not a simple matter for many whites—it's a matter of
whites learning how to live in a different way, truly accepting what is
coming which is black majority rule, and not fearing, not wanting
guarantees of group rights which will set them aside, set them apart,
mark them out forever. We've never had a Bill of Rights in South
Africa. I think if the rights of the individual are guaranteed, why do
you need to guarantee group rights? You're only keeping the
demarcation of color and class there forever. I think whites certainly
have a big part to play in the future, free, nonracial South Africa, but
they must learn to live differently. They can't be wanting to be the
boss and ordering other people around and doing their thinking for
them.

TG: I've heard some whites in South Africa who've done liberal or
radical works say that they fear that if there is a revolution there will
be so much unleashed rage, rage against white people, and understandably so; and this rage will not discriminate between white
people who've opposed apartheid and white people who've supported it. Do you ever worry about that?

NG: No, I must say I don't. I'm interested to hear that this should
have come to you from people who have been active, because this is
the kind of fear that comes from people who have never done
anything with blacks.

TG: I won't mention names here, but there's one person in
particular who said that to me.

NG: I think it might have been true; it was true in the '70s during the black separatist time. But now with the United Democratic Front—still operating under great difficulty, half banned—in the '80s there's been a great revival of democratic action across the color-line.

TG: Was there a moment or a period when you stopped fluctuating between staying in South Africa or leaving, and you just decided to stay?

NG: Oh, there's really only been in my life one or two moments when I thought at all of leaving South Africa.

TG: What were those moments?

NG: Well, actually they were in the '60s when, through personal circumstances, I could have gone to live in Zambia. I went, I'd been travelling quite a bit in Central Africa generally, Tanzania, Kenya, Zambia, and I had what I realized later was a romantic idea that I could then commit myself to an African country as an African. Whereas in South Africa, there was the struggle against white supremacists in the '60s—you must remember it was after Sharpeville, the African National Congress was banned, the other liberation movements were banned—and there was just a feeling of total stalemate, that the apartheid government was going to be there *forever.* And I didn't want to spend my life as a white living in the white laager, struggling to keep contact with blacks. But, I think fortunately for me, I discovered on visits to Zambia, much as I liked the country and the people, that there I was just regarded as a European. I was just a white person like expatriates from England working there, or from any other country. Whereas at home in my own country, there's never been a time when I felt I wasn't recognized as a white African.

TG: I believe three of your books have been censored; is that right?

NG: Three of my books have been banned over the years in South Africa, but lately nothing of mine has been banned; and I optimistically hope that nothing will be. I think there's a certain protection, I know there is, in being, becoming well known outside, as I've become better known in the outside world. It is seen hardly worthwhile for the government to ban a writer like myself, not a terribly easy writer to read. So that I think the calculation is that it's not worth the fuss that there is when a book of mine is banned, the fuss that there is in the outside world as well as at home. But in any case, censorship, the real clout of censorship, has moved from the censorship banning of books to that of muzzling the press. The real heat is on the press, the media generally.

TG: Is censorship almost a badge of honor . . . knowing that the government was so outraged by a book that they don't even want other people to read it?

NG: Yes, I suppose so in a way, but really for me that's offset by the fact that it cannot be read by your own people then. But, as I say, now very few works of fiction are banned, and even quite tough nonfiction works. This is also because, if they're on a certain level, they're not going to find a very large reading public. And you must remember there's complete control of television; it's all state television. People like myself don't write for television; we don't appear in discussion programs; we are muzzled in this way.

TG: Let me read to you a statement you once said about writing. You said that "the best way to write is to do so as if one were already dead, afraid of no one's reactions, answerable to no one's views." What led you to say that, and I guess I wonder if you've taken heat on both sides in South Africa?

NG: No, this was just a conviction that goes, really, deeper than that. I think that a writer must always maintain the independence, the artistic independence, to use his or her insights—something that a writer has beyond the insights of other people—without worrying whether you're going to offend your mother, your best friend, or whether your political confreres are going to decide that you have let down their side. A writer must never let herself become a propagandist. Propagandists have a place; agitprop has a place. But I'm not that kind; I'm not that person. I'm a writer; I have a certain ability, and I feel the first duty is to use that ability properly. The nearest you can get to the truth, you get through using that ability properly, not worrying what anybody's going to say. That's why I would stand by that old statement, you know, that you must write as if you were already dead and not worry about the consequences. Because as soon as you've got your eye on an audience, on people who are watching you, who are going to hear what you have to say, you're going to falsify that little extra vision you have that will bring you near to the truth. And in the end, if we look at your position, the writer's position in society, the essential gesture to society, in the end it is what you are going to be able to record and discover of the truth that is going to serve your society best.

TG: Do you feel that you've ever been expected to write books that would be more effective propaganda?

NG: Oh yes. Indeed.

TG: Where has that pressure come from?

NG: Well it hasn't really been pressure, and it hasn't usually come from quarters that bothered me very much. Because I feel that if I took no part in community life, lived in an ivory tower, then perhaps I might listen to it. But I'm also a human being, a citizen, and I know that I have a certain responsibility toward my society for what's happened there, what's happened in my name as a white, whether I had anything to do with it or not. So I have another part of my life where I put my life on the line for what I believe in; and I think, therefore, I have the freedom to write as I feel I must, as I please. I'm not retiring into an ivory tower because I am doing other things as a human being and a citizen.

TG: We talked a little earlier about how in the 1950s you became good friends with many black writers from South Africa. Is it any more difficult now to keep connections like that? What I mean is, do government restrictions make it really difficult to get together and to communicate?

NG: No, only insofar as you know that when you're in organizations like our new writers' organization, of which I was one of the founders—it's only just going to be two years old in July, it's very young still—we know that we are watched, because part of our preamble to our constitution is that we are committed to the liberation of South Africa; we are committed to working with and encouraging a grass-roots culture, which means working with the cultural groups in trade unions. We make no excuses for it; we *are* a political organization because culture is political. We want to create a new culture. We know that we are watched. When some of our members—not directly through their activities with us, but through other activities—have been detained, they're quite closely questioned about us. So that there isn't anything that you do across the color line, without racial division or even with racial division if it's against the regime, that doesn't bring you some kind of risk. But you can still mix as a writer with your black colleagues if you wish, as long as you have what is really in common: the desire, first of all, to do good work and, secondly, to understand your responsibility as a writer to other people who are struggling to learn to write, who have had fewer educational opportunities. And this applies to blacks as well as whites, because you have some of our black writers who teach in universities or run alternative educational establishments; in other words, they're white-collar people. And there are lots and lots of people in the trade unions, among mine workers, peasants in the country, who long to write and to read, who don't have the libraries, and they don't have the ability to express themselves. We feel it's part of our duty of being writers to work with them and help them.

TG: It's interesting; you see it as a political responsibility.

NG: Yes. It's a political and a professional and artistic responsibility.

TG: You mentioned a new organization of writers that you helped to found; what is it called?

NG: It's called the Congress of South African Writers, COSAW. It's really spreading out into the country. We try to get away from the concentration in the big cities with our readings and workshops, and we are about 95% black membership now. But by black I mean, we call black, people that you call coloured, people who are of Indian descent, people who are of mixed blood, and so on. But we have a 95% black membership.

TG: One last question: what do you need to do to make sure that the organization doesn't get banned and get forced underground?

NG: Well, we can't do anything, because then we would be stifling our real convictions. We simply go on doing what we think is right and we're prepared to take the consequences.

Index